International Relations Theory

International Relations Theory

A Bibliography

Edited by A.J.R.Groom and C.R.Mitchell

Frances Pinter Ltd. London
Nichols Publishing Co. New York

47566

Copyright © A.J.R. Groom and C.R. Mitchell 1978

First Published in Great Britain in 1978 by
Frances Pinter (Publishers) Limited
161 West End Lane, London NW6 2LG

ISBN 0 903804 17 4 Paperback
ISBN 0 903804 18 2 Hardback

Published in the U.S.A. in 1978 by
Nichols Publishing Company
Post Office Box 96
New York, N.Y. 10024

Library of Congress Cataloging in Publication:
International relations theory.

    Includes index.
    1. International relations-Research-Bibliography.
I. Groom, A.J.R. II. Mitchell, Christopher.
Z6461.I49 1978   [JX1291]   016.327'07'2   77-20896
ISBN 0-89397-026-3

Printed in Great Britain
A. Wheaton & Co. Ltd., Exeter

CONTENTS

INTRODUCTION

by The Editors

The printed word (or number) is a boon and a bane. It is a boon in that it has provided a necessary technological under-pinning to the tremendous growth and spread of knowledge that is so characteristic of the modern era. It is a bane in that the seemingly exponential growth of the literature threatens to overwhelm the intellect and to disenfranchise thought. Sometimes the choice seems stark indeed: that between reading books and writing them. Following the maxim 'publish or perish' those that can write do so only to perish on the publisher's treadmill. *Plus ça change, plus c'est la même chose.*

The purpose of an analytical and critical bibliography is to act as a (temporary) palliative: it sets priorities in terms of the interests of the compilers and the literature of the day. It is thus necessary to dwell briefly on both variables. This volume is confined to the theoretical and conceptual aspects of International Relations. While there is a concern with methodological issues in both their epistemological and technical aspects, case studies, history, reference works, data books and the like are firmly eschewed. The limitations are draconian in a further respect: very few articles and 'classics' in the field are included. Rather the aim has been to reflect and comment upon the present state of the literature in International Relations in what may be loosely defined as its theoretical and conceptual aspects and to point to both likely and desirable future directions. Most attention has been given to books and monographs despite the frequency with which innovative ideas first come to the attention in article form or may be succinctly presented in a journal only later to be laboriously filled-out to justify hard or soft covers (and generate fame and fortune!). Yet the number of journals proliferates as writers publish and readers perish. If the scope of a bibliography is too wide it runs the risk of compounding the problem of an abundance of material rather than alleviating it. Hence the concentration on books which, in turn, is largely restricted to those published in Britain or North America.

These quasi-technical criteria for selection are but one set of filters. Of greater moment for the reader is the intellectual filter. The contributors to this volume are all or have been associated with the Centre for the Analysis of Conflict. With the metamorphosis of the Centre their institutional affiliation has changed yet, for the most part, they have maintained close intellectual and personal ties. However, this bibliography is in no sense a manifesto although it reflects, hopefully, a degree of cohesion and consensus. While the contributors may in some respects appear to form a group with a particular set of interests and even a point of view which is reflected in their teaching and research, the differences between them are fierce, fundamental but friendly. Moreover, as a loosely-knit, informal group they have sought to develop ties in their area of interest throughout the English-language university world and in both eastern and western Europe. The focal point of the group has always been the study of conflict in the broadest context. Inter-state conflict, inter-communal conflict, industrial conflict, deviancy and the like in an adisciplinary framework are among the research interests of members of the group. But as teachers of International Relations others have delved into questions of organisation and development. Yet a consensus remains which can best be summarised as a 'world society approach'.

The 'world society approach' has no one generally accepted definition. Certainly its definition and its merits do not evoke agreement among the contributors except negatively in that they have a clear idea of what it is not; for example, it is not a concern with world government. However, there is some measure of agreement that the level of analysis is a function of the research problem, as is the unit of analysis. Thus the traditional demarcation line between Political Science and International Relations, that is between intra-state relations characterised by a large degree of consensus and orderly government and inter-state relations reflecting dissensus and anarchy, is erased. But it is not

10

merely a question of an interdisciplinary approach. Rather the focus is upon the adisciplinary treatment of universal phenomena such as conflict, decision-making, development, integration or identity seen in the context of world society as a whole. The basic organising concept is that of a system of transactions analysed in a cybernetic framework which points to the central importance of decision-making and to its behavioural characteristics. A further central focus is the degree of legitimacy which prevails in the structures and transactions of the system in question. It is assumed that although levels of analysis, units of analysis, systems boundaries, cultural context and the substantive content of transactions may vary, it is possible and profitable to approach phenomena such as conflict or development in a single framework. The question is, of course, ultimately an empirical one but, for the time being and in varying degrees, the world society approach is the dominant conceptual framework of the contributors.

A bibliography devoted entirely to the world society approach, however defined, would indeed be brief. Moreover, it would constitute more a 'future direction' than the present 'state of the field'. The contributors have therefore been asked to review the present literature with their conceptions of the future direction of International Relations in mind. They are both selective and critical with no pretence at a balanced and complete survey of the literature. They have been encouraged to recommend what they think is worthwhile. Their response has varied with some concentrating on the present literature and others giving more attention to their conception of future developments. In part the breakdown of the volume into chapters has put a premium on the present literature since the breakdown is essentially founded on the need to organise the material in such a way as to facilitate its use by teachers and, more particularly, students in the existing structure of courses in British and North American universities. Inevitably there has been some duplication of material but since the reader will refer only to particular sections at one time this presents some advantages. Equally, while the Editors suggested a standard format for presentation they see no great virtue in rigidity so that there are occasional variations in presentation.

A collaborative venture of this kind derives whatever merits it can muster from the individual talents and spirit of co-operation of the contributors. The Editors wish to pay great tribute to their friends for their intellectual and practical co-operation in a task that may at times have been burdensome or even seemed thankless. A volume of this nature is particularly dependent on painstaking secretarial assistance for which thanks are due to Fay Trager-Green and her colleagues at University College London; and to Dinah Hilton, Norah Vas and Gillian Lambert at The City University, London.

A.J.R. Groom
C.R. Mitchell
London, December 1977.

Chapter I

THE METHODOLOGY OF INTERNATIONAL RELATIONS

by Michael Nicholson
The Richardson Institute for Conflict and Peace Research

In most disciplines there are a group of scholars who ask questions
about the fundamental nature of the activity which is being followed.
Thus, while mathematicians do mathematics, some people ask questions
such as 'What is a valid proof?'. In the natural sciences scientists try to
establish theories, while a few ask what a theory is. Similarly, in the
social sciences most people carry out the activity in question, but a few
will ask such questions as 'What do explanations in the social sciences
consist of?'. These sorts of problems are the subject matter of the
'philosophy' of the various disciplines. International Relations is a
subset of the social sciences and is by and large subject to the questions
which can be raised about any analysis of social behaviour. However,
there is fundamental disagreement on some of these basic questions.
Whether International Relations can be regarded as scientific, even in
an extended sense, is very contentious. Hence it is necessary to glance,
if only briefly, at the major issues involved. These mirror some basic
disagreements in the philosophy of the social sciences as a whole, and
while there is some literature on the specific issues raised by Political
Science, and even more specifically in International Relations, the
fundamental problems are common to the social sciences as a whole.

The major disagreement concerns the legitimacy of scientific
methods in the analysis of social behaviour. Although this is a
simplistic way of putting it, and though there are a multitude of
efforts at reconciliation, an underlying division exists. Thus any

analysis of the philosophy of the social sciences has to be discussed in the context of the philosophy of the natural sciences: the would-be scientists regard this as the obvious starting point, while the opponents commonly take it as the point of attack. Hence the following note is divided into three, although at times with fairly arbitrary borderlines. First, mention is made of some books on the philosophy of science in general — primarily the philosophy of the natural sciences. The second part consists of books on the philosophy of the social sciences in general, with one or two particularly relevant works on particular social sciences other than International Relations. The third part is on the philosophy of Political Science, in particular International Relations.

The Philosophy of Science

There are a large number of books on the philosophy of science, each with their own emphases and some in substantial disagreement with each other. Personal taste is a significant factor in determining a selection from the mass which is available. Three introductory books with rather different emphases are Harré's THE PHILOSOPHIES OF SCIENCE (23), Hempel's PHILOSOPHY OF NATURAL SCIENCE (25), and Toulmin's PHILOSOPHY OF SCIENCE(56).

Rather more difficult, but rewarding for those who can stay the course, is R.B. Braithwaite's SCIENTIFIC EXPLANATION (4). In many ways, a careful reading of this book would provide a clearer and more thorough knowledge of the nature of laws and explanations in science than would a more superficial reading of a wider range of books. However, Popper is a name which appears before very long in any discussion of scientific method. THE LOGIC OF SCIENTIFIC DISCOVERY (44) is his major work where the philosophy of the natural sciences is concerned. Popper is particularly known in this area for his emphasis on falsifiability as the principle which demarcates scientific from non-scientific statements. This is regarded as too strong a criterion by some philosophers (for example, A.J. Ayer in THE PROBLEM OF KNOWLEDGE (2) — a more general topic than the philosophy of science alone). Readable, witty, but profound, is Bertrand Russell's HUMAN KNOWLEDGE: ITS SCOPE AND LIMITS (50).

The dependence of perception on changing conceptual frameworks is emphasized in Thomas Kuhn's THE STRUCTURE OF SCIENTIFIC REVOLUTIONS (33) which is one of the most widely quoted books in this area. Kuhn is interested in scientific change and discovery and is perhaps less clinical and detached than Popper. In a related vein is

14

PATTERNS OF DISCOVERY (21) by N.R. Hanson. Less widely read, and at times difficult, Hanson's book is rewarding and elegant.

Some of the disputes which have gone on in the philosophy of science were put together in Lakatos and Musgrave CRITICISM AND THE GROWTH OF KNOWLEDGE (34), a symposium in which both Popper and Kuhn have substantial contributions. An important essay here is Lakatos' own paper 'Falsification and the Methodology of Scientific Research Programmes'.

This is not a comprehensive list of the books on the philosophy of the science or anything remotely like it. However, they are helpful to anyone interested in the foundations of the discipline. Obviously the more one knows about the natural sciences (particularly physics) the better, but, except perhaps for Hanson's book, the arguments can be followed without any scientific training.

The Philosophy of the Social Sciences

The philosophy of the social sciences is deeply reft by totally inconsistent viewpoints, very crudely, between those who hold that social phenomena can be analysed, generally speaking, in a manner closely parallel to those of the natural sciences, and those who hold that this is totally out of the question.

Two introductory books on the philosophy of the social sciences are Alan Ryan THE PHILOSOPHY OF THE SOCIAL SCIENCES (52) and Richard Rudner THE PHILOSOPHY OF SOCIAL SCIENCE (48).

A defiant assertion of the validity of the scientific school is made by Carl Hempel with his paper on 'The Function of General Laws in History' in ASPECTS OF SCIENTIFIC EXPLANATION (26). (The paper was originally published in JOURNAL OF PHILOSOPHY, 1940.) This paper is well worth reading as it has the twin virtues of being a clear exposition of the 'Covering Law Model' of explanation while applying it to that discipline, History, which by common consent is one of the hardest to fit into this framework. If the model applies in History, then it applies to the rest of the social sciences without additional assumptions. The issues concerning explanation in History are argued in two excellent short books: one, by P.L. Gardiner THE NATURE OF HISTORICAL EXPLANATION (14), argues for scientific explanations in History, and the other by W.H. Dray, LAWS AND EXPLANATION IN HISTORY (10), contains a counter-argument. A collection of essays edited by P.L. Gardiner PHILOSOPHY OF HISTORY (15) provides a good survey of the controversies. The most vigorous, almost strident exponent of the view that social science as modelled on the natural sciences is impossible is Peter Winch (60). In some respects a curiously similar argument is presented from a Marxist point of view by Lucien Goldmann in THE HUMAN SCIENCES AND PHILOSOPHY (17). Charles Taylor's THE EXPLANATION OF BEHAVIOUR (55) is a more sober work and obligatory for anyone other than the dilettante. EXPLANATION AND UNDERSTANDING (58) by G.H. Von Wright contains the hardest but by far the most intellectually convincing version of the argument.

The general positivist case is most clearly stated by Milton Friedman with respect to Economics in ESSAYS IN POSITIVE ECONOMICS (13). This has had great influence amongst economists but also amongst other social scientists. An application of the methodology to a more tendentious field is THE LOGIC OF EXPLANATION IN PSYCHO-ANALYSIS (54) by Michael Sherwood. Along with History, it might be thought (although in my view incorrectly) that Psycho-Analysis is the area to which the deductivist approach is least applicable.

Political Science and International Relations

Whether International Relations and Political Science can usefully be separated is arguable. However, they do raise substantially the same methodological problems. The issues are largely the same as in the rest of the social sciences except that, historically, their development has been a little different. Rather crudely, the 'traditionalists' uphold a view compatible with that of Winch, and the 'behaviouralists' uphold a view compatible with Hempel. The issues are stated in a collection of essays edited by K. Knorr and J.N. Rosenau called CONTENDING APPROACHES TO INTERNATIONAL POLITICS (32). The classical or traditional view is defended in a well known essay in that collection by Hedley Bull. Charles Reynold's THEORY AND EXPLANATION IN INTERNATIONAL POLITICS (47) confines itself to International Relations while AN INTRODUCTION TO METAPOLITICS (19) by A. James Gregor deals with the Political Sciences as a whole.

Amongst those who are in some sense 'scientific' in their approach to International Relations there are inevitable controversies about method, even if the nature of the end product is broadly agreed upon. There is a question of emphasis on whether our relative lack of under-standing of the international system is due to a shortage of data or whether there is a shortage of theory. In particular, there is some disagreement about the significance to be given to quantitative studies.

16

The two contending attitudes are clearly stated in Oran Young's 'Professor Russett: Industrious Tailor to a Naked Emperor' (61) and Russett's reply 'The Young Science of International Politics' (51). Discussions on method are clearly grounded in debates on their presuppositions, but this leads us into the subject matter of our second chapter on methods.

Bibliography

1. Archibald, G.C., 'Refutation or Comparison', BRITISH JOURNAL FOR PHILOSOPHY OF SCIENCE, Volume 17, (4) February 1967, pp. 279–296
2. Ayer, A.J., THE PROBLEM OF KNOWLEDGE, Harmondsworth, Middx., Penguin, 1956. Also London & New York, Macmillan, 1956
3. Blaug, M., 'Kuhn versus Lakatos, or paradigms versus research programmes in the history of economics', HISTORY OF POLITICAL ECONOMY, Volume 7, Winter 1975, pp. 399–433
4. Braithwaite, R.B., SCIENTIFIC EXPLANATION, Cambridge, Cambridge University Press, 1953
5. Brodbeck, M. (ed.), READINGS IN THE PHILOSOPHY OF THE SOCIAL SCIENCES, New York, Macmillan, 1968
6. Brown, R., EXPLANATION IN SOCIAL SCIENCE, Chicago, Aldine Press, 1963
7. Charlesworth, J.C. (ed.), THE LIMITATIONS OF BEHAVIOUR-ALISM IN POLITICAL SCIENCE, Philadelphia, American Academy of Political and Social Science, 1962
8. Clarkson, G.P.E., THE THEORY OF CONSUMER DEMAND: A CRITICAL APPRAISAL, Englewood Cliffs, N.J., Prentice Hall, 1963 (Deals extensively with epistemological issues)
9. Deutsch, K.W., 'On Political Theory and Political Action', AMERICAN POLITICAL SCIENCE REVIEW, Volume 65, March 1971, pp. 11–27
10. Dray, W.H., LAWS AND EXPLANATIONS IN HISTORY, London, Oxford Classical and Philosophical Manuscripts, 1957
11. Feyerabend, P., AGAINST METHOD: OUTLINE OF AN ANARCHISTIC THEORY OF KNOWLEDGE, London, New Left Books, 1975
12. Frank, P.G. (ed.), THE VALIDATION OF SCIENTIFIC THEORIES, New York, Collier Books, 1961
13. Friedman, M. ESSAYS IN POSITIVE ECONOMICS, Chicago,

University of Chicago Press, 1953

14. Gardiner, P.L., THE NATURE OF HISTORICAL EXPLANATION, London, Oxford University Press, 1965. (First published in 1952)
15. Gardiner, P.L. (ed.), THE PHILOSOPHY OF HISTORY, London, Oxford University Press, 1974
16. Giddens, A. (ed.), POSITIVISM AND SOCIOLOGY, London, Heinemann, 1974
17. Goldmann, L., THE HUMAN SCIENCES AND PHILOSOPHY, (translated by Hayden V. White and Robert Anchor) London, Jonathan Cape, 1969
18. Goodman, N., FACT, FICTION AND FORECAST, (2nd Edition), Indianapolis, Bobbs-Merrill, 1965
19. Gregor, A.J., AN INTRODUCTION TO METAPOLITICS, New York, The Free Press, 1971
20. Gunnell, J.G., Goldberg, S. & Gregor, A.J., 'Symposium of Scientific Explanation in Political Science', AMERICAN POLITICAL SCIENCE REVIEW, Volume 63, December 1969, pp. 1233—1262
21. Hanson, N.R., PATTERNS OF DISCOVERY, Cambridge, Cambridge University Press, 1958
22. Hanson, N.R., OBSERVATION AND EXPLANATION: A GUIDE TO PHILOSOPHY OF SCIENCE, New York, Harper & Row, 1971
23. Harré, R., THE PHILOSOPHIES OF SCIENCE: AN INTRO-DUCTORY SURVEY, London, Oxford University Press, 1972
24. Harré, R. & Secord, P.F., THE EXPLANATION OF SOCIAL BEHAVIOUR, Oxford, Basil Blackwell, 1972
25. Hempel, C.G., PHILOSOPHY OF NATURAL SCIENCE, (Foundations of Philosophy Series), Englewood Cliffs, N.J., Prentice Hall, 1966
26. Hempel, C.G. (ed.), ASPECTS OF SCIENTIFIC EXPLANATION, AND OTHER ESSAYS, London and New York, Collier-Macmillan, 1965
27. Hempel, C.G., ASPECTS OF CONCEPT FORMATION IN EMPIRICAL SCIENCE, International Encyclopaedia of Unified Science, Chicago, University of Chicago Press, 1967
28. Hempel, C.G., 'The Function of General Laws in History' in ASPECTS OF SCIENTIFIC EXPLANATION, AND OTHER ESSAYS, London and New York, Collier-Macmillan, 1965
29. Hirschman, A.O., 'The Search for Paradigms as a Hindrance to Understanding', WORLD POLITICS, Volume XXII (3), April 1970, pp. 329—343

30. Hudson, L., THE CULT OF THE FACT, London, Jonathan Cape, 1972
31. Kalleberg, A.L., 'Concept Formulation in Normative and Empirical Studies: Toward Reconstruction in Political Theory', AMERICAN POLITICAL SCIENCE REVIEW, Volume 63, March 1969, pp. 26– 39
32. Knorr, K. & Rosenau, J.N. (eds.), CONTENDING APPROACHES TO INTERNATIONAL POLITICS, Princeton, N.J., Princeton University Press, 1970
33. Kuhn, T.S., THE STRUCTURE OF SCIENTIFIC REVOLUTIONS, (2nd Edition), (International Encyclopaedia of Unified Science), Chicago, University of Chicago Press, 1970
34. Lakatos, I. & Musgrave, A. (eds.), CRITICISM AND THE GROWTH OF KNOWLEDGE: PROCEEDINGS OF THE INTERNATIONAL COLLOQUIUM IN THE PHILOSOPHY OF SCIENCE, (International Colloquium in the Philosophy of Science 1965), Cambridge, Cambridge University Press, 1970
35. Louch, A.R., EXPLANATION AND HUMAN ACTION, Oxford, Basil Blackwell, 1966
36. Magee, B., POPPER, London, Fontana Modern Masters Series, 1973
37. Meehan, E.J., EXPLANATION IN SOCIAL SCIENCE, Homewood, Illinois, Dorsey Press, 1968
38. Miller, F., 'Positivism, Historicism and Political Inquiry', AMERICAN POLITICAL SCIENCE REVIEW, Volume 66, September 1972, pp. 796–873
39. Nagel, E., THE STRUCTURE OF SCIENCE: PROBLEMS IN THE LOGIC OF SCIENTIFIC EXPLANATION, London, Routledge & Kegan Paul, 1961
40. Nidditch, P.H. (ed.), PHILOSOPHY OF SCIENCE, London, Oxford University Press, 1968
41. Novak, G., AN INTRODUCTION TO THE LOGIC OF MARXISM, (5th Edition), New York, Pathfinder Press, 1971
42. Phillips, W.R., 'Where have all the theories gone?', WORLD POLITICS, Volume XXVI (2), January 1974, pp. 155–188
43. Popper, K.R., CONJECTURES AND REFUTATIONS: THE GROWTH OF SCIENTIFIC KNOWLEDGE, (3rd Edition), London, Routledge & Kegan Paul, 1969
44. Popper, K.R., THE LOGIC OF SCIENTIFIC DISCOVERY, London, Hutchinson, 1959. (Originally published in German as LOGIK DER FORSCHUNG, Vienna, 1935)

45. Popper, K.R., THE POVERTY OF HISTORICISM, New York, Harper & Row, 1957
46. Ravetz, J.R., SCIENTIFIC KNOWLEDGE AND ITS SOCIAL PROBLEMS, London, Oxford University Press, 1971. (Also Harmondsworth, Penguin University Books, 1973)
47. Reynolds, C., THEORY AND EXPLANATION IN INTERNATIONAL POLITICS, London, Martin Robertson, 1973
48. Rudner, R., PHILOSOPHY OF SOCIAL SCIENCE, (Foundations of Philosophy Series), Englewood Cliffs, N.J., Prentice Hall, 1966
49. Runciman, W.G., SOCIAL SCIENCE AND POLITICAL THEORY, Cambridge, Cambridge University Press, 1965
50. Russell, B., HUMAN KNOWLEDGE: ITS SCOPE AND LIMITS, London, Allen & Unwin, 1948. (Also New York, Simon & Schuster, 1948)
51. Russett, B.M., 'The Young Science of International Politics', WORLD POLITICS, Volume XXII, (1) October 1969, pp. 87–94
52. Ryan, A.P., THE PHILOSOPHY OF THE SOCIAL SCIENCES, London, Macmillan, 1970
53. Ryan, A.P. (ed.), THE PHILOSOPHY OF SOCIAL EXPLANATION, London, Oxford University Press, 1973
54. Sherwood, M., THE LOGIC OF EXPLANATION IN PSYCHOANALYSIS, New York and London, Academic Press, 1969
55. Taylor, C., THE EXPLANATION OF BEHAVIOUR, London and New York, Routledge and Kegan Paul, 1964
56. Toulmin, S., PHILOSOPHY OF SCIENCE, London, Hutchinson, 1953
57. Van Dyke, V., POLITICAL SCIENCE: A PHILOSOPHICAL ANALYSIS, Stanford, California, Stanford University Press, 1960
58. Von Wright, G., EXPLANATION AND UNDERSTANDING, London, Routledge and Kegan Paul, 1971
59. Walsh, W.H., AN INTRODUCTION TO PHILOSOPHY OF HISTORY, London, Hutchinson University Library, 1967
60. Winch, P., THE IDEA OF A SOCIAL SCIENCE, London, Routledge and Kegan Paul, 1970
61. Young, O.R., 'Professor Russett: Industrious Tailor to a Naked Emperor', WORLD POLITICS, Volume XXI (3), April 1969, pp. 486–511

Chapter II

RESEARCH METHODS IN INTERNATIONAL RELATIONS

by
John C. Fahy, University of Maryland (European Division) and
Nancy Wilshusen Fahy, University of Southern California

Introduction

The study of human behaviour, of which the discipline of International
Relations is only a part, relies heavily upon research for its development: research conducted in the laboratory, in the library, in the
classroom, or in the field. Research forms an integral part of any field
of knowledge. It facilitates learning by testing ideas, notions,
hypotheses and theories. The manner in which one undertakes a
research problem is up to the student; there is no one 'correct' or
'single' methodology. In many ways this is determined by the research
question itself.

Over the past two decades, much of the research in International
Relations has shared the characteristics of the other social sciences.
Scientific method is being applied to problems of international
behaviour; data are being gathered, coded, and stored for present and
future use by the academic community; and techniques heretofore
utilized primarily by the 'hard' sciences are being used in the analysis
of data. What follows is a brief overview of the literature that
addresses itself to the techniques being applied in International
Relations research today. It should be viewed as an indicative guide
from which a solid methodological foundation can be built; it is not
intended to be an exhaustive review of the literature.

Research Techniques — General Texts

The preliminary and perhaps most essential step of any research task is a careful definition of the research problem. A significant quantity of time and scarce resources can be saved if care is taken in framing the research problem first before collecting data. A careful reading of Ted Gurr's POLITIMETRICS (9) should convince the reader of the merits of this initial task. This short text is a valuable guide to the initial phases of problem selection and definition, specification and operationalization of concepts, data collection rules and processing. Although the text also contains cursory discussions of some statistical techniques, these discussions are useful only as superficial overviews of the various methods.

Somewhat more useful to the uninitiated researcher with little or no training in statistics might be Garson's HANDBOOK OF POLITICAL SCIENCE METHODS (7). This text alone is not sufficient to gain a command of many of the techniques discussed but it is un-complicated and well written and would be valuable as a companion to a more sophisticated statistical text.

Moroney's FACTS FROM FIGURES (15) provides an excellent foundation for statistical analysis and it is advisable that the neophyte begin here. The book was written for non-mathematicians and begins at 'Square One' — a discussion of probability and the laws of chance. Although the book neglects many of the more advanced statistical tools, too few texts can match this work in laying a solid foundation for building up to the more complex methods.

Blalock's SOCIAL STATISTICS (3) has long been recognized as a seminal work in its field. The author discusses probability, hypothesis testing, univariate descriptive statistics, bivariate and multivariate statistics, as well as sampling, significance tests, and analysis of variance. Although Blalock states in the preface that 'the text has been written so as to avoid mathematical derivations insofar as possible,' the reader is somewhat burdened by its dry approach, emphasizing theory and computational formulae and a concomitant lack of real world examples. Some of the more advanced methods such as factor analysis are beyond the scope of this book. Nevertheless, SOCIAL STATISTICS is highly recommended both as a textbook and reference source.

For the more advanced student, Galtung's THEORY AND METHODS OF SOCIAL RESEARCH (6) and Zinnes' CONTEM-PORARY RESEARCH IN INTERNATIONAL RELATIONS (22) are solid general texts. Galtung combines a discussion of philosophy of science with mathematical techniques. The book is divided into two sections: data collection and data analysis. The author is concerned more with what can be accomplished with social science methods than he is with mathematical formulae *per se*. A familiarity with elementary methods and techniques is assumed. Zinnes' book is valuable because of its rather different approach. She illustrates various research techniques through studies that have been conducted in International Relations. Three general categories are treated: 1) data collection, index construction, and concept measurement; 2) a study of hypothesis testing; 3) presentation of formal models that treat issues central to International Relations, (e.g. conflict models, simulation models). The book serves as a good illustration of what may be accomplished with diverse research tools.

Rounding out this discussion of general texts, mention must be made of the STATISTICAL PACKAGE FOR THE SOCIAL SCIENCES (SPSS) (16). Not only is this manual useful as a guide to data processing, but it is also valuable for its discussion of general statistical techniques. Most chapters include both a discussion of SPSS subprogrammes with respect to a *particular* technique and a discussion of the *general* applications of that technique, with diagrams and examples to illustrate major points. Those readers relatively unfamiliar with statistical methods should find this manual one of the more useful reference sources. Kenneth Janda's DATA PROCESSING (12) should be consulted by those wishing to acquaint themselves with the rudiments of this art. It contains many helpful suggestions for collecting, coding and managing data, and is a worthy example of Northwestern University Press' series HANDBOOKS FOR RESEARCH IN POLITICAL BEHAVIOUR.

Specific Techniques

Should research require the collapsing of a large number of variables into a smaller, more manageable number of underlying factors, Rummel's APPLIED FACTOR ANALYSIS (19) is highly recommended. Rummel has contributed a comprehensive, relatively non-technical treatment of factor analysis, geared to social science applications. General discussions of mathematical prerequisites are also included.

Thomas Bayes' theorem has proved to be useful to some research tasks, particularly those involving decision-making under conditions of uncertainty. This approach allows the making of inferences about a population based on a sample as opposed to the classical approaches which treat the population as fixed or given. It allows for a constant revision of probability estimates. McGowan's article, 'A Bayesian Approach to the Problem of Events Data Validity' (14) is especially well written and should serve as a firm introduction to the Bayesian approach. For a more comprehensive treatment the reader should refer to Bayes (2), or Box and Tiao (4).

Content analysis is a technique used to measure or describe the characteristics of either written or verbal communication with respect to a particular quality or attribute of that communication — usually one which is difficult to measure directly, or for which other data are inaccessible. The attempt to measure perceptions or attitudes of a particular leader through the coding and quantification of specific verbal or written cues is a familiar example. Ole Holsti has produced a convenient introduction and guide in CONTENT ANALYSIS FOR THE SOCIAL SCIENCES AND HUMANITIES (11). He explains when it may be used, offers helpful suggestions about coding, sampling, measuring validity and reliability of data, and provides many examples to elucidate his points. A very ample bibliography is also presented for those wishing to delve more deeply into particular topics. Robert North and his colleagues (including Holsti) provide another good general guide in their book, CONTENT ANALYSIS: A HANDBOOK WITH APPLICATIONS FOR THE STUDY OF INTERNATIONAL CRISES (17) especially in regard to coding and scaling methods.

For a thorough discussion of event interaction analysis consult Azar and Ben-Dak's THEORY AND PRACTICE OF EVENTS RESEARCH (1). In general, event interaction analysis is a research technique which attempts to identify typical or atypical interaction patterns among specified actors by categorizing and quantifying interactions among these actors across time as reported in public sources of information. McClelland and Young (13) should be consulted for the specifics of coding.

A number of available books spanning diverse disciplines describe and explain simulation as an experimental tool. Only a few will be mentioned here. Simulation is commonly employed when it is not possible to experiment directly with an actual situation or environment, or when one wishes to foresee how a hypothetical system might evolve. Quite simply, simulation affords greater control over experimental variables than would be otherwise possible in a non-modeled situation. Coplin (5), Guetzkow (8), and Hermann (10), taken individually or together, should furnish sufficient guidance to the potential advantages and limitations, as well as the mechanics, of simulation exercises.

Game theory is a burgeoning field of inquiry which had its theoretical origin with von Neumann and Morgenstern (21). At its simplest, game theory is a study of decision-making in a conflictual situation. It focuses on bargaining and choice within the context of attempting to define an optimal strategy to attain a desired (or acceptable) goal depending upon the rules of the game and the specified alternatives. The strategy requires mapping each player's set of alternative choices with those of his opponents, and assigning payoff and probability of occurrence values to each prospective outcome. Rapoport's STRATEGY AND CONSCIENCE (18) is a significant theoretical contribution to the literature, as he examines the application of game theory to military and defence strategies. Martin Shubik (20) is the editor of a collection of short articles which draws from psychological, sociological, and political perspectives as they apply to various bargaining, negotiation, and threat situations. In general, the JOURNAL OF CONFLICT RESOLUTION is an excellent source of articles for specific applications of game theory, as well as for many of the other research techniques discussed above.

Bibliography

1. Azar, E. and Ben-Dak, J.D. (eds.), THEORY AND PRACTICE OF EVENTS RESEARCH, New York, Gordon and Breach, 1975
2. Bayes, T., 'An Essay toward solving a Problem in the Doctrine of Chances: with a Biographical Note by G.A. Barnard', BIOMETRIKA, Volume 45, December 1958, pp. 293–315
3. Blalock, H.M., SOCIAL STATISTICS, (2nd Edition), New York, McGraw-Hill, 1972, (First published 1960)
4. Box, G.E.P. and Tiao, G.C., BAYESIAN INFERENCE IN STATISTICAL ANALYSIS, Reading, Mass., Addison-Wesley, 1972
5. Coplin, W.D., SIMULATION IN THE STUDY OF POLITICS, Chicago, Markham, 1968
6. Galtung, J., THEORY AND METHODS OF SOCIAL RESEARCH, London, George Allen and Unwin, 1967
7. Garson, G.D., HANDBOOK OF POLITICAL SCIENCE METHODS, Boston, Holbrook Press Inc., 1971
8. Guetzkow, H., SIMULATION IN INTERNATIONAL RELATIONS,

Englewood Cliffs, N.J., Prentice Hall, 1963

9. Gurr, T.R., POLITIMETRICS: AN INTRODUCTION TO QUANTITATIVE MACROPOLITICS, Englewood Cliffs, N.J., Prentice Hall, 1972

10. Hermann, C.F., CRISES IN FOREIGN POLICY: A SIMULATION ANALYSIS, Indianapolis, Bobbs-Merrill, 1969

11. Holsti, O.R., CONTENT ANALYSIS FOR THE SOCIAL SCIENCES AND HUMANITIES, Reading, Mass., Addison-Wesley, 1969

12. Janda, K., DATA PROCESSING: APPLICATIONS TO POLITICAL RESEARCH, Evanston, Illinois, Northwestern University Press, 1965

13. McClelland, C.A. and Young, R.A., WORLD EVENT/INTER-ACTION SURVEY HANDBOOK AND CODEBOOK, (WEIS Technical Report No. 1), Los Angeles, University of Southern California, 1969

14. McGowan, P.J., 'A Bayesian Approach to the Problem of Events Data Validity', in Rosenau J.N. (ed.), COMPARING FOREIGN POLICIES, New York, John Wiley, 1974

15. Moroney, M.J., FACTS FROM FIGURES, Harmondsworth, Middx., Penguin Books, 1951

16. Nie, N. et al, STATISTICAL PACKAGE FOR THE SOCIAL SCIENCES (SPSS), (2nd Edition), New York, McGraw Hill, 1975

17. North, R.C., et al, CONTENT ANALYSIS: A HANDBOOK WITH APPLICATIONS FOR THE STUDY OF INTERNATIONAL CRISES, Evanston, Illinois, Northwestern University Press, 1963

18. Rapoport, A., STRATEGY AND CONSCIENCE, New York, Harper and Row, 1964

19. Rummel, R.J., APPLIED FACTOR ANALYSIS, Evanston, Illinois, Northwestern University Press, 1970

20. Shubik, M. (ed.), GAME THEORY AND RELATED APPROACHES TO SOCIAL BEHAVIOUR, New York, John Wiley, 1964

21. Von Neumann, J., and Morgenstern, O., THE THEORY OF GAMES AND ECONOMIC BEHAVIOUR, (2nd Edition), Princeton, N.J., Princeton University Press, 1947

22. Zinnes, D.A., CONTEMPORARY RESEARCH IN INTERNATIONAL RELATIONS: A PERSPECTIVE AND CRITICAL APPRAISAL, New York, The Free Press, 1976

Chapter III

INTERNATIONAL RELATIONS TEXTBOOKS

by Frances Pinter
Oxford University

Textbooks reflect both the changing issue-areas of concern to
International Relations scholars, and the changing approaches thought
most appropriate and fruitful for studying the subject matter. Of
course, these two elements are related, but one would have difficulties
imagining Machiavelli using a computer to test his well-known maxims.
Although the study of inter-state relations has been with us for a long
time, the subject area took on new dimensions at the turn of the
century when academics in the United States tried to understand the
involvement of that country in European and Asian affairs. These
studies, as well as those carried out by European scholars, were on the
whole analyses of the ever increasing number of treaties and perceived
obligations under international law. After the First World War textbooks became increasingly moralistic. From the 'normative' school a
number of books emerged which were highly value laden, preaching
world peace through institutions, organizations, and international law.
Analysis was concerned with discovering how and why states had
made such tragic mistakes resulting in war. The rise of Hitler and
fascism resulting in the Second World War brought about disillusion-
ment with the normative approach.

In 1948 Hans Morgenthau published his famous POLITICS AMONG
NATIONS (28) which through many updated editions stands as the
definitive work on power politics. The post-war flock of textbooks
became more analytical and stressed the need for generalisations with

explantory power. On the whole these were still historical in their approach (see, for example, Schuman (40), Hartmann (15), Greene (14) or Palmer and Perkins (32)). By the early sixties, however, the behavioural sciences were even making inroads into International Relations, and while new research methods were being introduced there was also a change in focus from purely inter-state diplomacy to such areas as integration, patterns of trade, and interdependence. New conceptual tools were borrowed from other disciplines, refined, and applied to the now more diverse subject matter. Theories on conflict behaviour, communication, and perception, to name a few, were developed and utilised. The cobweb model (best developed as a text in John Burton's WORLD SOCIETY (3)) incorporated all transactions taking place in the world, including religious, ethnic, and functional interaction, as well as inter-state diplomatic behaviour. It was set in competition with the billiard-ball model which still proclaimed inter-state behaviour as paramount within the international system. A recent and valuable assessment of some of the more esoteric developments stemming from the former approach is Ralph Pettman's concise book HUMAN BEHAVIOUR AND WORLD POLITICS (33) which attempts to set the transdisciplinary approach to international studies into the broader context of more conventional International Relations scholarship and does so in a successful, but by no means uncritical fashion.

Most of the recent textbooks stress the teaching of concepts. One popular hybrid, however, bridging historical and behavioural approaches is K.J. Holsti's INTERNATIONAL POLITICS: A FRAMEWORK FOR ANALYSIS (17). According to a survey of 178 introductory courses in International Relations by James N. Rosenau et. al. (29) Holsti's book was the second most assigned text. (Morgenthau led by one point.)

William Coplin, in his INTRODUCTION TO INTERNATIONAL POLITICS: A THEORETICAL OVERVIEW (5), covers many of the traditional areas of concern, but through a social science perspective. He discusses the trends in the field, familiarising the reader with the conflicts within the discipline. It is a popular text in the United States today, and can be used as the core of an introductory course. Another attempt at an all-inclusive textbook is Ivo Duchacek's NATIONS AND MEN (8). Its particular strength lies in its ability to make complex processes understandable to the uninitiated student.

Karl Deutsch's THE ANALYSIS OF INTERNATIONAL RELATIONS (7) is an ideal companion to core material in an introductory course. Deutsch is particularly good at producing clear and succinct definitions, which students find helpful when reading other material. Charles McClelland, one of the leading figures in the development of quantitative methods, has written a short and concise book called THEORY AND THE INTERNATIONAL SYSTEM (25), now, unfortunately, out of print. While this is by no means a central text, it is one of the most popular statements on the use of theory in the field. David Edward's book INTERNATIONAL POLITICAL ANALYSIS (10) is a significant contribution to explaining the process of analysing within the field, rather than a guide to the field itself. While it may be too complex for an early undergraduate, it is essential reading for the student specialising in the field and carrying out post-graduate work. Robert Lieber's short THEORY AND WORLD POLITICS (24) explores the potential of scientific theory in International Relations. The format of the book is that of a compendium of analytic tools, rather than a collection of specific issue-related theories. For the person wanting concise guidance to the techniques of theory building, data-gathering, and testing, together with some applications in the international sphere, a handy little book has been published by Davis Bobrow called INTERNATIONAL RELATIONS: NEW APPROACHES (2).

Finally, a recent survey by Michael Sullivan looks back over more than a decade of behavioural research in International Relations, and examines the theories developed and tested during the period by behaviouralists using 'scientific' methods and techniques. While hardly a textbook in any conventional sense, INTERNATIONAL RELATIONS; THEORIES AND EVIDENCE (44) is nonetheless highly recommendable as an up-to-date report on the fruits of an extremely successful protest in international studies, and is essential reading for anyone interested in the 'how' of International Relations, as well as the 'what'.

The summary list below contains many books not mentioned above. Those selected for the discussion represent the wide range of textbook types available in a field where there is no general consensus as to the nature of the subject, nor the methods to be used in its study.

Bibliography

1. Axline, A.N. and Stegenga, J., THE GLOBAL COMMUNITY: A BRIEF INTRODUCTION TO INTERNATIONAL RELATIONS, New York, Dodd Mead, 1972
2. Bobrow, D., INTERNATIONAL RELATIONS: NEW

29

APPROACHES, London and New York, Collier-Macmillan, 1973

3. Burton, J.W., WORLD SOCIETY, London, Cambridge University Press, 1972

4. Cantor, R., INTRODUCTION TO INTERNATIONAL POLITICS, Itasca, Illinois, F.E. Peacock, 1976

5. Coplin, W., INTRODUCTION TO INTERNATIONAL POLITICS: A THEORETICAL OVERVIEW, Chicago, Markham Publishing Co., 1971

6. Crabb, C.V., NATIONS IN A MULTIPOLAR WORLD, New York, Harper and Row, 1968

7. Deutsch, K.W., THE ANALYSIS OF INTERNATIONAL RELATIONS, Englewood Cliffs, N.J., Prentice Hall, 1969

8. Duchacek, I.D., NATIONS AND MEN: AN INTRODUCTION TO INTERNATIONAL POLITICS, New York, Holt, Rinehart and Winston, 1971

9. Dougherty, J.E. and Pfaltzgraff, R., Jr., CONTENDING THEORIES OF INTERNATIONAL RELATIONS, Philadelphia, Lippincott, 1971

10. Edwards, D.V., INTERNATIONAL POLITICAL ANALYSIS, New York, Holt, Rinehart and Winston, 1969

11. Frankel, J., CONTEMPORARY INTERNATIONAL THEORY AND THE BEHAVIOUR OF STATES, London, Oxford University Press, 1973

12. Frankel, J., INTERNATIONAL POLITICS: CONFLICT AND HARMONY, Harmondsworth, Middlesex, Penguin Press, 1973

13. Frankel, J., INTERNATIONAL RELATIONS, (2nd edition), London, Oxford University Press, 1969

14. Greene, F., DYNAMICS OF INTERNATIONAL RELATIONS: POWER, SECURITY, AND ORDER, New York, Holt, Rinehart and Winston, 1964

15. Hartmann, F., THE RELATIONS OF NATIONS (4th Edition), London, Macmillan, 1974, (First published in 1962)

16. Hill, N., INTERNATIONAL POLITICS, New York, Harper and Row, 1963

17. Holsti, K.J., INTERNATIONAL POLITICS: A FRAMEWORK FOR ANALYSIS, (3rd Edition), Englewood Cliffs, N.J., Prentice Hall, 1976

18. Hopkins, R. and Mansbach, R.W., STRUCTURE AND PROCESS IN INTERNATIONAL POLITICS, New York, Harper and Row, 1973

19. Isaak, R.A., INDIVIDUALS AND WORLD POLITICS, North Scituate, Mass., Duxbury Press, 1975
20. Jordan, D.C., WORLD POLITICS IN OUR TIME, Lexington, Mass., D.C. Heath, 1970
21. Kulski, W.W., INTERNATIONAL POLITICS IN A REVOLUTION-ARY AGE, New York, Lippincott, 1964
22. Legg, K.R. and Morrison, J., POLITICS AND THE INTER-NATIONAL SYSTEM: AN INTRODUCTION, New York, Harper and Row, 1971
23. Levi, W., INTERNATIONAL POLITICS, Minneapolis, University of Minnesota Press, 1974
24. Lieber, R.J., THEORY AND WORLD POLITICS, London, Allen and Unwin, 1973
25. McClelland, C.A., THEORY AND THE INTERNATIONAL SYSTEM, New York, Macmillan, 1966
26. Modelski, G., PRINCIPLES OF WORLD POLITICS, New York, The Free Press, 1972
27. Morgan, P.M., THEORIES AND APPROACHES TO INTER-NATIONAL POLITICS, San Ramon, Calif., Consensus Publishers, 1972
28. Morgenthau, H.J., POLITICS AMONG NATIONS: THE STRUGGLE FOR POWER AND PEACE, (5th edition), New York, Alfred Knopf, 1973 (First published in 1948)
29. Northedge, F., THE INTERNATIONAL POLITICAL SYSTEM, London, Faber and Faber, 1976
30. Organski, A.F.K., WORLD POLITICS, New York, Alfred Knopf, 1968
31. Padelford, N. and Lincoln, G., THE DYNAMICS OF INTER-NATIONAL POLITICS, New York, Macmillan, 1967
32. Palmer, N.D. and Perkins, H.C., INTERNATIONAL RELATIONS: THE WORLD COMMUNITY IN TRANSITION, (3rd edition), Boston, Houghton Mifflin, 1969
33. Pettman, R., HUMAN BEHAVIOUR AND WORLD POLITICS: AN INTRODUCTION TO INTERNATIONAL RELATIONS, London, Macmillan, 1975
34. Puchala, D.J., INTERNATIONAL POLITICS TODAY, New York, Dodd, Mead, 1971
35. Purnell, R., THE SOCIETY OF STATES: AN INTRODUCTION TO INTERNATIONAL POLITICS, London, Weidenfeld and Nicholson, 1973

36. Reynolds, P.A., AN INTRODUCTION TO INTERNATIONAL RELATIONS, London, Longmans, 1972
37. Rosecrance, R.N., INTERNATIONAL RELATIONS: PEACE OR WAR, New York, McGraw-Hill, 1973
38. Rosen, S.J. and Jones, W.S., THE LOGIC OF INTERNATIONAL RELATIONS, Cambridge, Mass., Winthrop Publishers, 1974
39. Rosenau, J.N. et al, 'Of Syllabi, Texts, Students and Scholarship in International Relations', WORLD POLITICS, XXIX(2), January 1977, pp. 263–340
40. Schuman, F.L., INTERNATIONAL POLITICS: ANARCHY AND ORDER IN THE WORLD SOCIETY, (7th edition), New York, McGraw-Hill, 1969
41. Spanier, J., GAMES NATIONS PLAY: ANALYZING INTER-NATIONAL POLITICS, New York, Praeger, 1972
42. Spiro, H., WORLD POLITICS: THE GLOBAL SYSTEM, Homewood, Illinois, Dorsey Press, 1966
43. Sterling, R., MACROPOLITICS: INTERNATIONAL RELATIONS IN A GLOBAL SOCIETY, New York, Alfred Knopf, 1974
44. Sullivan, M.P., INTERNATIONAL RELATIONS: THEORIES AND EVIDENCE, Englewood Cliffs, N.J., Prentice Hall, 1976
45. Van Dyke, V., INTERNATIONAL POLITICS, (3rd edition), New York, Appleton-Century-Crofts, 1966

Chapter IV

SYSTEMS THEORY AND INTERNATIONAL RELATIONS

by C.R. Mitchell
The City University, London

One of the more interesting developments that has taken place in the
academic world since the end of the Second World War has been the
growth of the so-called 'systems approach' within a number of
ostensibly diverse fields and disciplines. This systems 'movement' is
varied, in the nature and sources of its basic concepts, in its applications,
as well as in the form it has taken in the different fields to which it has
been applied, which range from engineering to ecology, and from
biology to sociology. The systems approach arose from a number of
separate developments which came together in the late 1940's and
early 1950's to produce a somewhat confused but nevertheless exciting
amalgam of ideas, approaches, techniques and dogma. One of its
implicit starting points was the apparent inability of conventional
modes of analysis to cope with an increasingly complex and inter-
dependent world, where policy decisions designed to deal with one
(possibly technological) problem were subsequently found to have
undesired — or, at least, unforeseen — effects upon other (possibly
social or political) factors. Thus, any approach which took as its
basic watchword the need to deal with problems on a holistic basis,
rather than piecemeal, was sure of a welcome in the second half of
the 20th century, (no matter how difficult it might be, in many cases,
to draw a systems boundary with the certainty that all the major
relevant sub-systems were included within the boundary). In short,
the systems approach was initially seen as one possible 'cure for chaos',

to use the term initially employed by a systems engineer who was also a convinced advocate of the systems approach as a panacea for society's ills (45).

More specifically, a number of different in-puts from distinct fields contributed noticeably to the development of a body of systems doctrine over the past thirty years. One original impetus came from biologists, whose concern for the structure of living organisms as systems that inter-acted with an environment, (and in some cases responded to that environment by changing their internal structure and processes) led them to consider both the advantages of studying organisms together with their environment as a unit, and those of analyzing, in a similar fashion, inter-connected aspects of highly complex organisms (the respiratory or the central nervous system in the human body, for example). In a similar fashion, engineers became increasingly concerned with problems of complicated processes, involving the use of monitoring and informational feedbacks to control those processes within desired limits; and as the possibilities of building in some form of 'artificial intelligence' increased with the development of communications technology, the discipline of systems engineering became firmly established in research centres and, ultimately, in universities. In addition, the study of information processing and the growth of the discipline of cybernetics had developed in a separate but parallel fashion both to the growth of systems engineering and the analysis of living systems, and had been enormously boosted by the development of complex computers and analogies (or homologies) drawn between these entities and the human brain. (One of Ross Ashby's most famous works is entitled AN INTRODUCTION TO CYBERNETICS (1); another is called DESIGN FOR A BRAIN (2).) Thus, another in-put into the general systems movement came from cyberneticians, and those interested in information science, with its esoteric terms such as negative feedback, starvation or homeostasis. Finally, the war-time example of Operations Research in applying scientific techniques to immediate, practical problems of policy and decision making, made a profound impact upon the systems movement, and gave it an immediately pragmatic bent. Knowledge, theory and analytical techniques were to be applied to pressing contemporary problems, and a range of possible answers to problems found from which managers, bureaucrats and political leaders could choose.

However, if this had been all that 'the systems movement' had to offer, it would hardly have made the impact it did in the 1960's, despite the successes of the systems engineers in space technology or other fields of automatic control. Even at first sight, the concept of a 'system' as an arrangement of particular components or elements, so interrelated as to form a whole does not appear particularly electrifying or even new, a point admitted by Ludwig von Bertalanffy (50), one of the founding fathers of the systems approach. Nor can stunning originality be claimed for the idea that systems inter-act with their environments, or that there is an excellent chance that cross-boundary flows of energy, material or information can be delineated and measured, and transfer functions established for them. This hardly seems a sufficient basis to claim for the systems approach, as does George Klir (34), that it is 'a new and radical movement in science'.

What was new and radical, however, was the claim put forward by scholars interested in the philosophical underpinnings of the approach, that particular processes, patterns of behaviour, structural properties and developmental sequences could be found in all 'real' systems, whether these were biological, social, physical or man-made. In other words, the possibility was held out that an integrating general theory about the nature and behaviour of complex systems was attainable. This would act not merely as a source of simple analogies between different types of system, but as an over-arching and unifying grand theory to explain the behaviour of complex entities at any analytic level. Thus, the centre and the most intellectually stimulating aspect of the systems movement was the possibility of developing 'general systems theory', rather than just a systems approach to problems, or a set of useful systems techniques for analysing complexity and avoiding reductionism. An indication of the high hopes for 'GST' in the early days of the systems movement can be gauged by the enthusiastic activities of the members of the Society for the Advancement of General Systems Theory (founded in 1954 and drawing members from a hugely diverse range of conventional disciplines); and by the publication of many books and articles on the application of the systems approach or GST to systems drawn from diverse disciplines. (A flavour of this early enthusiasm and diversity can be gained from Roy Grinker's symposium, (26) whose revealing title is very much a reflection of its era.)

In time, the enthusiasm for GST (and the quest for over-arching theory applicable to engineering systems as well as human societies) has waned considerably, as the enormity of the analytical task became increasingly apparent. However, the general systems aspect of the over-all systems movement has had its effects upon Political Science in general as well as on the study of International Relations so that some background knowledge about this aspect of the systems movement is necessary in order to appreciate the manner in which the movement made an impact upon the development of International Relations theory. In fact, all of the diverse aspects of 'the systems approach' had some effect on the development of International Relations during the 1960's and 1970's, so that it is well to keep the complex and rather chaotic nature of the approach at the back of one's mind when considering the uses that International Relations scholars have made of 'the systems approach'.

Systems in International Relations

With such a varied range of concepts, approaches and frameworks available, it is not surprising that individual International Relations scholars selected different aspects of the systems movement to introduce into their field. Broadly speaking, writers using the systems approach in International Relations can be classified into two groups: those scholars with Political Science or International Relations backgrounds who have borrowed systems terms and concepts and attempted to use them to throw light upon the traditional subject matter of the field; and those scholars with Systems Science or Operations Research backgrounds who have entered the International Relations field in the hope that their techniques can be applied to systems involving human groups and organizations, and especially to human decision-making processes. We deal with this latter group in a later section of this Chapter. The former, have, as noted above, adopted a number of different elements in their overall systems 'package', including various aspects of communications theory derived from the cyberneticians; the systems engineers' technique of 'black-boxing' complex sub-systems and merely analyzing in-puts and out-puts therefrom; some aspects of structure-functionalism derived from the systems approach by way of sociology; and the basic concept of isolating a complex system from its environment and studying its structure and intra-system processes with a view to analyzing the conditions of system stability or change. A number of useful overviews exist for those interested in first obtaining a broad picture of the impact of the systems approach on International Relations. The best of these is Oran Young's admirably clear and concise survey, which can be recommended to anyone coming 'cold' to the field (55). Alternatively, Wiseman's survey, although a little dated, can be used as a substitute; it is very clear on David Easton's work (53). Both Young and Wiseman deal with the impact of the systems approach on Political

Science in general. A recent, highly critical survey by Weltman confines itself more closely to the use of the systems approach in International Relations (51), and is up-to-date. Potential readers should not be put off by the book's sub-title. Equally critical is Stephen's survey article (48), published a year before Weltman's work.

Of scholars using an in-put-out-put approach to political processes, undoubtedly the best known is David Easton. Easton has adopted insights from both systems engineers and communications theorists, and produced an impressive *corpus* of work analyzing the workings of the 'political system' as a set of processes for converting in-puts from the political community (demands) into decisions about the authoritative allocation of valued resources and roles for the society, so that these will affect other types of in-put (support) into the system. While admirable in its imagination and scope, and as a major intellectual innovation by a single scholar, Easton's work still leaves many people with the impression that it only works at the level of a complicated analogy, and that while the analogy remains a most fruitful one (the present author has derived enormous benefit from Easton's basic concepts), it remains an analogy. For those interested in discovering the quality of Easton's work for themselves, the best starting point is A FRAMEWORK FOR POLITICAL ANALYSIS (2); Easton's other two major works are more complex, but rewarding (21, 22).

For the International Relations student, a prime question is whether Easton's work can be applied to the international political system, with its decentralized, ad-hoc decision-making and its lack of any element of legitimized authority regarding the way in which values are allocated. Nicholson and Reynolds discuss this point in an article which also contains a good survey of the use of the systems concept in International Relations (41). They come to the conclusion that Easton's approach, while appropriate for national political systems (i.e. the state), is hardly applicable to the international system of states. However, even if this conclusion is a valid one — and the argument is convincing — Easton's adoption of the systems approach certainly remains helpful in the analysis of the foreign policy-making process, and its influence can be seen in much of the literature of foreign policy decision-making, for example in Brecher's work on Israel (9).

The systems approach has also influenced decision-making literature in International Relations through the gradual incorporation of ideas from communications theory into the overall processes of constructing a range of options from which decision-makers choose, and then

37

learning about environmental reactions that necessitate adaption of behaviour and 'steering'. This particular systems input has percolated into the literature almost by a process of osmosis, and it is difficult to point to any individual 'step functions' in the relevant literature. More directly, the cybernetic approach in International Relations is represented by Karl Deutsch's NERVES OF GOVERNMENT an innovative and remarkably original attempt to apply cybernetic concepts and principles to political behaviour (19). A key book of the 1960's, this now appears rather less electrifying than when it was first published, although the more solid virtues of Deutsch's other basic work (18) adopting a systems approach are now much easier to appreciate and value. In retrospect, NATIONALISM AND SOCIAL COMMUNI-CATION may come to be recognized as the foundation of many aspects of 'the systems movement' in International Relations. An interesting and extremely readable introduction to the whole communications view of political behaviour (from decision-making to the formulation and activity of public opinion) is Richard Fagen's POLITICS AND COMMUNICATION (24) which can be thoroughly recommended for its ability to explain complex processes clearly and without reverting to esoteric jargon.

A third major feature of the systems approach in International Relations has been the attempt by a number of scholars to explore various aspects of the structure and functioning of 'the' international system, and to apply systems ideas to traditional International Relations concerns, such as the effect of the number of elements in that system on its stability, or the ability of the elements to survive as independent units. Much of this work has tended to ignore the basic principle of systems analysis — that a system lies in the eye of the beholder, and that one separates a system-of-interest from its environment (and hence ignores innumerable other potentially isolatable systems) as a preliminary act of classification rather than a recognition of something that exists objectively in its own right. Hence, there often seems to be an assumption that it is proper to talk about 'the' international system as consisting of state-units, their inter-actions, and patterns of activity ('changes of state') — or some regional sub-set thereof — rather than regarding this as one possible set of units and relationships among many others that could be studied systemically or systematically. (This is a position rejected by other scholars, as we note below.) While this was certainly not intended by scholars adopting this approach to 'international systems analysis', nonetheless it is one effect of their work (which forms the bulk of systems research at the global level), even if an unintended effect.

Anyone approaching this third aspect of International Relations 'systems' scholarship for the first time would do well to begin with the relevant sections of Philip Reynolds' introductory textbook (46); these are by no means easy to read, but they offer a comprehensive and sophisticated discussion of the field for those with the determination to master it. Another good, if early, survey with many interesting ideas, is Knorr and Verba's symposium on the international system (35). Anyone more historically minded might care to attempt Rosecrance's survey of 19th century Europe from a systems perspective (47), although sections of this work have to be treated with some caution. By far the most intellectually rigorous of the earlier works on international systems analysis is Morton Kaplan's SYSTEM AND PROCESS IN INTERNATIONAL POLITICS, (31). Unfortunately, it is also the most unreadable, since it demands a thorough understanding of Kaplan's meta-language before the book can be read with any profit. Some of Kaplan's later work on delineating the structure of historic international systems is less difficult to decipher (32), and certainly his ideas have had a major impact on subsequent work on the structure of other types of international system (see, for example, the discussion on stratification in our next Chapter), or on the literature of regionalism and regional sub-systems, discussed in Chapter 4. (Note particularly the articles Banks (3), Bowman (7), Brecher (8) or Zartmann (56).) A further interesting effort to supply a systems approach to a somewhat traditionally conceived international system of state elements can be found in the work of Charles McClelland (37). In one sense, the entire World Event Inter-Action Study can be seen as an effort to take McClelland's original conception of the elements in the international system and the inter-action between them, and provide a systematic body of data about various flows between units, and the patterns which emerge over time in these flows.

Not all International Relations scholars have, however, been content to apply the systems approach to the most traditionally conceived of international systems. One article by Oran Young on recognizable discontinuities of exchange and interaction within global society (54) reveal him as a direct heir of the Deutsch of NATIONALISM AND SOCIAL COMMUNICATION. However, in the most thorough-going rejection of 'the' (conventionally conceived) international system John Burton has written a series of books rejecting the idea that the state itself is a system, and hence arguing that the idea of a system of state units is a contradiction in terms (12). Burton proposes a fully fledged Deutsch-ian approach to international systems analysis, in which global society is made up of whole series of interlocking systems, nesting one within another, rather like sets of Chinese boxes, and requiring the most careful delineation and analysis before the true complexity of any situation can be revealed. Burton's work — which is often couched in deceptively straightforward and jargon-free language — centres around the idea that a state-centric approach obscures the existence of systems which cross state or 'national' boundaries, and which form the limiting sub-structure with which networks of decision-makers must cope. Burton's claim that this structure of overlapping and inter-acting networks of relationships *determines* activity at the more conventionally defined level of international politics has been contested by more conventional scholars, although his influence upon the development of a linkage politics, or transnational approaches to International Relations cannot be denied.

These developments in the application of a systems approach to International Relations are covered very adequately in Weltman (51). The second major input into International Relations scholarship has come from the Operations Research wing of the systems movement, and has mainly taken the form of the use of a systems approach in the fields of policy studies, or defence analysis.

Systems Analysis for Decision Making*

The application of Operations Research techniques to military problems during the Second World War had proved to be most fruitful. Such techniques were further developed and applied to defence problems after the War. In particular, systems analysis was applied to the problem of choosing between rival weapons systems. The advantage of systems analysis in this respect lies in its holistic character which enables the problem to be approached in terms of the function to be performed and the cost-effectiveness of different ways of fulfilling that function. But it can also embody consideration of the functions being performed themselves. Its greatest advantage is perhaps the extent to which it allows the analyst to look at the inter-actions of several lines of development which may allow the identification of undesirable consequences and the revelation of unpredicted but beneficial developments. Such analyses are, however, only good as the information upon which they

*This section was contributed by A.J.R. Groom.

are based, much of which is dependent on political parameters which represent basic value judgements. Over these there is frequently little control, and they constitute the Achilles heel of systems analysis, since no matter how rigorous and scientific the analysis the result will be misleading if the function to be performed, parts of the data and the political parameters are imbued with erroneous judgements. In such cases the systems analyst is the dupe of the decision-maker who may only be looking for a cloak of scientific legitimacy for his preconceived ideas. Such dangers and distortions are, however, not inevitable and they are clearly spelled out in the literature on the subject.

Systems analysis became an integral part of the decision-making process in defence in the United States during the tenure in office of Secretary of Defence McNamara. Mr. Healey in Britain quickly followed suit and the practice is now widespread. Hitch and McKean were two of McNamara's 'whiz-kids' and their volumes are a clear representation of the influential thinking of that period (29, 30). These are admirably supplemented by the edited volumes of Bobrow (5), Peck and Scherer (42), Quade (43) and Quade and Boucher (44). These give a good account of what was attempted and what can be done, replete with examples and *caveats* concerning the advantages and limitations of the application of systems analysis to the decision-making process in defence, and especially weapons procurement.

Systems in the Social Sciences

It will be gathered from the foregoing discussion that the impact of the overall 'systems approach' on International Relations studies has generally been diffuse, rather than direct, save in the defence area; and that the results of any systems in-put into the field are difficult to delineate, at least with any certainty. However, the overall strength of the systems movement appears to be growing rather than diminishing, so that students of International Relations, and of the social sciences at large, might care to extend their own explorations of a vast and burgeoning field in order to sample for themselves what the approach might offer them or their discipline. To some degree, this exercise has already been undertaken for sociologists, and both the book and reader by Walter Buckley (10, 11) can be thoroughly recommended as stimulating reading for social scientists in general.

Anyone wishing to start on the systems literature itself might care to begin with Churchman's introductory THE SYSTEMS APPROACH (14), but for those who find this work over-simple and who wish to obtain a broad survey of the whole field, a better starting point might be the reader edited by Emery (23) or the Open University book by John Beishon and Geoff Peters (4). Alternatively, one could start at the beginnings of the systems movement itself and consult Von Bertalanffy on GST (50), Norbert Weiner (52) or either of the Ashby books mentioned previously for the cybernetics approach (1, 2). For a biological viewpoint, James Miller's series on 'Living Systems' can be thoroughly recommended (40).

Readers unpeturbed by mathematics could then move on to the literature stemming from the field of systems engineering, and examine the way in which systems analysis has been applied to technological and (sometimes) socio-technological systems. Hare has written a good inter-mediate level work in this field (28), which could be used in conjunction with Lee's SYSTEMS ANALYSIS FRAMEWORKS (36). At a more sophisticated level, George Klir's work on GENERAL SYSTEMS THEORY has much to recommend it (33). Klir has more recently pro-duced a useful reader on the same subject, presenting a progress report on the general systems movement, that contains excellent survey articles (couched in a retrospective vein) by such founder members of the approach as Anatol Rapoport, Churchman, Buckley and (of course) Von Bertalanffy himself (34). Another reader that deserves to be better known among social scientists is that by Bossel, Klaczko and Muller (6), which contains a number of articles highly critical of the way in which the systems approach has been applied to the social sciences, and casting doubts upon the intellectual foundations of the entire enterprise. The book is also interesting in that it gives some indication of the way in which the systems approach has been adopted in Eastern Europe and the Soviet Union. For those interested in the underlying philosophy of GST and of the systems movement itself, the best course of action might be to consult the pages of the GENERAL SYSTEMS YEARBOOK, produced annually by the Society for General Systems Research (the successor to S.A.G.S.T.); or, alter-natively, to dip into Sutherland's rather forbidding work on the general philosophy of systems science (49).

Finally, a major aspect of the overall systems approach to analyzing social and political processes involves the building and testing out of complex 'dynamical' models of complicated, inter-dependent systems. It is here that the systems movement begins to impinge more directly upon International Relations once again, for many of these complex socio-technological models tend to be either regional or global models, and hence to have some intrinsic interest for International Relations scholars concerned with the structure of international systems, or some aspect thereof. Unfortunately, from an International Relations perspective, the major omission from many of the available systems models is a substantial political dimension. Most of them appear politically naive, to put criticism at its mildest. What is one to say about models that aggregate world resources, population and industrial pollution on a global basis, and where no effort is made to recognize even regional differences in distribution or political control? Efforts are currently being made to build political variables into some of the 'second generation' global models (for example, the Mesarovic-Pestel model being jointly developed in the U.S.A. and West Germany). However, a crying need at present is for some form of continuous co-operation between systems scientists and International Relations scholars. From such co-operation could come an illuminating and realistic political in-put into world modelling on the one hand, and on the other a recognition of the long term economic, human and ecological constraints within which political behaviour is not unlikely to occur.

Anyone interested in this aspect of the systems movement, and in the possibility of some form of fruitful future co-operation, has an increasing body of literature from which to choose. Probably the best known (even notorious) example of the world modelling approach remains the famous investigation into the 'limits of growth' commissioned, by the Club of Rome and carried out by Denis Meadows, (39). However, a better starting point might well be the original work by Forrester on INDUSTRIAL DYNAMICS (25), which is readable (in spite of its size); clear even to the non-specialist; and provides a methodological background with which to understand Meadows' somewhat alarming conclusions. The best critique of Meadows' work has been produced by Cole and his colleagues at the Science Policy Research Unit in Sussex University, (16) a work which can be read both as a critique of one specific model and as a warning about the process of developing complex models in general. The same source has more recently produced a comparative survey of world models, (15) mentioning both the work by Meadows and the Mesarovic-Pestel nine region inter-active model; and the work being carried out at the Fundacion Bariloche in Buenos Aires on the modelling of desirable futures, and the patterns of activity required in order to reach such futures. For up-to-date information on the state of the modelling 'art' interested scholars should consult the quarterly, FUTURES.

A final comment from the point of view of International Relations scholarship is that it is fascinating to compare the present world modelling movement with the development of simulation studies in International Relations during the 1960's. Many of the same problems can be seen as emerged in constructing such models as that used in Guetzkow's Inter-Nation Simulation, and its later derivatives (27). In this connection, it is instructive to compare Coplin's assessment of the theories and assumptions built into I.N.S. (17) with those built into Meadows' model; and to wonder whether we have progressed or regressed — at least as far as the political dimension is concerned — since the late 1950's.

Bibliography

1. Ashby, W. Ross, AN INTRODUCTION TO CYBERNETICS, New York, John Wiley, 1956
2. Ashby, W. Ross, DESIGN FOR A BRAIN, (2nd edition), New York, John Wiley, 1960
3. Banks, Michael, 'Systems Analysis and the Study of Regions', INTERNATIONAL STUDIES QUARTERLY, XIII(4) December 1969, pp. 335–360
4. Beishon, John and Peters, Geoff (eds.), SYSTEMS BEHAVIOUR, London, Harper & Row, 1972
5. Bobrow, Davis B. (ed.), WEAPONS SYSTEM DECISIONS, New York, Praeger, 1969
6. Bossell, Hartmut, Klaczko, Saloman and Muller, Norbert (eds.), SYSTEMS THEORY IN THE SOCIAL SCIENCES, Basel/Stuttgart, Birkhauser, 1976
7. Bowman, Larry W., 'The Sub-Ordinate State System of Southern Africa', INTERNATIONAL STUDIES QUARTERLY, XII(3), September 1968, pp. 231–261
8. Brecher, Michael, 'International Relations and Asian Studies; the Subordinate State System of Southern Asia', WORLD POLITICS, XV(2), January 1963, pp. 213–235
9. Brecher, Michael, THE FOREIGN POLICY SYSTEM OF ISRAEL: SETTING, IMAGES, PROCESS, London, Oxford University Press, 1972
10. Buckley, Walter, SOCIOLOGY AND MODERN SYSTEMS THEORY, Englewood Cliffs, N.J., Prentice Hall, 1967

11. Buckley, Walter (ed.), MODERN SYSTEMS RESEARCH FOR THE BEHAVIOURAL SCIENCES, Chicago, Aldine Pub. Co., 1968

12. Burton, J.W., SYSTEMS, STATES, DIPLOMACY AND RULES, Cambridge, Cambridge University Press, 1968

13. Cherry, Colin, ON HUMAN COMMUNICATION, New York, John Wiley, 1961

14. Churchman, C. West, THE SYSTEMS APPROACH, New York, Dell Pub. Co., 1968

15. Clark, John and Cole, Sam, GLOBAL SIMULATION MODELS: A COMPARATIVE STUDY, New York, John Wiley, 1975

16. Cole, H.S.D. et al (eds.), THINKING ABOUT THE FUTURE: A CRITIQUE OF 'LIMITS OF GROWTH', London, Chatto & Windus, 1973

17. Coplin, William D., 'Inter-Nation Simulation and Contemporary Theories of International Relations', AMERICAN POLITICAL SCIENCE REVIEW, LX (3), September 1966, pp. 462–478

18. Deutsch, Karl W., NATIONALISM AND SOCIAL COMMUN-ICATION, Cambridge, Mass., M.I.T. Press, 1953

19. Deutsch, Karl W., NERVES OF GOVERNMENT: MODELS OF POLITICAL COMMUNICATION AND CONTROL, New York, The Free Press, 1963

20. Easton, David, A FRAMEWORK FOR POLITICAL ANALYSIS, Englewood Cliffs, N.J., Prentice Hall, 1965

21. Easton, David, A SYSTEMS ANALYSIS OF POLITICAL LIFE, New York, John Wiley, 1965

22. Easton, David, THE POLITICAL SYSTEM, New York, Alfred Knopf, 1953

23. Emery, F.E. (ed.), SYSTEMS THINKING, Harmondsworth, Middlesex, Penguin Books, 1969

24. Fagen, Richard R., POLITICS AND COMMUNICATION, Boston, Little, Brown, 1966

25. Forrester, J.W., INDUSTRIAL DYNAMICS, Cambridge, Mass., M.I.T. Press, 1961

26. Grinker, Roy R. (ed.), TOWARDS A UNIFIED THEORY OF HUMAN BEHAVIOUR, New York, Basic Books, 1956

27. Guetzkow, H., 'A Decade of Life with the Inter-Nation Simulation' in Ralph M. Stogdill (ed.), THE PROCESS OF MODEL BUILDING IN THE BEHAVIOURAL SCIENCES, Columbus, Ohio, Ohio State University Press, 1970

28. Hare, Van Court, SYSTEMS ANALYSIS: A DIAGNOSTIC APPROACH, New York, Harcourt Brace and World, 1967

29. Hitch, C.J., DECISION-MAKING FOR DEFENCE, Berkeley, California, University of California Press, 1965

30. Hitch, C.J. and McKean, R.N., THE ECONOMICS OF DEFENSE IN THE NUCLEAR AGE, New York, Atheneum, 1965

31. Kaplan, Morton A., SYSTEM AND PROCESS IN INTERNATIONAL POLITICS, New York, John Wiley, 1957

32. Kaplan, Morton A. (ed.), NEW APPROACHES TO INTER-NATIONAL RELATIONS, New York, St. Martins Press, 1968

33. Klir, George J., AN APPROACH TO GENERAL SYSTEMS THEORY, New York, Von Nostrand, 1969

34. Klir, George J. (ed.), TRENDS IN GENERAL SYSTEMS THEORY, New York, John Wiley, 1972

35. Knorr, Klaus and Verba, Sidney (eds.), THE INTERNATIONAL SYSTEM: THEORETICAL ESSAYS, Princeton N.J., Princeton University Press, 1961

36. Lee, Alec M., SYSTEMS ANALYSIS FRAMEWORKS, London, Macmillan, 1970

37. McClelland, Charles A., THEORY AND THE INTERNATIONAL SYSTEM, New York, Macmillan, 1966

38. McKean, R.N. (ed.), ISSUES IN DEFENCE ECONOMICS, New York, Columbia University Press, 1967

39. Meadows, Donella H., Meadows, Dennis et al, THE LIMITS TO GROWTH, London, Pan Books, 1972

40. Miller, James G., LIVING SYSTEMS, New York, McGraw Hill, forthcoming*

41. Nicholson, M.B. and Reynolds, P.A., 'General Systems, The International System and the Eastonian Analysis', POLITICAL STUDIES, XV(1), February 1967, pp. 12–31

42. Peck, Merton J. and Scherer, Frederic M., THE WEAPONS ACQUISITION PROCESS: AN ECONOMIC ANALYSIS, Cambridge, Mass., Harvard University Press, 1962

43. Quade, E.S. (ed.), ANALYSIS FOR MILITARY DECISIONS, New York, North-Holland, 1970

44. Quade, E.S. and Boucher, W.I. (ed.), SYSTEMS ANALYSIS AND

*Several sections of Miller's *magnum opus* have been published in various issues of BEHAVIOURAL SCIENCE; see, particularly Volume 10, 1965, pp. 193–237 and 337–411; Volume 16, 1971, pp. 277–301; Volume 17, 1972, pp. 1–182; Volume 20, 1975, pp. 366–535; and Volume 21, 1976, pp. 320–468,

POLICY PLANNING, New York, Elsevier Scientific Publishing Co., 1968

45. Ramo, Simon, CURE FOR CHAOS: FRESH SOLUTIONS TO SOCIAL PROBLEMS THROUGH THE SYSTEMS APPROACH, New York, David McKay & Co., 1969
46. Reynolds, P.A., AN INTRODUCTION TO INTERNATIONAL RELATIONS, London, Longmans, 1971
47. Rosecrance, Richard N., ACTION AND REACTION IN WORLD POLITICS, Boston, Little, Brown, 1963
48. Stephens, J., 'An Appraisal of Some Systems Approaches to International Relations', INTERNATIONAL STUDIES QUARTERLY, XVI (3), September 1972, pp. 321–349
49. Sutherland, John W., A GENERAL SYSTEMS PHILOSOPHY FOR THE SOCIAL AND BEHAVIOURAL SCIENCES, New York, George Braziller, 1973
50. Von Bertalanffy, Ludwig, GENERAL SYSTEMS THEORY, New York, George Braziller, 1969
51. Weltman, John J., SYSTEMS THEORY IN INTERNATIONAL RELATIONS; A STUDY IN METAPHORIC HYPERTROPHY, Lexington, Mass., D.C. Heath & Co., 1973
52. Wiener, Norbert, CYBERNETICS, (2nd edition), Cambridge, Mass., M.I.T. Press, 1961
53. Wiseman, H.V., POLITICAL SYSTEMS: SOME SOCIOLOGICAL APPROACHES, New York, Frederick Praeger, 1966
54. Young, Oran R., 'Political Discontinuities in the International System', WORLD POLITICS, XX(3), April 1968, pp. 369–392
55. Young, Oran R., SYSTEMS OF POLITICAL SCIENCE, Englewood Cliffs, N.J., Prentice Hall, 1968
56. Zartman, I. William, 'Africa as a Subordinate State System in International Relations', INTERNATIONAL ORGANISATION, 21(3), Summer 1967, pp. 545–564

Chapter V

INTERNATIONAL STRATIFICATION

by Richard Little
The Open University

Stratification can be identified whenever there is inequality among the members of a group. According to Littlejohn (51) the concept is associated, therefore, with 'the unequal distribution of goods and services, rights and obligations, power and privilege'. Although the concept has been examined most extensively in terms of inequality among individuals in a closed society, there has now developed a diffuse body of literature, falling within an area identified by Etzioni as the 'sociology of international relations' (22), which examines stratification at the level of the international system.

A recent analysis of stratification by Luard (53) from the perspective of the historical sociologist illustrates that the international system has been stratified in many different ways. The range extends from the Roman Empire, where tributary states were subordinated to a central power, to the Chinese multi-state systems where power was unevenly spread amongst a large group of states. Despite this variation, however, stratification has not been extensively used as a variable to explain international behaviour. To a large extent, this is a consequence of the dominating influence of the realist approach to international relations. Realists assert that the balance of power represents the ubiquitous mode of organization for inter-state relations. And in Morgenthau's terminology, the balance of power represents 'an actual state of affairs in which power is distributed among several nations with approximate equality' (60). Such a definition, however, does not necessarily deny the existence of a stratified international system. Indeed, Gulick (35) argues that one of the major virtues attributed to the balance of power is the capacity of the system to deter the Great Powers from absorbing the smaller, defenceless states. Nevertheless, the importance attributed to the balance of power has meant that attention is almost invariably focused on the Great Powers. As a consequence, not only is the foreign policy of small states largely unexplored, but also the relationship between large and small states is comparatively neglected. The frequently abortive attempts by the US to influence the behaviour of small states since the Second World War has been matched by the absence of theories and concepts to understand and explain the resilience and independence of small states. There is now, however, a growing literature which is examining the relationship between small and large states, including works by Spiegel (84), Singer (83), Mathisen (55), Vital (89), Richardson (70), and Kaufman (44).

The distinction between large and small states tends to rest on the concept of power capabilities. But in the contemporary world, distinguishing states on this basis appears crude and restrictive. Using power criteria to compare countries, it is clear that the US and China will be designated as large states and Sweden as a small state. However, on the basis of a wide range of alternative criteria, it is equally apparent that Sweden and the US have much more in common than China and the US. With decolonization and the burgeoning of new states which followed, it has become evident that any consideration of a stratified international system must take development as well as power into consideration. In fact, it was in the context of underdevelopment that Lagos (47) put forward the proposition that the international system can be considered as a social system which is subject to stratification. He argued moreover, that whereas in the past the inequalities between states were insufficient to disturb the idea of formal equality, inherent in the notion of sovereignty, the newly emerged states have undergone an atimic process, indicating a loss of status, and this has resulted in a substantial gap developing between the formal and real status of these states.

While Lagos has been credited with establishing a new approach to international relations, his work did little to advance the ideas associated with stratification already established in sociology. Sociologists have never been content simply to describe the way in which society is stratified. They have been anxious, in addition, to explain why stratification develops, to examine the extent to which behaviour is influenced by stratification and to explore the consequences of stratification for society. Two very different perspectives — one conservative and the other radical — have emerged on stratification, reflecting divergent traditions in sociology.

The conservative perspective, closely associated with a version of functionalism, considers stratification to be both necessary and desirable. It is argued that society becomes stratified because the positions to which a high value are attached are rewarded in terms of either power, privilege or prestige. As a consequence, individuals are motivated to strive for these positions, with the result that important positions will be occupied by the best qualified individuals. Davis and Moore provide a clear exposition of this view of stratification, although the thesis has been subjected to subsequent revision by Simpson (79), Wrong (96) and Moore (59). The conservative approach, therefore, considers that stratification occurs as a consequence of functional specialization. It presupposes that the integration of society and the persistence of social order are a product of stratification and furthermore, the cohesion of society must reflect the existence of a 'value consensus' among the members of the society.

The radical perspective, on the other hand, does not accept that the stratification of society reflects an underlying legitimacy. Nor does it accept that stratification is an immutable facet of society, necessary for the maintenance of social cohesion. The radical view has, in fact, been most clearly enunciated by Marxist writers from whom it can be inferred that there are different types of stratification, each associated with distinct stages in a process of economic development. The relationship between master and slave, landlord and servant, capitalist and labourer, characterize different types of stratification and can be identified at various stages in the evolving economic structure of society. The radicals deny that stratification has at any of these stages served to optimize the benefits for the members of society as a whole. On the contrary, it is argued that the division of society into strata has always been accompanied by a process such that the power, privilege and prestige associated with one stratum has been achieved and maintained by the systematic exploitation of another. Social order therefore, has, according to this view, always been based on and maintained by some form of coercion.

In addition to advocates of these two conflicting perspectives, there is a third group of writers who consider, either; that the two perspectives are complementary and need to be considered in conjunction, or; that it is necessary to establish a synthesis between the two views, although there is considerable scepticism about the possibility of achieving a real synthesis. Nevertheless, both Ossowski (66) and Lenski (49) have advocated the need for a synthesis, with Dahrendorf (13) espousing the complementarity of the two perspectives.

The debate between the radical and conservative approaches to stratification has never been carried over to international relations. The international system is almost invariably considered to be anarchic and there has never been any support for the idea that states are functionally differentiated. Although the concept of a 'balancer' in the balance of power literature suggests some degree of functional differentiation, the idea is insufficient to disturb the general contention that states are not related to each other on a functional basis. The stability and order identified in the international system, therefore, is attributed to the power structure and not to a 'value consensus'. Given this orientation, it is not surprising to find that International Relations writers have been unattracted by the conservative approach to stratification. Instead, there has been a tendency to relate stratification to exploitation and conflict in the international system. Most of the ideas associated with stratification in the international system, therefore, have been derived from the radical perspective.

Despite the existence of a common perspective, the literature on stratification in the international system divides into two distinct areas. The first covers writers who can be characterized as interaction theorists. They assume that the actors in the international system are largely autonomous and that the interactions between these actors are rank dependent. In other words, the behaviour of states can be explained by their position in a stratified international system. The state, therefore, is treated as a concrete entity which can be described along a series of dimensions, thereby permitting all states to be compared and ranked with one another. For the sake of simplifying the analysis, the states are frequently classified into one of a number of groups or strata. However, in principle, it is accepted that each state can be individually ranked along a continuum. As a consequence, it becomes of interest to see how the behaviour of a state is affected by both its position and mobility on the continuum.

The second area of literature embraces historians and economists as well as specialists in International Relations. For these writers, the state is no longer an autonomous unit and capitalism has developed on a worldwide basis. One consequence of this development is, for example, that there is now an international division of labour: a line of argument which leads to the functional conclusion that states perform different roles in the international capitalist system. This area of literature associates these roles with two strata in the international system, designated as the centre and the periphery and containing, respectively, top dogs and underdogs. The objective of writers in this area is to discover why this type of stratification occurred and the consequences for the individuals living in both the centre and the peripheral regions. They argue that there is a structural relationship between these two regions, and, as a consequence, they will be referred to as structural theorists in a subsequent section which examines the literature in more detail. But first, we shall examine the literature associated with the interaction theorists.

Stratification and the Interaction Theorists

Three distinct, but related models have been used by the interaction theorists to explain the relationship between stratification and the behaviour of states in the international system. The first is based on the contention that international behaviour is affected by the distribution of power among the international actors. The second, drawing heavily on the frustration-aggression hypothesis advanced by psychologists, relates international behaviour to rank, or status, discrepancy experienced by states. The third relates international behaviour to the position of the actors in the stratified international system.

Although it is conventional to argue that stability in the international system is maximized when there is an even distribution of power among the major actors, there has always been a school of thought including Organski (65), for example, which associates stability with hegemony. This disagreement among power theorists was compounded when the early behaviouralists, such as Kaplan (43) and Rosecrance (73), adopting a systemic approach, identified a range of systems in which power was not distributed in accordance with the dictates of the balance of power theory. A debate was soon initiated between theorists like Waltz (94) who considered that a bipolar distribution of power promoted stability and those, such as Deutsch and Singer (16), who believed that stability was most likely to be stimulated when the distribution of power reflected multipolarity.

When the behaviouralists initiated a quantitative approach to International Relations, therefore, this debate prompted them to

52

investigate whether there is any empirical relationship between the distribution of power and the incidence of conflict in the international system. To examine the distribution of power, states are first ranked on the basis of a power index. When this is done, it becomes immediately apparent that the position of states on the power dimension has continuously changed and that the distribution of power in the international system has altered substantially over time. The work of Ferris (24), is interesting in this respect. In a study by Singer, Bremer and Stuckey (82) specifically designed to test the conflicting theories found in the balance of power literature, it was discovered, however, that there is no straightforward relationship between the level of conflict in the international system and the distribution of power. Although a persistent relationship is identified, the nature of the relationship alters in different time periods. So far, no adequate explanation of this finding has been advanced. It can be argued, however, that the level of conflict may be affected by the uncertainty induced amongst states by changes in the distribution of power. The factors precipitating uncertainty may change with, for example, the nature of technology.

The second area of theory used by the interaction theorists to explain conflict in the international system has been derived from the frustration-aggression hypothesis advanced by Dollard, Doob and Miller (17) which stipulated that aggression is always a consequence of frustration. Although some psychologists insist that frustration is not the only source of aggression, and despite subsequent criticisms and revisions by Berkowitz (6) and Yates (97), for example, the thesis has persisted and has frequently been extended from the individual to the societal level of analysis, by Gurr (36) among others.

The frustration-aggression hypothesis is reflected in two approaches to the study of international conflict. The first derives from the literature which argues that the socio-economic development process promotes frustration within a population. The frustration arises when the pace of economic development cannot accommodate the escalating demands encouraged by the process of development. According to this thesis, therefore, states are most likely to experience revolution during the period when modernization occurs. This phenomenon can be related to international conflict through the medium of the decision-making process. It is often suggested, for example, that decision makers precipitate international conflict in order to deflect attention from internal problems. According to this thesis, therefore, modernizing states will tend to be more aggressive than both the more and the less developed states. The Feierbends (23), who have developed an indicator of social frustration, have given some empirical support to this thesis.

A more extensive body of literature relates the frustration-aggression hypothesis to the conception of status or rank disequilibrium. The theoretical implications of this concept have been extensively examined by Galtung (29), who was also one of the first writers to apply the concept to International Relations (28, 30). He argues that states, like individuals, can be compared along a number of dimensions. In theory, the number of dimensions is infinite, although in practice, only a few will be considered critical. For the purposes of simplifying the analysis, Galtung considers that an actor can be identified on any dimension as a top dog or an underdog. At one extreme, therefore, an actor can be a top dog on all dimensions, while at the other, an actor may be an underdog on all dimensions. Status disequilibrium occurs at all points between these two extremes, when the actor is a top dog on some dimensions and an underdog on the remaining dimensions. Galtung stipulates that this disequilibrium creates frustration and can lead to aggression.

The most straight forward application of this theory has been to take the power dimension and examine the changing position of states on this dimension over time. When the power status of a state changes then a form of status disequilibrium is experienced. Ferris (24) has found that there is no relationship between changes in power status and the propensity of a state to engage in conflict. However, he did find a correlation at the systemic level between the total amount of conflict and the aggregated amount of change in the relative power capabilities of the states in the international system.

More complex applications of the status disequilibrium thesis have been based on the idea of frustration being precipitated by the disequilibrium occurring between two dimensions at a particular point in time. Considerable interest has been shown in the situation where there is a disequilibrium between the power capabilities possessed by a state and the prestige accorded to the state by other actors in the international system. In order to measure the prestige of a state, an index devised by Singer and Small (81) has frequently been employed. The assumption underlying the index is that prestige of a state is reflected in the number of foreign diplomats sent to its capital. In other words, the state possessing the most foreign diplomats is taken

54

to be the state possessing the greatest prestige, or ascribed status, in the international system. This variable contrasts with the measure of potential power or the achieved status of the state.

The results of research in this area are complex and conflicting. Wallace has shown that there is a relationship between international conflict and status inconsistency, but his results do not fit any clear or well-established model of international relations. Ray (68) has found no relationship, while Rosecrance (74) has suggested that the relationship is much more complex than is allowed for by the theory associated with status inconsistency. He argues, moreover, that it is the willingness to exercise power, rather than either the ascribed or achieved power status which provides a better indicator of conflict. However, neither of these authors makes allowance for a time-lag between status inconsistency and conflict. In contrast, Wallace (90) finds that his results are dramatically improved when a fifteen year time-lag is allowed for between status inconsistency and conflict. This phenomenon could arise, according to Wallace, because there is only an indirect relationship between the emergence of status inconsistency and the onset of war.

Finally, the interaction theorists have established a model based on the hierarchical relationship which exists among states. Galtung (30, 32) has argued that international relations are conducted in the context of a hierarchical feudal system. Such a system possesses two major characteristics. First, rankings tend to be concordant, in other words, the rank which an actor possesses on one dimension corresponds to the rank possessed on other dimensions. Secondly, interaction has a tendency to be rank dependent, that is, the nature of the interaction between two actors is dependent upon their respective rank in the stratified system. Galtung argues that in a feudal system there is a high level of interaction among a group of central actors: the central actors will each interact with a group of peripheral actors and there will be an absence of interaction among these peripheral actors. According to the theory, this pattern of interaction will be reflected along all dimensions of activity.

Although one major piece of research by Wallensteen (92) has used this model to examine conflictual interaction between states, much of the research in this area has concentrated on cooperative rather than conflictual interactions. Gleditsch (34) has examined the pattern of air traffic in Latin America; Galtung (31) has looked at diplomatic interaction among NATO and Warsaw Pact countries; Addo (1) has explored trade relations; and Schwartzman and Araujo (77) have examined the stratification of Latin America from the perspective of individual perceptions. All the research tends to confirm the basic outline of the model. It is significant, however, that a group of Rummel's associates (88) have found that rank can only be used to predict cooperative and not conflictual interactions between states.

Despite the empirical support, Galtung's model has been attacked for its rigidity. Dominguez (18) has argued that the international system is much more loosely structured than Galtung's model would suggest. He argues that the patterns of interaction among centre and peripheral countries are not isomorphic along different dimensions. Christopherson (11) has examined the two approaches from the perspective of trade and diplomatic visits. His findings tend to support Dominguez rather than Galtung.

Stratification and the Structuralist Theories

For the interaction theorists, the state represents the major unit of analysis. The structural theorists, on the other hand, are primarily concerned with the relationship between the centre and periphery in a world system and, as a consequence, the state is frequently not taken as the unit of analysis. This divergence of approach corresponds to a debate found in the sociological literature on stratification, where the nature of the unit of analysis provides one of the major differences between the conservative and radical perspectives on stratification. Conservatives consider that the state can be treated as an autonomous entity and stratification, therefore, refers to a phenomenon within the state. As a consequence, functionalists consider it to be highly significant, for example, that when the prestige of occupations in the developed world was studied by Inkeles and Rossi (41), a high degree of agreement was observed in six countries on the relative prestige accorded to a variety of occupations. Littlejohn (51) has noted, however, that for Marxists, this finding is unremarkable because these politically independent units are considered to exist within a common society of developed states. The state, according to this view, does not represent the critical unit of analysis.

The radical perspective, therefore, does not see the international system divided according to power criteria but rather according to levels of economic development. Although there have been realists in International Relations such as Carr (10) who have argued that the division between developed and underdeveloped countries can provide

a source of conflict in the international system, they explain the
division in terms of factors internal to the state, whereas the structuralists consider that the existence of developed and underdeveloped
states must be explained in terms of a world system. The structural
approach to the analysis of this world system embraces two distinct
areas of literature. The first, following in the steps of the early
Marxists, attempts to explain the reasons why it is necessary for
the developed countries to penetrate underdeveloped regions. The
second, examines the consequences for the centre and periphery of
the world system of the structural relationship which exists between
the two strata.

The first area of literature is often associated with the concept of
imperialism. Lichtheim has argued that 'if a country is invaded by a
stronger power and its political institutions are destroyed or re-
moulded, that country is under imperial domination' (50). This
conception of imperialism was originally shared by both conservatives
and radicals and the phenomenon was associated with the acquisition
of colonies. Since decolonization, however, radicals, who consider that
imperialism is still in evidence, are no longer prepared to define imperialism in political terms. Some liberal historians, examining Britain's
overseas relations in the nineteenth century, have adopted a similar
position. It is argued that both liberal and Marxist analysts at the
beginning of the twentieth century failed to appreciate that a distinction
can be made between a formal and an informal element to imperialism;
both elements are covered when imperialism is seen, as Gallagher and
Robinson (27) put it, to represent a 'process of integrating new regions
into the expanding economy'. This formulation provides a common
framework for literature examining imperialism in the past and the
present.

The inspiration for the ideas which are now being developed to
explain the penetration of peripheral regions by central countries, can
be traced to an earlier group of writers who wished to explain the
upsurge of interest in colonies at the end of the nineteenth century.
J.A. Hobson (38), an English liberal, argued that the need for colonies
was precipitated by underconsumption in the metropolitan country.
He believed, moreover, that while benefiting a class of people, the
overall effect of imperialism was harmful; and he stipulated that a
redistribution of income would eliminate the underconsumption and
thereby remove the factor precipitating imperialism. In contrast to
this liberal conception of imperialism, the Marxists who explored the

57

idea of imperialism at that time, saw it as a necessary stage in the development of capitalism. The colonies, therefore, were considered to be playing a crucial role in the existing capitalist economic structure. However, the Marxists were not agreed on either the nature or the consequences of this role. At one extreme, it was argued by Lenin (48) and Bukharin (9), amongst others, that imperialism would lead to conflict amongst the capitalist states; and at the other, it was believed by Kautsky (45), for example, that imperialism would lead to increased cooperation.

For a variety of reasons, most social scientists were unimpressed by these early attempts to establish a structural explanation of imperialism. In the first place, many of the facts contradicted the essential features of the models. For example, Britain, far from suffering from a surplus of capital when the colonies were established, was a net importer of capital. Secondly, most social scientists possessed, according to Barratt Brown (8), an uncritical acceptance of the liberal classical economic framework, which advocated laissez-faire and depicted phenomena such as imperialism and monopolies as 'unfortunate but temporary deviations from the true beliefs of Adam Smith'. As a consequence, they were more inclined to accept the explanation of imperialism offered by Schumpeter (75), a neo-classical economist, who believed that capitalism would encourage anti-imperialism, and that the brief period of imperialism at the end of the nineteenth century was an atavistic feature of the social system which would soon be eliminated. Finally, with decolonization, after the Second World War, events appeared unequivocally to vindicate the liberal perspective and negate the structural arguments which had been developed by the Marxists.

Since decolonization, however, the course of events has encouraged the growth of a widespread scepticism about the validity and relevance of the classical economic model. Its basic tenets are being undermined, for example, by the growing disparity between the developed and underdeveloped countries and the dramatic growth of the multinational corporations. The classical economic model is clearly inadequate to explain such developments and this has led to increasing interest in the structural models of the early Marxists. The interest has infused the recent literature examining the formation of British colonies in Africa. Non-structuralists, such as Gallagher and Robinson (27), and Semmel (78), have argued that Britain derived most of the economic benefits associated with imperialism through the medium of free trade. The establishment of the African colonies, which in any event it is suggested had no economic value, cannot consequently be attributed to a necessary economic structural relationship between the metropolitan and colonial countries. Robinson and Gallagher (71) argued, therefore, that the explanation must be expressed in terms of strategy and power politics, Recently, however, an alternative, or additional line of argument has been developed by economic historians who explicitly or implicitly accept a structural orientation. Reynolds (69), for example, has attempted to demonstrate that following the termination of slavery, traders in West Africa sought alternative sources of trade, undermining the existing political structure and precipitating colonization. A comparative study in Latin America by Monteon (58), where similar trading relationships did not give rise to colonization, has also been carried out. See also Low (52), Brett (7), Uzoigwe (87), Rodney (72), and Wolff (95).

A comparable debate between the radicals and the power politicians has also developed in the analysis of contemporary imperialism, although this literature, of course, concentrates on the US rather than Britain. It associates interventionist behaviour with imperialism, and suggests that this is not a new development, but reflects an historical tradition of expansionism. This view is propagated by revisionist historians, such as Fleming (25), Horowitz (39) and Kalb and Abel (42), as well as left-wing critics of American foreign policy, for example, Barnet (5) and Kolko (46). Such literature documents the history of US foreign policy. Other writers, Baran and Sweezy (3) and Magdoff (54), for example, have attempted to show, at a more theoretical level, that there is a structural relationship between the US and the developing countries. Baran and Sweezy stipulate that the international system is hierarchical 'with one or more of the leading metropoles at the top, completely dependent colonies at the bottom, and many degrees of super-ordination and subordination in between'. The centre countries attempt to maintain this situation, it is argued, because of the role the peripheral countries play in the economic structure of the centre. US foreign policy, therefore, has been designed to preserve the existing hierarchical situation by preventing either internal political changes or external control of Western oriented states by the communists. Even when the US has no direct economic interest in a country, as for example, in the case of Vietnam, the argument is sustained on the basis of a sophisticated application of the domino thesis. It is maintained that a defeat for the US in any country could have long-term detrimental effects on countries where there are US economic interests. The structural approach has, in addition, been applied by Sunkel (85), to the relationship between the multi-national corporations and the developing countries.

The external behaviour of the US, however, is not always related to the hierarchical structure of the international system. For example, it is also suggested that the steady expansion of the military in the US represents one of the 'counteracting tendencies' identified by Marx, available to a capitalist society to delay the onset of problems caused by the tendency for the potential productive capacity to exceed the potential capacity for consumption in a capitalist mode of production. External conflict, according to this argument, is encouraged in order to justify the expanding expenditure on military hardware. This argument is often used, for example by Melman (56), to provide additional support for the structural model.

Not surprisingly, the attempts to explain US foreign policy using the structural model have run into considerable criticism. In the first place, the academic credibility of much of the work by the revisionist historians has been opened to question by Tucker (86). But, more important, in this context, the whole approach has been attacked. Cohen (12) believes that the arguments advanced by the structuralists are unsound and are not supported by the facts. He insists that there is no necessary structural link between the centre and periphery countries. Instances of imperialism, which he accepts as an important phenomenon in the contemporary international system, can be explained only on the basis of a strategic model of international relations. It is interesting to note that Barratt Brown (8), who is sympathetic to the Marxist orientation, argues that instances of Soviet imperialism are also best explained on the basis of a power political or strategic model.

The second area of literature employing a structural model encompasses attempts to provide an explanation for the continuing gap which exists between the developed and underdeveloped countries. These explanations lie at the opposite extreme of explanations associated with the laissez-faire model of development. The laissez-faire model dictates that development is an option available to all states. The failure of some countries to develop must be explained, therefore, by internal cultural factors. Deutsch (15), for example, distinguishes between proto-industrial countries, where there is a culture which teaches the value of saving and thrift, and counter-industrial countries, defined by areas influenced by Islam. Despite making this distinction, however, there is a strong assumption underlying this model that eventually all states will become developed. But, in any event, failure to develop according to the laissez-faire model must be explained in terms of factors internal to the underdeveloped state.

Soon after decolonization, however, liberal economists began to question this assumption. Prebisch (67), who, according to Morse (61), was one of the first writers to draw the distinction between central and peripheral countries, recognized along with others, such as Myrdal (62), Singer (80), and Nurske (64), that market forces were not effecting an optimum distribution of resources, but by a process of 'circular cumulative causation' were widening the gap between rich and poor countries. This approach has been extended by the structuralists who argue, further, that underdevelopment arises from the same historical process which generates development. The development process, in other words, precipitates underdevelopment as well as development. This idea has been explored in its historical context by Wallerstein (93), who has looked at the emergence of the world economy in the sixteenth century, and at the division of labour which developed between the core states and the peripheral areas.

Structural analyses of the contemporary international system have centred on the idea that there is a division of labour between the developed and the underdeveloped states. Frank (26) and his associates have developed the idea with specific reference to the Latin American states, while Galtung (33) has examined it in the context of the European Community's relations with the underdeveloped countries. Galtung's thesis rests primarily on the idea that the division of labour occurs along the line of primary and manufactured goods. The existence of a number of wealthy, developed countries which are primary producers, however, is consistent with this model and cannot be explained by it. Emmanuel (21) has provided a controversial solution. He argues that while capital is mobile in the world economy, labour is, effectively, immobile. As a consequence, it is the cost of labour which determines the price of goods on the world market. Although Emmanuel does not offer any explanation for the current disparity in wage levels found in the developed and the underdeveloped countries, he is able to use the disparity to provide an explanation for the inability of the underdeveloped countries to develop. He argues that if underdeveloped countries start to produce goods currently produced by developed countries, the latter will move into new areas of production and the price of the goods will fall to the level dictated by the wage level in the underdeveloped countries. But even this model does not account for another critical problem posed for the structuralists: the demonstrated capacity of some underdeveloped states to develop. Amin (2) has argued, deductively, however, that the ability of these countries to develop indicates that they were never part of the peripheral area. He identifies them as 'young capitalist' countries. Critics have found this an unsatisfactory solution, and the debate amongst these writers continues.

Bibliography

1. Addo, H., 'Structural Basis of International Communication', PAPERS OF PEACE SCIENCE SOCIETY (INTERNATIONAL), 23, 1974, pp. 81–100
2. Amin, S., ACCUMULATION ON A WORLD SCALE: A CRITIQUE OF THE THEORY OF UNDERDEVELOPMENT, (2 Vols.), New York, Monthly Review Press, 1973
3. Baran, P.A. and Sweezy, P.M., MONOPOLY CAPITALISM, New York, Monthly Review Press, 1966
4. Barbera, H., RICH NATIONS AND POOR IN PEACE AND WAR: CONTINUITY AND CHANGE IN THE DEVELOPMENT HIERARCHY OF SEVENTY NATIONS FROM 1913 THROUGH 1952, Lexington, Mass., D.C. Heath & Co., 1973
5. Barnet, R.J., INTERVENTION AND REVOLUTION: THE UNITED STATES IN THE THIRD WORLD, New York, World Publishing Co., 1968
6. Berkowitz, L., AGGRESSION: A SOCIAL PSYCHOLOGICAL ANALYSIS, New York, McGraw Hill, 1962
7. Brett, E.A., COLONIALISM AND UNDERDEVELOPMENT IN EAST AFRICA: THE POLITICS OF ECONOMIC CHANGE, 1919–1939, New York, Nok, 1973
8. Brown, M.B., THE ECONOMICS OF IMPERIALISM, Harmondsworth, Middx., Penguin Books, 1974
9. Bukharin, N.I., IMPERIALISM AND WORLD ECONOMY, London, The Merlin Press, 1970
10. Carr, E.H., THE TWENTY YEARS' CRISIS: 1919–1939: AN INTRODUCTION TO THE STUDY OF INTERNATIONAL RELATIONS, (2nd edition), London, Macmillan, 1946
11. Christopherson, J.A., 'Structural Analysis of Transaction Systems', JOURNAL OF CONFLICT RESOLUTION, 20 (4), December 1976, pp. 637–662

12. Cohen, B.J., THE QUESTION OF IMPERIALISM, London, Macmillan, 1973
13. Dahrendorf, R., CLASS AND CLASS CONFLICT IN INDUSTRIAL SOCIETY, Stanford, Stanford University Press, 1959
14. Davis, K. and Moore, W.E., 'Some Principles of Stratification', AMERICAN SOCIOLOGICAL REVIEW, 10, April 1945, pp. 242–9
15. Deutsch, K.W., 'Theories of Imperialism and Neo-imperialism' in Steven J. Rosen and James R. Kurth, TESTING THEORIES OF ECONOMIC IMPERIALISM, Lexington, Mass., D.C. Heath & Co., 1974
16. Deutsch, K.W. and Singer, J.D., 'Multipolarity, Power Systems and International Stability', WORLD POLITICS, 16(3), April 1964, pp. 390–406
17. Dollard, John et al., FRUSTRATION AND AGGRESSION, New Haven, Yale University Press, 1939
18. Dominguez, J.I., 'Mice that do not Roar: Some Aspects of World Politics in the Peripheries', INTERNATIONAL ORGANIZATION, 25 (2), Spring 1971, pp. 175–208
19. East, M.A., 'Stratification in the International System: An Empirical Analysis' in James N. Rosenau, et al., (eds.), THE ANALYSIS OF INTERNATIONAL POLITICS, New York, The Free Press, 1971
20. East, M.A., 'Rank-dependent Interaction and Mobility: Two Aspects of International Stratification', PEACE RESEARCH SOCIETY PAPERS, 14, 1969, pp. 113–27
21. Emmanuel, A., UNEQUAL EXCHANGE: A STUDY OF THE IMPERIALISM OF TRADE, (Trans., B. Pearce), London, N.L.B., Monthly Review Press, 1972. (First published in French in 1969)
22. Etzioni, A., Review of Lagos's 'International Stratification and Underdeveloped Countries', AMERICAN JOURNAL OF SOCIOLOGY, 70, July 1964, pp. 114–5
23. Feierbend, I.K. and R., 'Levels of Development and International Behaviour' in Richard Butwell, FOREIGN POLICY AND THE DEVELOPING NATIONS, Lexington, University of Kentucky Press, 1969
24. Ferris, W.H., THE POWER CAPABILITIES OF NATION STATES: INTERNATIONAL CONFLICT AND WAR, Lexington, Mass., D.C. Heath & Co., 1973
25. Fleming, D.F., THE COLD WAR AND ITS ORIGINS, (2 Vols.), London, Allen & Unwin, 1961

26. Frank, A.G., LATIN AMERICA: UNDERDEVELOPMENT OR REVOLUTION, New York, Monthly Review Press, 1969
27. Gallagher, J. and Robinson, R., 'The Imperialism of Free Trade', ECONOMIC HISTORY REVIEW, 6 (1), 1953, pp. 1—15
28. Galtung, J.,'A Structural Theory of Aggression', JOURNAL OF PEACE RESEARCH, 1, 1964, pp. 95—119
29. Galtung, J., 'Rank and Social Integration: A Multidimensional Approach' in Joseph Berger, Morris Zelditch and Bo Anderson (eds.), SOCIOLOGICAL THEORIES IN PROGRESS, (Vol. 1), New York, Atlanta, 1965
30. Galtung, J., 'International Relations and International Conflicts: A Sociological Approach', International Sociological Association, TRANSACTIONS OF THE SIXTH WORLD CONGRESS OF SOCIOLOGY, Geneva, 1966
31. Galtung, J., 'East West Interaction Patterns', JOURNAL OF PEACE RESEARCH, 3, 1966, pp. 146—177
32. Galtung, J., y Araujo, M. and Schwartzman, S., 'The Latin American System of Nations: A Structural Analysis' in Bengt Hoglund and Jorgen W. Ulrick (eds.), CONFLICT CONTROL AND CONFLICT RESOULTION, Copenhagen, Munksgaard, 1972 and Atlantic Highlands, N.J., Humanities Press, 1972
33. Galtung, J., THE EUROPEAN COMMUNITY: A SUPERPOWER IN THE MAKING, London, Allen & Unwin, 1973
34. Gleditsch, N.P., 'World Airline Patterns', JOURNAL OF PEACE RESEARCH, 4, 1967, pp. 366—407
35. Gulick, E.V., EUROPE'S CLASSICAL BALANCE OF POWER, Ithaca, Cornell University Press, 1955 and New York, W.W. Norton, 1967
36. Gurr, T.R., 'Psychological Factors in Civil Violence', WORLD POLITICS, 20 (2), January 1968, pp. 245—78
37. Heintz, P., A MACROSOCIOLOGICAL THEORY OF SOCIETAL SYSTEMS WITH SPECIAL REFERENCE TO THE INTERNATIONAL SYSTEM, (2 Vols.), Bern, Hans Huber, 1972
38. Hobson, J.A., IMPERIALISM: A STUDY, Ann Arbor, University of Michigan Press, 1967 (First published in 1902)
39. Horowitz, D., THE FREE WORLD COLOSSUS: A CRITIQUE OF AMERICAN FOREIGN POLICY IN THE COLD WAR, London, Cox & Wyman Ltd., 1965
40. Horowitz, I.L., THREE WORLDS OF DEVELOPMENT: THE THEORY AND PRACTICE OF INTERNATIONAL

STRATIFICATION, (2nd edition), London, Oxford University Press, 1972

41. Inkeles, A. and Rossi, P.H., 'National Comparisons of Occupational Prestige', AMERICAN JOURNAL OF SOCIOLOGY, 61, May 1956, pp. 329–339

42. Kalb, M. and Abel, E., ROOTS OF INVOLVEMENT: THE US IN ASIA 1784–1971, New York, W.W. Norton, 1971

43. Kaplan, M.A., SYSTEM AND PROCESS IN INTERNATIONAL POLITICS, New York, John Wiley, 1957

44. Kaufman, E., THE SUPERPOWERS AND THEIR SPHERES OF INFLUENCE, London, Croom Helm, 1976

45. Kautsky, K., 'Ultra Imperialism', NEW LEFT REVIEW, 59, 1970, pp. 40–8

46. Kolko, G., THE ROOTS OF AMERICAN FOREIGN POLICY, Boston, Beacon Press, 1969

47. Lagos, G., INTERNATIONAL STRATIFICATION AND UNDER-DEVELOPED COUNTRIES, Chapel Hill, University of North Carolina Press, 1963

48. Lenin, V.I., IMPERIALISM, THE HIGHEST STAGE OF CAPITALISM, Collected Works, Vol. 2, Moscow, 1968, (First published in 1917)

49. Lenski, G., POWER AND PRIVILEGE: A THEORY OF SOCIAL STRATIFICATION, New York, McGraw Hill, 1966

50. Lichtheim, G., IMPERIALISM, Harmondsworth, Middx., Penguin Books, 1971

51. Littlejohn, J., SOCIAL STRATIFICATION, London, Allen & Unwin, 1972

52. Low, D.A., LION RAMPANT: ESSAYS IN THE STUDY OF BRITISH IMPERIALISM, London, Frank Cass, 1973

53. Luard, E., TYPES OF INTERNATIONAL SOCIETY, New York, The Free Press, 1976

54. Magdoff, H., THE AGE OF IMPERIALISM: THE ECONOMICS OF US FOREIGN POLICY, London, Monthly Review Press, 1969

55. Mathsen, T., THE FUNCTION OF THE SMALL STATE IN THE STRATEGIES OF THE GREAT POWERS, Oslo, Universitets-florlaget, 1971

56. Melman, S., PENTAGON CAPITALISM: THE POLITICAL ECONOMY OF WAR, New York, McGraw Hill, 1970

57. Midlarsky, M.I., ON WAR: POLITICAL VIOLENCE IN THE

INTERNATIONAL SYSTEM, New York, The Free Press, 1975

58. Monteon, M., 'The British in the Atacama Desert: The Cultural Bases of Economic Imperialism', JOURNAL OF ECONOMIC HISTORY, 35, March 1975, pp. 117–133

59. Moore, W.E., 'But Some Are More Equal Than Others', AMERICAN SOCIOLOGICAL REVIEW, 28, February 1963, pp. 13–18

60. Morgenthau, H.J., POLITICS AMONG NATIONS: THE STRUGGLE FOR POWER AND PEACE, (5th edition), New York, Alfred Knopf, 1973

61. Morse, E.L., MODERNIZATION AND THE TRANSFORMATION OF INTERNATIONAL RELATIONS, New York, The Free Press, 1976

62. Myrdal, G., ECONOMIC THEORY AND UNDERDEVELOPED COUNTRIES, London, Methuen, 1963

63. Nettl, J.P. and Robertson, R., INTERNATIONAL SYSTEMS AND THE MODERNIZATION OF SOCIETIES: THE FORMATION OF NATIONAL GOALS AND ATTITUDES, London, Faber and Faber, 1968

64. Nurske, R., EQUILIBRIUM AND GROWTH IN THE WORLD ECONOMY, Cambridge, Mass., Harvard University Press, 1962

65. Organski, A.F.K., WORLD POLITICS, (2nd edition), New York, Alfred Knopf, 1968

66. Ossowski, S., CLASS STRUCTURE IN THE SOCIAL CONSCIOUSNESS, London, Routledge & Kegan Paul, 1963

67. Prebisch, R., THE ECONOMIC DEVELOPMENT OF LATIN AMERICA AND ITS PRINCIPAL PROBLEMS, New York, United Nations, 1950

68. Ray, J., 'Status Inconsistency and War Involvement in Europe 1816–1970', PAPERS OF THE PEACE SCIENCE SOCIETY, (International), 23, 1974, pp. 69–79

69. Reynolds, E., 'Economic Imperialism: The Case of the Gold Coast', JOURNAL OF ECONOMIC HISTORY, 35, March 1975, pp. 94–116

70. Richardson, N.R., 'Political Compliance and US Trade Dominance', AMERICAN POLITICAL SCIENCE REVIEW, 70 (3), September 1976, pp. 1098–1109

71. Robinson, R. and Gallagher, J. (with Alice Denny), AFRICA AND THE VICTORIANS; THE OFFICIAL MIND OF IMPERIALISM, London, Macmillan, 1961

72. Rodney, W., HOW EUROPE UNDERDEVELOPED AFRICA, Dar es Salaam, Tanzania Publishing House, 1972
73. Rosecrance, R., 'Bipolarity, Multipolarity and the Future', JOURNAL OF CONFLICT RESOLUTION, 10 (3), September 1966, pp. 314–27
74. Rosecrance, R. et al., 'Power, Balance of Power and Status in Nineteenth Century International Relations', SAGE PROFESSIONAL PAPERS IN INTERNATIONAL RELATIONS, 1974, 02–029
75. Schumpeter, J., IMPERIALISM, New York, Meridian Books, 1955. (First published in 1919)
76. Schwartzman, S., 'International Development and International Feudalism: The Latin American Case', PROCEEDINGS OF THE IPRA INAUGURAL CONFERENCE, Assen, Van Gorcum, 1966
77.. Schwartzman, S. and y Araujo, M., 'The Images of International Stratification in Latin America', JOURNAL OF PEACE RESEARCH, 3, 1966, pp. 225–243
78. Semmel, B., THE RISE OF FREE TRADE IMPERIALISM: CLASSICAL POLITICAL ECONOMY, THE EMPIRE OF FREE TRADE AND IMPERIALISM 1770–1850, Cambridge, Cambridge University Press, 1970
79. Simpson, R., 'A Modification of the Functional Theory of Stratification', SOCIAL FORCES, 35, December 1956, pp. 132–7
80. Singer, H.W., STRATEGY OF INTERNATIONAL DEVELOP- MENT, New York, International Arts and Science Press, 1975
81. Singer, J.D. and Small, M., 'The Composition and Status Ordering of the International System', WORLD POLITICS, 18 (2), January 1966, pp. 236–282
82. Singer, J.D., Bremer, S. and Stuckey, J., 'Capability Distribution, Uncertainty, and Major Power War, 1920–1965' in Bruce M. Russett (ed.), PEACE, WAR AND NUMBERS, Beverley Hills, Calif., Sage Publications, 1972
83. Singer, M.R., WEAK STATES IN A WORLD OF POWERS: THE DYNAMICS OF INTERNATIONAL RELATIONSHIPS, New York, The Free Press, 1972
84. Spiegel, S.L., DOMINANCE AND DIVERSITY: THE INTER- NATIONAL HIERARCHY, Boston, Little, Brown, 1972
85. Sunkel, O., 'The Pattern of Latin American Dependence' in Victor L. Orquidi and Rosemary Thorp, LATIN AMERICA IN THE INTERNATIONAL ECONOMY, London, Macmillan, 1973
86. Tucker, R.W., RADICAL LEFT AND AMERICAN FOREIGN

POLICY, Baltimore, Johns Hopkins Press, 1971
87. Uzoigwe, G.U., BRITAIN AND THE CONQUEST OF AFRICA: THE AGE OF SALISBURY, Ann Arbor, University of Michigan Press, 1974
88. Vincent, J.E. et al., 'Empirical Tests of Attribute, Social Field, and Status Field Theories on International Relations Data', INTERNATIONAL STUDIES QUARTERLY, 17 (4), December 1973, pp. 405–43
89. Vital, D., THE INEQUALITY OF STATES, London, Oxford University Press, 1967
90. Wallace, M.D., WAR AND RANK AMONG NATIONS, Lexington, Mass., D.C. Heath, 1973
91. Wallace, M.D., 'Status, Formal Organisation and Arms Levels as Factors Leading to the Onset of International War 1820–1964' in B.M. Russett (ed.), PEACE, WAR AND NUMBERS, Beverly Hills, Calif., Sage Publications, 1972
92. Wallensteen, P., STRUCTURE AND WAR: ON INTERNATIONAL RELATIONS 1920–1968, (Publications of the Political Science Association), Stockholm, Räben and Sjögren, 1973
93. Wallerstein, I., THE MODERN WORLD-SYSTEM, New York, Academic Press, 1974
94. Waltz, K., 'International Structure, National Force and the Balance of World Power', JOURNAL OF INTERNATIONAL AFFAIRS, 21 (2), 1967, pp. 215–231
95. Wolff, R., THE ECONOMICS OF COLONIALISM, New Haven, Conn., Yale University Press, 1974
96. Wrong, D.H., 'The Functional Theory of Stratification: Some Neglected Considerations', AMERICAN SOCIOLOGICAL REVIEW, 24, December 1959, pp. 772–782
97. Yates, A.J., FRUSTRATION AND CONFLICT, London, Methuen, 1962

Chapter VI

THEORIES OF POWER, INFLUENCE AND AUTHORITY

by A.V.S. de Reuck*
University of Surrey*

It has been widely held that as wealth is to economics, so power is to
politics, and Hans J. Morgenthau expressed the classical view that
'International politics, like all politics, is a struggle for power'.
Nevertheless, power has proved as difficult to conceptualize as it is to
quantify.

Power Politics in International Relations

The major 'realist' school of thought has developed employing power
as the key explanatory concept in the study of International Relations
and many scholars have accepted power as the organizing principle
for the whole discipline of Political Science. It is generally conceded
that the most comprehensive and systematic treatment of international
studies within this framework is by Hans J. Morgenthau (POLITICS
AMONG NATIONS) (23) which has gone through many editions. To
this one should add the works of Raymond Aron (1), Georg
Schwarzenberger (30) and Harold and Margaret Sprout (36, 37), as well
as the penetratingly critical assessment of the whole 'power politics'
school of international theorists carried out by Inis Claude in his by
now classic study, POWER AND INTERNATIONAL RELATIONS (12).
The classical concept of the 'Balance of Power' has been subjected to
systems analysis by Morton Kaplan (19) and Richard Rosencrance (27),
and to game theory analysis by Thomas Schelling (29), while J. David
Singer has made a sustained attempt both to establish an historical

quantitative data bank and to test empirically the propositions derived from Balance of Power theory, with inconclusive results (34). He finds, for example, that during the nineteenth century peace depended on parity between coalitions, whereas in the twentieth century, preponderance of the leading coalition was the condition for international stability (32, 35).

For those interested in surveying the whole range of power approaches in International Relations, a number of useful readers exist including a good survey by Bell (8) and, more recently, by Barry (7). The recent literature on the modern doctrine of nuclear deterrence is later reviewed in the chapter on STRATEGY.

The primacy of power both as motivating principle and as explanatory concept in political theory has been challenged by some (but not all) authors of the 'behavioural' school, who treat 'legitimacy' (in the sociological rather than the juridical sense) as the prime concept, and regard power politics as the pathological outcome of failures of legitimacy, both in domestic and in international affairs. Preeminent among these authors is John Burton (INTERNATIONAL RELATIONS: A GENERAL THEORY (10) and SYSTEMS, STATES, DIPLOMACY AND RULES (11)). The greater complexity of the legitimacy paradigm and the fact that much history has been written, implicitly or explicitly, in the power political mode, renders these works difficult to grasp, but the power political position, whether as a policy prescription or as a theoretical framework, is now on the defensive and may in due course be relegated as an aspect of strategic studies.

It is not proposed to dwell at greater length on these relatively familiar developments.

Power nevertheless remains one of several concepts of central importance in Political Science in general and International Relations in particular. It is remarkable that although power was for so long accorded pride of place at the political table, it is to sociology rather than to political science that one must go for the most significant analyses of the nature of power. The remainder of this introductory note will be devoted to tracing a path through this branch of the literature, toward a better understanding of the modern concept of power compatible with the newer behavioural paradigm. It will be shown that a coherent thread runs through what at first sight is liable to appear as a bewildering array of disparate notions.

Community Power

A classical paper by Bachrach and Baratz (4) attempted a semantic clarification. They noted that the word 'power' had been used indiscriminately by different authors to describe the capacity of actors to secure compliance from other actors by a variety of means, and urged that the following vocabulary (given in parenthesis) should be adopted in order to distinguish instances where compliance is sought by threat of sanctions (power), by persuasion or expectation of reward (influence), by violent coercion (force), by covert misdirection or misinformation (manipulation), or by consent in the joint pursuit of common aims (authority). Note that whereas power (threat), if it succeeds in its objective is costless in the short term, successful influence (reward) involves debts to be paid. On the other hand, threats that fail are likely to be costly, since they then call for sanctions which are usually costly to impose. In the longer term, the exercise of power, force or manipulation breeds enmity and destroys legitimacy whereas influence and authority, rewardingly exercised, breed trust and enhance legitimacy for the future.

Traditional International Relations analysis proceeds to describe power (to threaten credible sanctions) as the possession by an actor of capability, assessed in terms of tangible assets such as military forces, manpower potential, productive capacity, resource endowment and geographical situation, together with intangible factors which include strategic situation, national morale, levels of technical skill, and political and economic stability.

A later paper, Bachrach and Baratz (2), expanded the concept of power to embrace control over the premises (and hence the processes) of decision-making; and introduced the dubious concept of the 'nondecision' to indicate situations where no overt exercise of authority, influence, power or force is necessary to achieve desired ends, as no challenge to those ends is contemplated by potential adversaries.

Both the above papers, as well as the same authors' study of the exercise of political power in an American city (3), were originally intended as a challenge to Robert Dahl's efforts to conceptualize an operationalized version of political power (13) as a basis for empirically delineating 'the powerful' in the American community of New Haven (14). The debate between 'pluralists' and 'neo-elitists' in the analysis of community power has centred around the crucial matter of the existence of a permanent and self-perpetuating power elite in American society, a debate that has its roots in Wright Mills' original enquiry into that topic (21). It is a debate that has reverberated through the pages of the AMERICAN POLITICAL SCIENCE REVIEW, and for those interesting in following the 'state of play' there are a number of papers that usefully summarize and augment this fascinating if rather inconclusive series of exchanges. Apart from the papers by Bachrach and Baratz, the articles by Merelman (20), Riker (26), Wolfinger (39), Frey (18), and Debnam (15), can be particularly recommended, while a book by a convinced pluralist to be set against Bachrach and Baratz's POWER AND POVERTY (3) is Nelson Polsby's COMMUNITY POWER AND POLITICAL THEORY (25).

Exchange and Power

Sociological analysis by Talcott Parsons (24) abruptly switches our attention to power as a generalized medium of exchange in political transactions, analogous to credit in economic affairs (see an admirable account by Mitchell (22) which contains an exhaustive bibliography). Parsons' detailed and sophisticated exploration of this analogy (or homology as he insists) which refers to power in the domestic polity rather than in international affairs, is briefly outlined by Karl Deutsch (NERVES OF GOVERNMENT, CHAPTER 7 (17)). To comprehend its significance it is necessary to appreciate two points. First, that it refers as much or more to legitimate power (rewarding influence) as to the power of threat, so that henceforth the traditional emphasis on power as military credibility must be replaced by an even stronger emphasis on influence derived from proven capability to provide collective satisfactions. Second, that power, like credit, depends upon past performance and present reputation both to execute threats and to reward compliance. The traditional analyses of capability (above) remain relevant as a checklist of assets that render credible both threats and promises, expressed or implied. But it requires augmentation by the inclusion of the past record of reliability of the actor concerned — a point indeed never neglected by traditional analysts.

Parsons' analysis (24) brings out two further aspects of the nature of power. First, that like credit, power is a relational attribute rather than a possession of an actor, and since it inheres in the attitudes of the related actors, it may be highly specific to the context and issues involved. Second, that power, like credit, injudiciously overextended, may result in political inflation, homologous in most respects with economic inflation, arising for instance from homologous causes and subject to homologous remedies. This is one of the most important insights offered by the new conceptualization, and it is capable of extensive elaboration. It promises to lead to a more rigorous explication of the consequences of 'exports' and 'imports' between the economic and social systems and the political system   The crucial importance of political legitimacy is another aspect of the concept of power as political credit.

Peter Blau (9) made a valuable but superficially contradictory formulation of the concept of power as arising from a monopolistic situation. If actor A is in a position to grant or withhold (political) services from another actor B which the latter considers essential and does not know how to obtain elsewhere, then A has power over B, particularly if B commands nothing that A vitally needs in return. In general, the party less dependent on an exchange relationship is in the more powerful position.

Again, this emphasizes that power is an attribute of a structural relationship rather than a possession of an actor, although universal needs afford universal power to monopolists of 'essential' services (e.g. nuclear powers). Blau shows that the theory of monopoly (or of oligopoly) applies to the resulting relationships. For example:

(1) if the service supplied is inelastic, the introduction of new clients will enhance the power of the supplier (Malta's relations with Nato and the Warsaw Pact),

(2) suppliers who club together to create a monopoly increase their power (OPEC),

(3) clients' ignorance of alternative sources of supply enhance the power of the supplier, in whose interest it is therefore to keep clients separated and ignorant (divide and rule).

Subordinate actors can escape from the powerful only by learning to do without the 'essential' service, or by finding viable substitute services or alternative suppliers.

Parsons and Blau are not inconsistent; they are complementary. Whereas Parsons conceptualizes power *in* a competitive 'market', resulting from a combination of a reliable reputation, a productive base, good (legitimate) relationships and scarce political talents, Blau emphasizes oligopolistic power *over* a 'market': that is to say, the power to dictate one's own terms in transactions. Political 'markets' of both sorts exist. The oligopolistic situation more closely resembles the international system, although as the number of actors increases, whether they be states or transnational agencies or corporations, the competitive market model becomes increasingly relevant. Power as

73

political credit rests upon legitimacy; monopoly power stresses threat.

The task of reducing this concept of power, whether *in* or *over* a 'market', to an operational definition, so that it may be measured on an ordinal or (ultimately) an interval scale, has not been completed. Deutsch (ANALYSIS OF INTERNATIONAL RELATIONS, Chapter 3 (16)) distinguishes the following dimensions: power potential (material and human resources capable of mobilization to secure compliance), weight (the probability that a decision will be followed by the appropriate outcome), domain (the institutional actors, persons, territory or resources controlled), scope (the number of sectors, e.g. political, military, economic, social or cultural, subject to control), and range (the difference between the highest reward or 'indulgence' and the worst penalty or 'deprivation' which the powerful actor can bestow or inflict within his domain). In NERVES OF GOVERNMENT (17) Deutsch remarks that since power affords an ability to impose the costs of change on others and to resist the attempts of others to impose the costs of change on oneself, the net power differential between pairs of actors may be assessed as the ratio of costs imposed to costs accepted.

No discussion of legitimate power can neglect Max Weber's classical analysis in terms of traditional, legal-rational and charismatic modes of authority (33). Charismatic authority tends to arise when either the traditional 'divine right' or the rational 'bureaucratic' modes break down in crises. Some men are born great, some achieve greatness and some have greatness thrust upon them. Notwithstanding all appearances to the contrary, charisma lies in the eye of the beholder and is thrust upon leaders in times of crisis. In the final analysis, all (legitimate) authority is conferred by those over whom it is exercised.

Bibliography

1. Aron, R., PEACE AND WAR: A THEORY OF INTERNATIONAL RELATIONS, London, Weidenfeld and Nicholson, 1967
2. Bachrach, P. and Baratz, M.S., 'Decisions and Non-Decisions; An Analytical Framework', AMERICAN POLITICAL SCIENCE REVIEW, 57(3), September 1963, pp. 632–642
3. Bachrach, P. and Baratz, M.S., POWER AND POVERTY: THEORY AND PRACTICE, London, Oxford University Press, 1970
4. Bachrach, P. and Baratz, M.S., 'Two Faces of Power', AMERICAN POLITICAL SCIENCE REVIEW, 56(4), December 1962,

pp. 947—952

5. Baldwin, D.A., 'Foreign Aid, Intervention and Influence', WORLD POLITICS, XXI (3), April 1969, pp. 425—447

6. Baldwin, D.A., 'The Power of Positive Sanctions', WORLD POLITICS, XXIV (1), October 1971, pp. 19—38

7. Barry, B. (ed.), POWER AND POLITICAL THEORY: SOME EUROPEAN PERSPECTIVES, New York, John Wiley, 1976

8. Bell, R., Edwards, D.V. and Wagner, R.H. (eds.), POLITICAL POWER: A READER IN THEORY AND RESEARCH, New York, The Free Press, 1969

9. Blau, P.M., EXCHANGE AND POWER IN SOCIAL LIFE, New York, John Wiley, 1964

10. Burton, J.W., INTERNATIONAL RELATIONS: A GENERAL THEORY, Cambridge, Cambridge University Press, 1965

11. Burton, J.W., SYSTEMS, STATES, DIPLOMACY AND RULES, Cambridge, Cambridge University Press, 1968

12. Claude, I.L., POWER AND INTERNATIONAL RELATIONS, New York, Random House, 1962

13. Dahl, R.A., 'The Concept of Power', BEHAVIOURAL SCIENCE, 2, July 1957, pp. 201—215

14. Dahl, R.A., WHO GOVERNS? DEMOCRACY AND POWER IN AN AMERICAN CITY, New Haven, Conn., Yale University Press, 1961

15. Debnam, G., 'Non-decisions and Power; The Two Faces of Bachrach and Baratz', AMERICAN POLITICAL SCIENCE REVIEW, 69(3), September 1975, pp. 889—899

16. Deutsch, K.W., THE ANALYSIS OF INTERNATIONAL RELATIONS, Englewood Cliffs, N.J., Prentice Hall, 1968

17. Deutsch, K.W., THE NERVES OF GOVERNMENT: MODELS OF POLITICAL COMMUNICATION AND CONTROL, New York, The Free Press, 1963

18. Frey, F.W., 'On Issues and Non-issues in the Study of Power', AMERICAN POLITICAL SCIENCE REVIEW, 65(4), December 1971, pp. 1081—1101

19. Kaplan, M.A., SYSTEM AND PROCESS IN INTERNATIONAL POLITICS, New York, John Wiley, 1967

20. Merelman, R.M., 'On the Neo Elitist Critique of Community Power', AMERICAN POLITICAL SCIENCE REVIEW, 62(2), June 1968, pp. 451—60

21. Mills, C.W., THE POWER ELITE, London, Oxford University Press,

1956

22. Mitchell, W.C., SOCIOLOGICAL ANALYSIS AND POLITICS: THE THEORIES OF TALCOTT PARSONS, New York, The Free Press, 1967

23. Morgenthau, H.J., POLITICS AMONG NATIONS: THE STRUGGLE FOR POWER AND PEACE, (Fifth edition), New York, Alfred Knopf, 1973

24. Parsons, T., POLITICS AND SOCIAL STRUCTURE, New York, The Free Press, 1969

25. Polsby, N.W., COMMUNITY POWER AND POLITICAL THEORY, New Haven, Yale University Press, 1963

26. Riker, W.H., 'Some Ambiguities in the Notion of Power', AMERICAN POLITICAL SCIENCE REVIEW, 58(2), June 1964, pp. 341–349

27. Rosecrance, R.N., ACTION AND REACTION IN WORLD POLITICS, Boston, Little, Brown, 1963

28. Russell, B., POWER: A NEW SOCIAL ANALYSIS, London, Allen & Unwin, 1962

29. Schelling, T.C., THE STRATEGY OF CONFLICT, New York, Oxford University Press, 1963

30. Schwarzenberger, G., POWER POLITICS: A STUDY OF WORLD SOCIETY, (3rd edition), London, Stevens, 1964, (First published in 1941)

31. Singer, J.D., 'Inter-Nation Influence: A Formal Model', AMERICAN POLITICAL SCIENCE REVIEW, 57(2), June 1963, pp. 420–430

32. Singer, J.D. and Small, M., 'National Alliance Commitments and War Involvement', PEACE RESEARCH SOCIETY (INTER-NATIONAL) PAPERS, Vol. 5, 1966, pp. 109–140

33. Singer, J.D. and Small, M., 'Patterns of International Warfare: 1816–1965', ANNALS OF THE AMERICAN ACADEMY OF POLITICAL AND ECONOMIC SCIENCE, Vol. 391, September 1970, pp. 145–155

34. Singer, J.D. and Small, M., THE WAGES OF WAR: 1816–1965, New York, John Wiley, 1972

35. Singer, J.D., Bremer, S. and Stuckey, J., 'Capability Distribution, Uncertainty and Major Power War; 1816–1965' in Bruce M. Russett (ed.), PEACE, WAR AND NUMBERS, Beverly Hills, California, Sage Publications, 1972

36. Sprout, H. and M., FOUNDATIONS OF INTERNATIONAL

POLITICS, Princeton, N.J., Van Nostrand, 1962
37. Sprout, H. and M., THE ECOLOGICAL PERSPECTIVE ON HUMAN AFFAIRS, Princeton, N.J., Princeton University Press, 1965
38. Weber, M., THE THEORY OF SOCIAL AND ECONOMIC ORGANIZATION, New York, The Free Press, 1966, (First published in 1925)
39. Wolfinger, R.E., 'Non-decisions and the Study of Local Politics', AMERICAN POLITICAL SCIENCE REVIEW, 65(4), December 1971, pp. 1063–80

Chapter VII

CONFLICT AND WAR

by C.R. Mitchell
The City University, London

One of the most long-lasting and traditional concerns of International
Relations scholarship has been the explanation of large scale, lethal
violence at the international level; and the development of theories or
explanatory schemes to account for the fact that national governments
wage, or become involved in, war, almost irrespective of the nature of
nation or government. Hence, this Chapter surveys a very substantial
sub-field within International Relations theory. The format adopted
involves first considering the literature on conflicts in general, much
of which has been developed within the 'conflict research' movement;
and then surveying work more specifically directed towards illuminating the phenomenon of international war, its causes, course and
settlement.

Conflict Analysis

The impact of the 'conflict research' movement of the late 1950's and
1960's on the study of International Relations has been considerable,
if diffuse, and many of the insights provided by conflict researchers
have been incorporated in the main body of International Relations
theory in subtle and by no means obvious ways. Hence, the quickest
way of assessing the debt International Relations owes to conflict
research is often to return directly to those writers who unambiguously
take the position that international conflict is merely one sub-category
of a general phenomenon consisting of goal incompatibility between

groups or organizations, and the behaviour or psychological states that arise from the existence of such conflict situations. This part of the Chapter will, therefore, briefly review works of relevance to International Relations but focussed mainly upon the sources, processes and management of social conflict. Works dealing specifically with international war will be dealt with in the second section.

Writing introductory surveys of a field as vast as that of social conflict presents almost unsurmountable problems, so that the paucity of readable, comprehensive introductions should be no surprise. Anatol Rapoport's recent paperback (114) is a good starting point for those new to the field, although they might be slightly deterred by the author's taste for formal analyses of conflict situations. In a rather different vein, Juergen Dedring's survey (32) of conflict research 'in progress' has the great advantage that it contains information on conflict research and findings from non-English speaking sources (mainly West German), although it suffers from the disadvantage of being something of an 'insider's' book, intended for those already working in the field. For the rest, there are a number of books of readings, the best of which is still probably Zawodny's two volume review of conflict and integration (165). Smith's collection (139) relies very heavily on the JOURNAL OF CONFLICT RESOLUTION, while Brickman's (16) is probably of more interest to psychologists and sociologists than students of international conflicts. McNeil's THE NATURE OF HUMAN CONFLICT (93) is now over 10 years old, and probably of only historical interest, but there remains much interesting material in the collections edited by Fisher (49) or by de Reuck and Knight (34).

For those interested in formal approaches to analyzing conflict situations and processes, and in efforts to utilize deductive logic, mathematical models or game theory, the most representative and comprehensive work remains Kenneth Boulding's CONFLICT AND DEFENSE (14), very much influenced by the author's background as an economist familiar with topographical and economic models. Less formidable, and probably more relevant to the non-technical reader, is Rapoport's FIGHTS, GAMES AND DEBATES (115), although the easiest, but by no means least sophisticated, introduction to the formal side of conflict research is that by Michael Nicholson (102). Anyone interested in pursuing this rather esoteric aspect should consult the pages of recent editions of the JOURNAL OF CONFLICT RESOLUTION which have abounded with examples of the genre;

while further formal analysis can be found in the annual volumes of GENERAL SYSTEMS YEARBOOK and the PEACE SCIENCE SOCIETY (INTERNATIONAL) PAPERS.

Works concerned with the sources and effects of social conflict are many and varied, reflecting divergent ideas about whether the major sources of social conflict are psychological and educational, or social and structural. One large sub-category of works on sources of competition and conflict is that dealing with — perhaps 'debating about' is a better description — the nature of human aggression. This body of literature contains familiar names such as Lorenz (86), Montagu (100), Storr (147), Dollard (37), Scott (126) and Berkowitz (8). However, the best introductory work to the whole subject is undoubtedly John Gunn's VIOLENCE IN HUMAN SOCIETY (58), while an excellent reader, which traces a careful path among the debates about aggressive drives, frustration-aggression, and behaviour as a learned response, is that edited by Megargee and Hokkansen (94). Finally, Erich Fromm's THE ANATOMY OF HUMAN DESTRUCTIVENESS (55) provides an up to date, if idiosyncratic, survey of individual aggression from the viewpoint of a distinguished psycho-analyst.

An even vaster collection of books can be subsumed under the category concerned with conflict arising from the structure of particular societies. Conflict can arise from class divisions, caste cleavages or other types of religious, ethno-linguistic or regional differences that give rise to the search for a sense of security, to competing claims on resources, or to efforts to build up protected or influential positions in the social structure. An interesting analysis of stable and unstable social systems is Chalmers Johnson's REVOLUTIONARY CHANGE (75), which makes an important link between the incidence of widespread, lethal conflict and the speed and extent of social change, a link echoed in much conflict research literature. More specifically directed towards connections between conflict and the structure of modern industrial society is Dahrendorf's famous study (31) which might be regarded as an up-dating of Marxist analysis of the bases of social conflict. Still relevant in this respect is Georg Simmel's classic work on conflict and on the 'web of group affiliations' (131), while Coser's later re-consideration of Simmel's propositions links the debate about the fundamental sources of conflict to the question of its effects, and thence to the debate about whether conflict is functional or dysfunctional for a society (or 'productive or destructive' in Morton Deutsch's terms). Coser's THE FUNCTIONS OF SOCIAL CONFLICT (27) remains the classic discussion of this topic, and should be read together with his later collection of essays (26), and the relevant chapters of Deutsch's THE RESOLUTION OF CONFLICT (36). An interesting attempt to apply some of Coser's ideas to international conflict is Siddiqui's study of Pakistan (130), which is a useful corrective to the impression to be gained from some proponents of the doctrine of functional conflict that conflict is always 'a good thing'. Robert Merton reminds us that we need always ask: 'Functional for whom?' when discussing beneficial aspects of conflict situations, processes and outcomes. Industrial conflict, for example, might be functional for a union in highlighting organizational weaknesses in its structure, but highly dysfunctional for losing strikers.

The approach to social conflict through political socialization is an interesting, but patchily covered aspect of conflict research. As anthropologists point out, who we are, who are our enemies and how we can, (or should) behave towards them, are all very much socially defined factors; and yet this particular approach to the sources of social and international conflict has yet to be worked through in any systematic fashion. At best, some connections are implied in the recent work on political socialization by Hess and Torney (63), by Greenstein (57), by Easton and Dennis (42) and (in an interesting comparison between the U.S.A. and the Soviet Union) by Bronfenbrenner (17). Other studies exist which specifically try to relate children's up-bringing and socio-cultural background to their attitude to war, personal heroism or other social groups and nations (for example CHILDREN AND WAR (152) by Howard Tolley); and there is a continuing series of relevant articles in the JOURNAL OF PEACE RESEARCH. Similarly, those approaching the question from the opposite pole of education for peace have produced a number of isolated works on bringing up children for a peaceful world, rather than for a competitive or conflict-ridden one. (Notably the UNESCO sponsored handbook edited by Wulf (162) and Barbara Stanford's recent handbook on PEACEMAKING (144).) However, there is no single book that systematically sets out to explore connections between socialization processes and social conflict.

In comparison with the literature on socialization, that dealing with a related subject, the contribution of psychological factors to the creation or exacerbation of a conflict situation, is comprehensive and wide-ranging, (perhaps reflecting the original focus of the conflict research movement). Much conventional psychological analysis of perceptions and attitudes is relevant in this regard. Kenneth Boulding's THE IMAGE (15), although old, remains the simplest introduction to the role of perception in conflicts. Gordon Allport's classic THE NATURE OF PREJUDICE (1) remains a classic, as does Rokeach's work on the open and closed mind (117), while Robert Jervis's THE LOGIC OF IMAGES IN INTERNATIONAL RELATIONS (74) applies insights on perceptual processes to the realm of international politics. More recently, Milgram's experiments on individual tendencies towards obedience have produced interesting, (if alarming) insights into how the talents and energies of individual group members might best be mobilized for participation in a conflict (98), especially one involving extremes of violence towards dehumanized adversaries.

Works more specifically concerned with the psychology of being 'in conflict' include Stagner's lively and readable PSYCHOLOGICAL ASPECTS OF INTERNATIONAL CONFLICT (142) (now unfortunately out of print, as is his major work on the psychology of industrial conflict (141)); Jerome Frank's SANITY AND SURVIVAL (53), recently issued as a paperback; and the coherent and comprehensive CONFLICT AMONG HUMANS by Robert Nye (106), probably the best single volume introduction to the subject now available. Works concerned more directly with conflict at the international level range from Kelman's rather dated but still useful reader (78), (and a narrower, more issue orientated collection by Farrell and Smith (45)) to Ralph White's analysis of the psychology of the Vietnam struggle (106) and Finlay, Holsti and Fagen's study of the role of adversaries and rivals, ENEMIES OF POLITICS (47). Somewhat in the same tradition is Rona Field's eye-witness analysis of the psychology of contemporary Northern Ireland (46), a work suffused with a fine level of indignation based on personal experiences. An unusual addition to works on the psychological aspects of conflict is Pelton's THE PSYCHOLOGY OF NON-VIOLENCE (108), in which the author adopts the novel approach of examining the central tenets and tactics of non-violent action in the light of psychological theory, to discover whether non-violent behaviour during conflicts is theoretically likely to have (at least) the psychological effects necessary for success. A remarkably fresh approach to the subject.

Moving away from works about how people perceive, think, feel and evaluate when involved in conflict, the next major concern is how

82

they behave. Again, there is a wide variety of work dealing with various aspects of conflict behaviour, a variety which matches the diverse behaviour patterns open to those seeking to win their dispute. Much of the work in this area consists of the analysis of violence as a strategy; or of coercive tactics designed to make adversaries abandon their goals, or at least negotiate a settlement. Among the former group, Hannah Arendt's thoughtful essay ON VIOLENCE (2) is a useful introduction to the subject, while the uses of coercion to deter or compel are analyzed in Thomas Schelling's two books (124, 125), (of which ARMS AND INFLUENCE is the more readable, and probably the more misleading in its view of how parties in conflict behave, given their actual structure and decision-making processes). In addition, much of the literature reviewed in the Chapter on Strategic Studies is relevant here. A somewhat less coercively orientated analysis of behaviour in conflicts is Roger Fisher's jocularly titled INTERNATIONAL CONFLICT FOR BEGINNERS (48) (published in Britain as BASIC NEGOTIATING STRATEGY), while a similar approach to the narrower field of arms control negotiations is adopted in Jeremy Stone's STRATEGIC PERSUASION (146). Out of the literature on non-violence as a strategy for gaining one's ends, Gene Sharp's massive THE POLITICS OF NON-VIOLENT ACTION (128) is undoubtedly the most comprehensive survey, but more interesting is the careful analysis of the limits of non-violence as a strategy by Boserup and Mack (13). Both books contain adequate bibliographies for anyone interested in pursuing the ethical and practical, as well as the tactical, aspects of non-violent behaviour.

Until recently, little scholarly attention had focussed on the general problems of ending a dispute, making a bilateral peace, or terminating conflict — the notable exception being an early article by Coser (28). The U.S. Government's struggles to escape from Vietnam 'with honour' changed this situation somewhat, and recent years have seen the publication of Ikle's anecdotal but insightful monograph (69); Randle's large scale, comparative study THE ORIGINS OF PEACE (113) (which somehow leaves a reader with no very clear impression of any peacemaking process); and a volume of the A.A.P.S.S. Papers devoted to the difficulties of ending conflicts (51). In this area, however, one of the best studies of the dilemmas of making peace remains Kecskemeti's work on 'Strategic Surrender' (77), even though this is now nearly twenty years old and deals with the problem mainly from the viewpoint of the vanquished. On the more general problem of negotiating an end to a dispute, the best introduction remains Ikle's HOW NATIONS NEGOTIATE (70), although a more comprehensive analytical framework is provided by Sawyer and Guetzkow's article in Kelman's INTERNATIONAL BEHAVIOUR (78). Zartmann's recent reader (164) provides some interesting articles, ranging from the descriptive to the formally analytical, while a good survey of recent experimental investigations into psychological aspects of negotiation can be found in Druckman's Sage Paper (40). For anyone interested in a diplomat's analysis of the business of ending conflicts through negotiation, there is always Arthur Lall's MODERN INTERNATIONAL NEGOTIATION (81) although, perversely, more insights can be gained from a book dealing with negotiation in an industrial setting, namely Walton and McKersie's A BEHAVIOURAL THEORY OF LABOUR NEGOTIATIONS (157).

Literature in the general area of managing conflicts, (by avoiding, channelling, suppressing or resolving them) is again heterogeneous, and yet to be organized into a coherent body of theories or findings. Perhaps the best starting place might be some of the anthropological literature on conflict in simple societies discussed in the Chapter XIV of this bibliography. Certainly, Lucy Mair's PRIMITIVE GOVERN-MENT (89) provides a useful introduction to the manner in which simpler societies develop devices for coping with internal conflicts through the establishment of mechanisms for informal mediation; of rules and norms; of rule-making structures and processes; and (finally), of institutions for interpreting and enforcing rules. Works directly concerned with the problem of conflict management tend to be disappointing. Pirage's recent MANAGING POLITICAL CONFLICT (110) never gets to grips with any of the central problems of conflict management, while Thomas and Bennis's reader (151), is mainly concerned with conflict within formal organizations rather than within society at large. Matthew Melko's 52 PEACEFUL SOCIETIES (95) adopts an interesting comparative approach, but ultimately is only a beginning. Both Nordlinger's CONFLICT REGULATION IN DIVIDED SOCIETIES (103) and Nardin's attack on the assumption that the state is solely a conflict manager rather than a party to many conflicts (101) are interesting, but inevitably more narrowly conceived. A good general survey of conflict management remains to be written, although Lynn McDonal's recent work on the sociology of 'law and order' (92) is a broader treatment than its title might suggest, as well as being subtle and readable.

On specific aspects of the process, however, a number of works can be highly recommended. Barkun's study of LAW WITHOUT SANCTIONS (5) is a useful introduction to the whole subject of the institutionalization of conflict behaviour within a set of rules or a legal system, while for those seeking a more conventional approach Wolfgang Friedman's LAW IN A CHANGING SOCIETY (54), or Aubert's reader (3) remain well worth reading. Of books more directly concerned with the problem of establishing some set of rules for international conflict, Rosalyn Higgins' introductory CONFLICT OF INTERESTS (64) is clear and concise, while Thomas Franck's THE STRUCTURE OF IMPARTIALITY (52) tackles one of the central issues in the functioning of any legal system. On the related subject of complementary values helping to off-set, or minimize, conflict between groups or governments, Sherif's conception of 'super-ordinate goals' is best discussed in his well-known INTER-GROUP CONFLICT AND CO-OPERATION (129), although this approach rapidly leads into the literature on 'functionalism', 'functional co-operation' and conflict management in international organizations (for example, Nye's excellent PEACE IN PARTS (105)) which is discussed in Chapter X.

A final body of literature in conflict analysis deals with efforts to settle or resolve conflicts once they have reached the stage of open coercion or violence; and particularly once tacit bargaining or bilateral negotiation have failed to produce some form of solution, whether this be defeat, victory, or a negotiated compromise. At their most straight-forward such efforts involve processes of peacekeeping or peace enforce-ment and relate to the vast literature on international peacekeeping. (See Chapter VIII.) More generally, they involve a wide variety of activities by third parties to end, at least, conflict behaviour and at most the existence of a conflict situation. In this area, the most com-prehensive theoretical survey of third party activity remains Oran Young's book (163) which could be supplemented by Cot's less readable and more descriptive INTERNATIONAL CONCILIATION (29). An interesting and reflective account of a number of personal experiences can be found in Adam Curle's MAKING PEACE, which deals with this Quaker intermediary's own efforts at interpersonal, intergroup and international peacemaking (30). Interesting parallels can be drawn between settling conflicts in organizations or in industry, and similar activities at the international level. Anyone interested in these can do no better than begin with the Walton and McKersie volume mentioned above, or Blake, Shepherd and Mouton's MANAGING

INTER-GROUP CONFLICT IN INDUSTRY (11). (Ann Douglas's
INDUSTRIAL PEACEMAKING (39) also remains relevant in this area.)
Richard Walton has also dealt with interpersonal conflicts within
organizations in his INTERPERSONAL PEACEMAKING (156), a work
that combines detailed descriptions of case studies with a summary
that analyzes and illuminates the genesis and development of individual
conflicts and antagonisms.

Recent efforts to apply non-directive (or case work) methods of
conflict resolution to a number of varied disputes have yet to be
systematically treated in any book length study, but some ideas of the
process can be gained from summary articles by Kelman in Merritt's
COMMUNICATION IN INTERNATIONAL POLITICS (79) or by
Fisher in the JOURNAL OF CONFLICT RESOLUTION (50). Two
attempts to use this general approach in resolving international conflicts
are reported in John Burton's CONFLICT AND COMMUNICATION
(19), which also contains a highly critical review of more conventional
intermediary processes and their lack of any real or lasting impact on
disputes; and Leonard Doob's RESOLVING CONFLICT IN AFRICA
(38). The more conventional approach attacked by Burton is well
represented in the UNITAR 'Peaceful Settlement' series, the volumes by
Pechota (107) and by Edmead (44) being the most interesting of an
admittedly not very distinguished collection. Finally, a symposium
with an interesting central theme but a disappointing set of papers, is
Jandt's CONFLICT RESOLUTION THROUGH COMMUNICATION
(71).

War and the Theory of War
Separating the study of war from the general study of International
Relations may initially appear slightly unreal. (Similarly, many
scholars in the field of conflict research would argue that to separate
war from other forms of conflict is equally unreal.) War is, as we are
frequently reminded, politics (or conflict) carried on by 'other' means,
and certainly most modern International Relations scholars, both
classical and behavioural, would agree that wars lie at one extreme of
a continuum of influence behaviours used by governments for a variety
of purposes; to gain resources, to increase their perceived security, to
avoid having to change themselves or their society (and thus forcing
change on others), or even to survive. However, a body of literature has
developed within the general field of International Relations theory that
concerns itself primarily with the nature and origins of war as a

distinctive phenomenon in international society. Moreover, this study is both conceived and carried out on a systematic and comparative basis, often using large scale data gathering schemes, and computing facilities for aggregate data analysis. Hence, the work is very directly the heir of two previous, classic works on the subject; Quincy Wright's massive A STUDY OF WAR (161), first published in its complete form in 1942; and Lewis Fry Richardson's STATISTICS OF DEADLY QUARRELS (116), a pioneering attempt to establish a body of statistical information about the number, nature and intensity of lethal conflicts involving national governments.

For the newcomer, however, it might be wise to begin with some less esoteric introduction to the subject before proceeding to the latest, quantitatively based studies of war and its correlates. Undoubtedly the best introduction, a summary of thinking about war over the last 2,000 years, is Kenneth Waltz's MAN, THE STATE AND WAR (159), which has, by now, achieved almost the status of a classic in its own right. More recent, but extremely readable is Geoffrey Blainey's THE CAUSES OF WAR (9), a book that appears anecdotal at first, but which proves to contain frequent flashes of insight and wisdom the more closely it is read. In the same tradition, though less distinguished and rather derivative, are Evan Luard's CONFLICT AND PEACE IN THE MODERN INTERNATIONAL SYSTEM (87), and Alastair Buchan's WAR IN MODERN SOCIETY (18).

An alternative way of starting to study the phenomenon of war is to enquire what sorts of activities constitute 'a war', and how many wars have taken place in recent history. Both questions are confronted by J. David Singer's massive 'Correlates of War' project, which initially involved describing and cataloguing all international wars since 1815; and in the publications resulting from this work (132, 133), most notably THE WAGES OF WAR (136). Also concerned with this, initial, descriptive, aspect of the study of war is an article by Denton (33) attempting to discern cyclical patterns in the occurence of large scale international conflicts; and a short review by Beer (7).

Moving from efforts to define, describe and then count wars to works that seek to explain them by references to empirical and comparative analysis, Pruitt and Snyder's early reader (112) attempts to give the impression of a coherent body of theory (or, at least, a progression of ideas) about the long term structural and more immediate decisional causes of wars. However, THEORY AND RESEARCH ON THE CAUSES OF WAR ultimately remains a rather diverse collection of papers or extracts, of very variable quality. More traditional in format, and in assumptions about the sources of international conflict, is John Stoessinger's WHY NATIONS GO TO WAR (145), while another reader that attempts to deal broadly with the sources of disputes and war is Russett's PEACE, WAR AND NUMBERS (123), a work which, as its title suggests, takes us firmly into the empirico-quantitative school of analysis but (unfortunately) no nearer a comprehensive or comprehensible general theory about wars. More traditional in style, but still far from proposing any general theories about war, is Northedge and Donelan's INTERNATIONAL DISPUTES: THE POLITICAL ASPECTS (104).

Various recent works have attempted to consider and test out in a systematic way a number of theories about the origins of war, often using somewhat esoteric language, aggregate or over-time data, and a variety of statistical techniques for establishing the presence or absence of relationships, (possibly casual) between key variables. The most interesting of these is Choucri and North's NATIONS IN CONFLICT (23), a study of 'lateral pressure' on countries and their governments in late 19th and early 20th century Europe, and a project that stemmed from North's early interest in the origins and outbreaks of the First World War. A more systematic treatment of wars in general, as opposed to one war-prone historical period, is Michael Haas's INTERNATIONAL CONFLICT (59), admirable in its coherence and single-mindedness, but difficult to plough through and emerge with a clear grasp of significant substantive findings. In a similar vein is Midlarsky's ON WAR (97), which takes virtually a Waltzian framework, and then proceeds to test hypotheses empirically by surveying existing evidence for wars being the result of man, state or system. A similar approach, using data from a much shorter time span, is Richard Barringer's WAR: PATTERNS OF CONFLICT (6), which provides one volume of analysis and findings and another on the data used in that analysis. The short time span covered tends to vitiate the wider applicability of any findings.

Most of the rest of recent theoretical work on the sources of war tends to concentrate upon single approaches or theories to explain why wars take place, leading one to suspect that we may be dealing with a phenomenon for which there are a large number of sufficient conditions, which might not be necessary. One body of literature takes up the question of the relationship between domestic conflicts (or high levels of internal instability) and involvement in international war. Two lines of thought are pursued here. The first is whether (or how) actual civil strife 'spills over' into international society, so that the two levels of conflict become intermingled, either through outsiders being drawn in, willy nilly, to a large scale, violent domestic conflict; or through purposive intervention by regional or global powers with an interest in the outcome of the internal struggle. James Rosenau's INTERNATIONAL ASPECTS OF CIVIL STRIFE (121) remains an excellent collection of theoretical articles on this subject, while Eckstein's INTERNAL WAR (43), of similar vintage, is less successful but contains some papers of interest, notably those by Deutsch and Thornton. A collection of papers published by the International Institute for Strategic Studies, CIVIL VIOLENCE AND THE INTERNATIONAL SYSTEM (24), contains much of interest, mainly from the point of view of the traditionalist or the practitioner. An interesting article by Istvan Kende emphasizes the recent frequency of this unstable phenomenon of internal war (80), and a paper by the present writer challenges conventional wisdom about the roots of intervention (99). The magnitude of the phenomenon is again emphasized in Bloomfield and Leiss's study CONTROLLING SMALL WARS (12), which surveys recent 'small' wars and which, as its title suggests, is very much written with a 'great Power' policeman's role in mind. An interesting work applying a theoretical framework to four historical cases of intervention is Richard Little's INTERVENTION (85).

The other main approach to the relationship between domestic and international phenomena is that which investigates whether there is any truth in the conventional wisdom about governments diverting attention from domestic unrest, policy failure, disunity or major grievance, by creating (or activating) an external threat, and thus bringing about a high probability of international conflict, and ultimately war. This is an old problem (Wright devotes a chapter to it in THE STUDY OF WAR), and new methods of analysis and techniques for large scale comparative analysis have revealed no clear answers, except that a straightforward relationship between internal disunity and external conflict does not exist. There is, unfortunately, no comprehensive treatment of the question, and those interested will have to consult articles by Haas or Rummel in Singer's QUANTITATIVE INTERNATIONAL POLITICS (138), or by Rummel and Tanter in various journals (122, 149). A good critique of the shortcomings of much of this aggregate analysis is the article by Mack (88), who points out that overall aggregation can mask significant sub-sets of cases where there is, indeed, a strong connection between external conflict and internal unrest — although the casual path may run in the opposite way to that posited by conventional hunches!

Two other major sets of ideas about the origins of war recently explored are those dealing with the activities of revisionist, revolutionary (or merely pro-change) states and their governments in international society; and those dealing with the constraining effects of the structure of that society on the incidence of war and peace. Two rather old, but still interesting books on the way in which wars are related to change in international society, (either technological, structural or to do with governmental capabilities and the international 'pecking order') are John Herz's INTERNATIONAL POLITICS IN THE ATOMIC AGE (62) (still packed with interesting insights, even though the promised demise of the territorial state has yet ot occur); and John Burton's PEACE THEORY (20), with its conceptions of 'primary' and 'secondary' change, and the necessity of adjusting to the former if wars are to be avoided. Much recent work in this latter tradition has taken up the idea of pro-change states and governments and combined it with Gerhardt Lenski's concept of 'status disequilibrium' to explain why states (as well as individuals and social groups) experience a need to alter their positions and statuses in the international social order; and might, as a last resort, employ war to bring about such a change. Midlarsky devotes two chapters to testing out this idea in ON WAR (97) (although one may take considerable exception to his method of operationalizing concepts such as 'achievement' or 'aspiration'). Galtung anecdotally applies Lenski's ideas at the international level in his article 'A Structural Theory of Aggression' (56). However, the most comprehensive testing out of the idea is that carried out by Michael Wallace, to be found in a number of articles (153), and in his WAR AND RANK AMONG NATIONS (154). An alternative approach, looking at the effects of rank disequilibrium within the international system itself, is by East (41). In spite of all the empirical work, however, the form and status of the theory remains highly unsatisfactory, and while it remains persuasive at the individual and group level, it sits uneasily at the international level, even in comparison with other existing 'theories' about the sources of war.

Writing about the relationship between the 'structure' of the international system and the propensity for wars to occur has a long history, going back to 19th century discussions of the operations of the balance of power, and its dampening effects upon a country's willingness to contemplate war as a strategy to gain desired ends. The tradition has been carried on in recent literature, although much of this (for example, Kaplan's SYSTEM AND PROCESS IN INTERNATIONAL POLITICS (76) or Rosecrance's ACTION AND REACTION IN WORLD POLITICS (118)) deals with a generally broader set of problems. In the later 1960's, discussion switched to the effects of a changing bipolarity in international society on stability and on the likelihood of war. Three key articles by Waltz (158), by Rosecrance (119), and by Deutsch and Singer (35) were collected by Rosenau for his 1969 reader, INTERNATIONAL POLITICS AND FOREIGN POLICY (120). More recently, an input from radical and Marxist scholars has switched attention from the conventional state and political power structure of international society to the underlying, and often neglected, economic-dependency structure of that society, and the relationship between this structure and the development of conflicts and war. This newer work has departed from classical Marxist views about the linkage between the capitalist system, imperialism and the likelihood of wars occurring over markets, raw materials or captive outlets for capital investment, long discredited in its classic form in Lenin's or Hobson's work. Instead, writers such as Jenkins (73), Hveem (68), Senghaas (127), and Langholm (82) argue that the crucial 'structural' aspects of international society making for conflicts and war are relationships of dominance and dependency between 'centre' and 'periphery'. To such theorists, the 'conflict formations' in international society are basically economic and have been neglected in conventional, state-centric International Relations literature, a neglect they have attempted to correct in a series of critical articles. Targ's recent article in the INTERNATIONAL STUDIES QUARTERLY is an excellent summary (150). The most sustained argument of this school of thought is in Wallensteen's book, STRUCTURE AND WAR (155), which reviews the pattern of conflict between 'centre' countries and their attached 'peripheries' since the end of World War I. (This literature is more fully discussed in Chapter V.)

A final aspect of recent work on the origins of war deals not with long and medium term factors that work to create disputes and conflicts between states and governments, but with behaviour at the brink of war, and with the circumstances that push decision-makers over that brink and into open warfare. In some respects, this work is concerned with the old problem of 'accidental' war, and the factors contributing towards leaders blundering into a war which they would rather have avoided, could they have seen a satisfactory way out. In others, it is a branch of general decision-making theory, and more specifically of the study of crisis behaviour by individuals and small groups. The best current overview of this aspect of the outbreak of wars is Charles Hermann's collection of papers, INTERNATIONAL CRISES; INSIGHTS FROM BEHAVIOURAL RESEARCH (61), which presents a useful, and long, inventory of propositions about crisis behaviour as an appendix. (The same author's CRISES IN FOREIGN POLICY (60) investigates efforts to learn about crisis behaviour through simulation exercises.) The Stanford University project on the study of international crises has produced a large number of assorted papers and articles by North, Holsti, Brody or Zinnes (66, 67, 166) as the main researchers, but the best summary of this work (concentrating heavily on the crisis of July–August 1914) is Ole Holsti's CRISIS, ESCALATION, WAR (65), which can be read in conjunction with the slightly more technical papers in the Pruitt and Snyder (112) and the Rosenau (120) readers mentioned above. The general literature on crisis behaviour is more fully discussed in our Chapter on foreign policy analysis and decision-making but two books that treat aspects of the complex process particularly well should be mentioned here. One is Irving Janis's VICTIMS OF GROUPTHINK (72), a social psychologist's analysis of factors making for an unwillingness to reconsider crucial decisions taken under crisis conditions by a close-knit group of decision-makers; and Ernest May's 'LESSONS' OF THE PAST (91). This is a historian's account of how recent history 'taught' key decision-makers fundamental 'lessons' about international disputes by setting up often erroneous models in their minds, thus leading to a number of decisions that were designed to deal with situations that had once existed in the past, rather than the reality that was confronting decision-makers currently. Both these books are disturbing in their implications for behaviour at the brink of war, and quite properly belong to any comprehensive survey of theoretical works on the sources of international conflicts and war.

Bibliography

1. Allport, Gordon W., THE NATURE OF PREJUDICE, Reading, Mass., Addison Wesley, 1954
2. Arendt, Hannah, ON VIOLENCE, New York, Harcourt Brace, 1969
3. Aubert, Vilhelm (ed.), SOCIOLOGY OF LAW, Harmondsworth, Middx., Penguin Books, 1969

4. Bailey, Sydney D., PEACEFUL SETTLEMENT OF DISPUTES: IDEAS AND PROPOSALS FOR RESEARCH, (Unitar Peaceful Settlement Series P.S. No. 1), New York, Unitar, 1971
5. Barkun, Michael, LAW WITHOUT SANCTIONS: ORDER IN PRIMITIVE SOCIETIES AND THE WORLD COMMUNITY New Haven, Conn., Yale University Press, 1968
6. Barringer, Richard E., WAR: PATTERNS OF CONFLICT, (2 volumes), Cambridge, Mass., M.I.T. Press, 1972
7. Beer, Francis A., HOW MUCH WAR IN HISTORY: DEFINITIONS, ESTIMATES, EXTRAPOLATIONS AND TRENDS, Beverly Hills, Calif., Sage Publications, 1974
8. Berkowitz, Leonard, AGGRESSION: A SOCIAL-PSYCHOLOGICAL ANALYSIS, New York, McGraw Hill, 1962
9. Blainey, Geoffrey, THE CAUSES OF WAR, London, Macmillan, 1973
10. Blake, R.R., Shepherd, H.A. and Mouton, J.S., INTERGROUP CONFLICT IN ORGANISATIONS, Ann Arbor, Mich., Foundation for Research on Human Behaviour, 1964
11. Blake, R.R., Shepherd, H.A. and Mouton, J.S., MANAGING INTER-GROUP CONFLICT IN INDUSTRY, Houston, Tex., Gulf Publishing Co., 1964
12. Bloomfield, Lincoln P. and Leiss, Amelia C., CONTROLLING SMALL WARS, London, Allen Lane, 1970
13. Boserup, Anders and Mack, Andrew, WAR WITHOUT WEAPONS: NON VIOLENCE IN NATIONAL DEFENCE, London, Frances Pinter, 1974
14. Boulding, Kenneth E., CONFLICT AND DEFENSE: A GENERAL THEORY, New York, Harper & Row, 1962
15. Boulding, Kenneth E., THE IMAGE: KNOWLEDGE IN LIFE AND SOCIETY, Ann Arbor, Mich., University of Michigan Press, 1961
16. Brickman, Philip (ed.), SOCIAL CONFLICT; READINGS IN RULE STRUCTURE AND CONFLICT RELATIONSHIPS, Lexington, Mass., D.C. Heath, 1974
17. Bronfenbrenner, Urie, TWO WORLDS OF CHILDHOOD: U.S. AND U.S.S.R., London, Allen & Unwin, 1971
18. Buchan, Alastair, WAR IN MODERN SOCIETY, London, Collins, 1968
19. Burton, John W., CONFLICT AND COMMUNICATION: THE USE OF CONTROLLED COMMUNICATION IN INTER-

NATIONAL RELATIONS, London, Macmillan, 1969

20. Burton, John W., PEACE THEORY; PRE-CONDITIONS OF DISARMAMENT, New York, Alfred Knopf, 1962

21. Butterworth, Robert L., MANAGING INTER-STATE CONFLICT 1945–74: DATA WITH SYNOPSES, Pittsburgh, U.C.I.S. Publications, 1976

22. Chase, Stuart, ROADS TO AGREEMENT, New York, Harper & Row, 1951

23. Choucri, Nazli and North, Robert C., NATIONS IN CONFLICT: NATIONAL GROWTH AND INTERNATIONAL VIOLENCE, San Francisco, Freeman, 1975

24. CIVIL VIOLENCE AND THE INTERNATIONAL SYSTEM, London, International Institute for Strategic Studies, 1971

25. Cohen, R. and S., PEACE CONFERENCES: THE FORMAL ASPECTS, (Jerusalem Papers on Peace Problems: No. 1), Jerusalem, The Hebrew University, 1974

26. Coser, Lewis A., CONTINUITIES IN THE STUDY OF SOCIAL CONFLICT, New York, The Free Press, 1967

27. Coser, Lewis A., THE FUNCTIONS OF SOCIAL CONFLICT, London, Routledge & Kegan Paul, 1956

28. Coser, Lewis A., 'The Termination of Conflict', JOURNAL OF CONFLICT RESOLUTION, V(4), December 1961, pp. 347–353

29. Cot, J.P., INTERNATIONAL CONCILIATION, London, Europa, 1972, (First published in French in 1968)

30. Curle, Adam, MAKING PEACE, London, Tavistock Publications, 1971

31. Dahrendorf, Ralf, CLASS AND CLASS CONFLICT IN INDUSTRIAL SOCIETY, London, Routledge & Kegan Paul, 1959

32. Dedring, Juergen, RECENT ADVANCES IN PEACE AND CONFLICT RESEARCH: A CRITICAL SURVEY, Beverly Hills, Calif., Sage Publications, 1976

33. Denton, F.H., 'Some Regularities in International Conflict 1820–1949', BACKGROUND, IX(4), February 1966, pp. 283–296

34. de Reuck, A.V.S. and Knight, Julie (eds.), CONFLICT IN SOCIETY, (A CIBA Foundation Symposium), London, J & A Churchill, 1966

35. Deutsch, Karl W. and Singer, J. David, 'Multipolar Power Systems and International Stability', WORLD POLITICS, XVI(3), April

1964, pp. 390–406

36. Deutsch, Morton, THE RESOLUTION OF CONFLICT, New Haven, Conn., Yale University Press, 1973

37. Dollard, John et al., FRUSTRATION AND AGGRESSION, New Haven, Conn., Yale University Press, 1968, (First published in 1939)

38. Doob, Leonard W. (ed.), RESOLVING CONFLICT IN AFRICA: THE FERMEDA WORKSHOP, New Haven, Conn., Yale University Press, 1970

39. Douglas, Ann, INDUSTRIAL PEACEMAKING: A REPORT ON UNION-MANAGEMENT NEGOTIATIONS, New York, Columbia University Press, 1962

40. Druckman, Daniel, HUMAN FACTORS IN INTERNATIONAL NEGOTIATIONS: SOCIAL-PSYCHOLOGICAL ASPECTS OF INTERNATIONAL CONFLICT, Beverly Hills, Calif., Sage Publications, 1973

41. East, Maurice A., 'Status Discrepancy and Violence in the International System', in J.N. Rosenau, V. Davis and M.A. East (eds.), THE ANALYSIS OF INTERNATIONAL POLITICS, New York, The Free Press, 1972

42. Easton, David and Dennis, Jack, CHILDREN IN THE POLITICAL SYSTEM: ORIGINS OF POLITICAL LEGITIMACY, New York, McGraw Hill, 1969

43. Eckstein, H. (ed.), INTERNAL WAR, New York, The Free Press, 1964

44. Edmead, Frank, ANALYSIS AND PREDICTION IN INTER-NATIONAL MEDIATION, (Unitar Peaceful Settlement Series P.S. No. 2), New York, Unitar, 1971

45. Farrell, John C. and Smith, Asa P. (eds.), IMAGE AND REALITY IN WORLD POLITICS, New York, Columbia University Press, 1968

46. Fields, Rona N., A SOCIETY ON THE RUN, Harmondsworth, Middx., Penguin Books, 1973

47. Finlay, J., Holsti, Ole R. and Fagen, Richard R., ENEMIES IN POLITICS, Chicago, Rand McNally, 1967

48. Fisher, Roger, BASIC NEGOTIATING STRATEGY, London, Allen Lane, 1970, (Published in the U.S.A. as INTERNATIONAL CONFLICT FOR BEGINNERS, New York, Harper & Row, 1969)

49. Fisher, Roger (ed.), INTERNATIONAL CONFLICT AND THE BEHAVIOURAL SCIENCES: THE CRAIGSVILLE PAPERS,

New York, Basic Books, 1964

50. Fisher, Ronald J., 'Third Party Consultation', JOURNAL OF CONFLICT RESOLUTION, XVI (1), March 1972, pp. 67—94

51. Fox, W.T.R. (ed.), 'How Wars End', ANNALS OF THE AMERICAN ACADEMY FOR POLITICAL AND SOCIAL SCIENCES, Volume 392, November 1970

52. Franck, Thomas M., THE STRUCTURE OF IMPARTIALITY: TOWARDS THE ORGANISATION OF WORLD LAW, New York, Macmillan, 1968

53. Frank, Jerome D., SANITY AND SURVIVAL: PSYCHOLOGICAL ASPECTS OF WAR AND PEACE, New York, Random House, 1968

54. Friedman, Wolfgang, LAW IN A CHANGING SOCIETY (2nd edition), London, Stevens & Sons, 1972

55. Fromm, Erich, THE ANATOMY OF HUMAN DESTRUCTIVE-NESS, London, Jonathan Cape, 1974

56. Galtung, Johan, 'A Structural Theory of Aggression', JOURNAL OF PEACE RESEARCH, Volume 1, 1964, pp. 95—119

57. Greenstein, Fred I., CHILDREN AND POLITICS, (revised edition), New Haven, Conn., Yale University Press, 1969

58. Gunn, John, VIOLENCE IN HUMAN SOCIETY, Newton Abbot, David & Charles, 1973

59. Haas, Michael, INTERNATIONAL CONFLICT, Indianapolis, Bobbs Merrill, 1974

60. Hermann, Charles F., CRISES IN FOREIGN POLICY, New York, The Free Press, 1970

61. Hermann, Charles F. (ed.), INTERNATIONAL CRISES: INSIGHTS FROM BEHAVIOURAL RESEARCH, New York, The Free Press, 1973

62. Herz, John H., INTERNATIONAL POLITICS IN THE ATOMIC AGE, New York, Columbia University Press, 1959

63. Hess, Robert D. and Torney, Judith V., THE DEVELOPMENT OF POLITICAL ATTITUDES IN CHILDREN, Chicago, Aldine Pub. Co., 1967

64. Higgins, Rosalyn, CONFLICT OF INTEREST, London, The Bodley Head, 1965

65. Holsti, Ole R., CRISIS, ESCALATION, WAR, Montreal, Queens-McGill University Press, 1972

66. Holsti, Ole R., 'The 1914 Case', AMERICAN POLITICAL SCIENCE REVIEW, LIX (2), June 1965, pp. 365—378

67. Holsti, Ole R., North, Robert C. and Brody, Richard A.,

'Perception and Action in the 1914 Crisis' in J. David Singer (ed.), QUANTITATIVE INTERNATIONAL POLITICS, New York, The Free Press, 1968

68. Hveem, H., 'The Global Dominance System', JOURNAL OF PEACE RESEARCH, Volume 10, 1973, pp. 319–340

69. Iklé, Fred Charles, EVERY WAR MUST END, New York, Columbia University Press, 1971

70. Iklé, Fred Charles, HOW NATIONS NEGOTIATE, New York, Harper & Row, 1964

71. Jandt, Fred E. (ed.), CONFLICT RESOLUTION THROUGH COMMUNICATION, New York, Harper & Row, 1973

72. Janis, Irving L., VICTIMS OF GROUPTHINK, New York, Houghton Mifflin, 1972

73. Jenkins, Robin S., EXPLOITATION; THE WORLD POWER STRUCTURE AND THE INEQUALITY OF NATIONS, London, McGibbon & Kee, 1970

74. Jervis, Robert, THE LOGIC OF IMAGES IN INTERNATIONAL RELATIONS, Princeton, N.J., Princeton University Press, 1970

75. Johnson, Chalmers, REVOLUTIONARY CHANGE, Boston, Little, Brown, 1964

76. Kaplan, Morton A., SYSTEM AND PROCESS IN INTERNATIONAL POLITICS, New York, John Wiley, 1957

77. Kecskemeti, Paul, STRATEGIC SURRENDER, Stanford, Calif., Stanford University Press, 1958

78. Kelman, H.C. (ed.), INTERNATIONAL BEHAVIOUR: A SOCIAL-PSYCHOLOGICAL ANALYSIS, New York, Holt, Rhinehart & Winston, 1965

79. Kelman, H.C., 'The Problem-Solving Workshop in Conflict Resolution' in R.L. Merritt (ed.), COMMUNICATION IN INTERNATIONAL POLITICS, Urbana, University of Illinois Press, 1972

80. Kende, Istvan, 'Twenty-Five Years of Local Wars', JOURNAL OF PEACE RESEARCH, Volume 8, 1971, pp. 5–22

81. Lall, Arthur, MODERN INTERNATIONAL NEGOTIATION, New York, Columbia University Press, 1966

82. Langholm, Siv, 'On the Concepts of Centre and Periphery', JOURNAL OF PEACE RESEARCH, Volume 8, 1971, pp. 273–278

83. Lee, Robert and Marty, Martin E. (eds.), RELIGION AND SOCIAL CONFLICT, New York, Oxford University Press, 1964

84. Levine, R.A. and Campbell, D.T., ETHNOCENTRISM: THEORIES OF CONFLICT, ETHNIC ATTITUDES AND GROUP BEHAVIOUR, New York, John Wiley, 1972
85. Little, Richard, INTERVENTION, London, Martin Robertson, 1975
86. Lorenz, Konrad, ON AGGRESSION, New York, Harcourt Brace and World, 1966, (First published as DAS SOGENNANTE BOSE, Vienna, 1963)
87. Luard, Evan, CONFLICT AND PEACE IN THE MODERN INTERNATIONAL SYSTEM, Boston, Little, Brown, 1968
88. Mack, Andrew J.R., 'Why Big Nations Lose Small Wars: The Politics of Asymmetric Conflict', WORLD POLITICS, XXVII(2), January 1975, pp. 175—200
89. Mair, Lucy, PRIMITIVE GOVERNMENT, Harmondsworth, Middx., Penguin Books, 1962
90. Masters, Roger D., 'World Politics as a Primitive Political System', WORLD POLITICS, XVI(4), July 1964, pp. 595—619
91. May, Ernest R., 'LESSONS' OF THE PAST: THE USE AND MISUSE OF HISTORY IN AMERICAN FOREIGN POLICY, New York, Oxford University Press, 1973
92. McDonald, Lynn, THE SOCIOLOGY OF LAW AND ORDER, London, Faber & Faber, 1976
93. McNeil, Elton B., THE NATURE OF HUMAN CONFLICT, Englewood Cliffs, N.J., Prentice Hall, 1965
94. Megargee, Edwin I. and Hokansen, Jack E. (eds.), THE DYNAMICS OF AGGRESSION, New York, Harper & Row, 1970
95. Melko, Matthew, 52 PEACEFUL SOCIETIES, Oakville, Ontario, Canadian Peace Research Institute Press, 1973
96. Merritt, Richard L. (ed.), COMMUNICATION IN INTER-NATIONAL POLITICS, Urbana, Ill., University of Illinois Press, 1972
97. Midlarsky, Manus, ON WAR; POLITICAL VIOLENCE IN THE INTERNATIONAL SYSTEM, New York, The Free Press, 1975
98. Milgram, Stanley, OBEDIENCE TO AUTHORITY: AN EXPERIMENTAL VIEW, London, Tavistock Publications, 1974 and New York, Harper & Row, 1974
99. Mitchell, C.R., 'Civil Strife and the Involvement of External Parties', INTERNATIONAL STUDIES QUARTERLY, XIV(2), June, 1970, pp. 166—194
100. Montagu, M.F. Ashley (ed.), MAN AND AGGRESSION, London,

Oxford University Press, 1968
101. Nardin, Terry, VIOLENCE AND THE STATE: A CRITIQUE OF EMPIRICAL POLITICAL THEORY, Beverly Hills, Calif., Sage Publications, 1971
102. Nicholson, M.B., CONFLICT ANALYSIS, London, English Universities Press, 1970
103. Nordlinger, Eric A., CONFLICT REGULATION IN DIVIDED SOCIETIES, Camb., Mass., Harvard University Centre for International Affairs, 1972
104. Northedge, F.S. and Donelan, M.D., INTERNATIONAL DISPUTES: THE POLITICAL ASPECTS, London, Europa, 1971
105. Nye, J.S., PEACE IN PARTS: INTEGRATION AND CONFLICT IN REGIONAL ORGANISATIONS, Boston, Little, Brown, 1971
106. Nye, Robert D., CONFLICT AMONG HUMANS: SOME BASIC PSYCHOLOGICAL AND SOCIAL-PSYCHOLOGICAL CONSIDERATIONS, New York, Springer Pub. Co., 1973
107. Pechota, Vratislav, COMPLEMENTARY STRUCTURES IN THIRD PARTY SETTLEMENT OF INTERNATIONAL DISPUTES, (Unitar Peaceful Settlement Series P.S. No. 3), New York, Unitar, 1971
108. Pelton, Leroy H., THE PSYCHOLOGY OF NON-VIOLENCE, New York, Pergamon Press, 1974
109. Pickus, Robert and Woits, Robert (eds.), TO END WAR: AN INTRODUCTION TO THE IDEAS, ORGANISATIONS AND CURRENT BOOKS, New York, Harper & Row, 1970
110. Pirages, Dennis, MANAGING POLITICAL CONFLICT, Sunbury-on-Thames, Middx., Nelson, 1976
111. Prosterman, Roy L., SURVIVING TO 3000: AN INTRODUCTION TO THE STUDY OF LETHAL CONFLICT, Belmont, Calif., Duxbury Press, 1972
112. Pruitt, Dean G. and Snyder, Richard C. (eds.), THEORY AND RESEARCH ON THE CAUSES OF WAR, Englewood Cliffs, N.J., Prentice Hall, 1969
113. Randle, Robert F., THE ORIGINS OF PEACE: A STUDY OF PEACEMAKING AND THE STRUCTURE OF PEACE SETTLEMENTS, New York, The Free Press, 1973
114. Rapoport, Anatol, CONFLICT IN MAN-MADE ENVIRONMENT, Harmondsworth, Middx., Penguin Books, 1974
115. Rapoport, Anatol, FIGHTS, GAMES AND DEBATES, Ann Arbor, Mich., University of Michigan Press, 1960

116. Richardson, Lewis F., STATISTICS OF DEADLY QUARRELS, London, Stevens, 1960

117. Rokeach, Milton, THE OPEN AND CLOSED MIND, New York, Basic Books, 1960

118. Rosecrance, Richard N., ACTION AND REACTION IN WORLD POLITICS, Boston, Little, Brown, 1963

119. Rosecrance, Richard N., 'Bipolarity, Multipolarity and the Future', JOURNAL OF CONFLICT RESOLUTION, X(3), September 1966, pp. 314–327

120 Rosenau, James N. (ed.), INTERNATIONAL POLITICS AND FOREIGN POLICY, (2nd edition), New York, The Free Press, 1969

121. Rosenau, James N. (ed.), INTERNATIONAL ASPECTS OF CIVIL STRIFE, Princeton, N.J., Princeton University Press, 1965

122. Rummel, Rudolph J., 'The Relationship Between National Attributes and Foreign Conflict Behaviour' in J. David Singer (ed.), QUANTITATIVE INTERNATIONAL POLITICS, New York, The Free Press, 1968

123. Russett, Bruce M. (ed.), PEACE, WAR AND NUMBERS, Beverly Hills, Calif., Sage Publications, 1972

124. Schelling, Thomas C., ARMS AND INFLUENCE, New Haven, Conn., Yale University Press, 1966

125. Schelling, Thomas C., THE STRATEGY OF CONFLICT, New York, Oxford University Press, 1963

126. Scott, J.P., AGGRESSION, (2nd edition), Chicago, University of Chicago Press, 1975

127. Senghaas, Dieter, 'Conflict Formations in Contemporary International Society', JOURNAL OF PEACE RESEARCH, Volume X, 1973, pp. 163–184

128. Sharp, Gene et al (eds.), THE POLITICS OF NON-VIOLENT ACTION, Boston, Porter Sargent, 1973

129. Sherif, M. et al, INTER-GROUP CONFLICT AND CO-OPERATION: THE ROBBERS CAVE EXPERIMENT, Norman, Oklahoma, Oklahoma University Book Exchange, 1961

130. Siddiqui, Kalim, THE FUNCTIONS OF INTERNATIONAL CONFLICT, London, News and Media Ltd., 1976

131. Simmel, Georg, CONFLICT, (printed with THE WEB OF GROUP AFFILIATIONS), New York, The Free Press, 1955, (First published in 1908)

132. Singer, J. David, 'The Correlates of War Project; Continuity, Diversity and Convergency' in Francis W. Hoole and Dinna A. Zinnes (eds.), QUANTITATIVE INTERNATIONAL POLITICS: AN APPRAISAL, New York, Praeger, 1976

133. Singer, J. David, 'The Correlates of War Project; Interim Report and Rationale', WORLD POLITICS, XXIV(2), January 1972, pp. 243–270

134. Singer J. David (ed.), HUMAN NATURE AND INTER-NATIONAL RELATIONS, New York, Rand McNally, 1965

135. Singer J. David and Small, Melvin, 'Alliance Aggregation and the Onset of War: 1815–1945' in J. David Singer (ed.), QUANTITATIVE INTERNATIONAL POLITICS, New York, The Free Press, 1968

136. Singer, J. David and Small, Melvin, THE WAGES OF WAR: 1816–1965 A STATISTICAL HANDBOOK, New York, John Wiley, 1972

137. Singer, J. David, Bremer, Stuart A. and Stuckey, John, 'Capability Distribution, Uncertainty and Major Power War; 1820–1965' in Bruce M. Russett (ed.), PEACE, WAR AND NUMBERS, Beverly Hills, Calif., Sage Publications, 1972

138. Singer, J. David (ed.), QUANTITATIVE INTERNATIONAL POLITICS: INSIGHTS AND EVIDENCE, New York, The Free Press, 1968

139. Smith, Clagett G. (ed.), CONFLICT RESOLUTION: CON-TRIBUTIONS OF THE BEHAVIOURAL SCIENCES, Notre Dame, Ind., University of Notre Dame Press, 1971

140. Sperlich, Peter W., CONFLICT AND HARMONY IN HUMAN AFFAIRS: A STUDY OF CROSS-PRESSURES AND POLITICAL BEHAVIOUR, Chicago, Rand McNally, 1971

141. Stagner, Ross, PSYCHOLOGY OF INDUSTRIAL CONFLICT, New York, John Wiley, 1956

142 Stagner, Ross, PSYCHOLOGICAL ASPECTS OF INTER-NATIONAL CONFLICT, Belmont, Calif., Brooks/Cole Pub. Co., 1967

143. Stagner, Ross (ed.), THE DIMENSIONS OF HUMAN CONFLICT, Detroit, Wayne State University Press, 1967

144. Stanford, Barbara (ed.), PEACEMAKING: A GUIDE TO CONFLICT RESOLUTION FOR INDIVIDUALS, GROUPS AND NATIONS, New York, Bantam Books, 1976

145. Stoessinger, John G., WHY NATIONS GO TO WAR, New York,

St. Martins Press, 1974

146. Stone, Jeremy J., STRATEGIC PERSUASION: ARMS LIMIT-
ATION THROUGH DIALOGUE, New York, Columbia University
Press, 1967

147. Storr, Anthony, HUMAN AGGRESSION, London, Allen Lane,
1968

148. Strachey, John, ON THE PREVENTION OF WAR, London,
Macmillan, 1962

149. Tanter, Raymond, 'Dimensions of Conflict Behaviour Within and
Between Nations', JOURNAL OF CONFLICT RESOLUTION,
X(1), March 1966, pp. 41–64

150. Targ, Harry R., 'Global Dominance and Dependence, Post-
Industrialism and International Relations Theory: A Review',
INTERNATIONAL STUDIES QUARTERLY, 20(3), September
1976, pp. 461–482

151. Thomas, John M. and Bennis, Warren G. (eds.), MANAGEMENT
OF CONFLICT AND CHANGE, Harmondsworth, Middx., Penguin
Books, 1972

152. Tolley, Howard S., CHILDREN AND WAR: POLITICAL
SOCIALISATION TO INTERNATIONAL CONFLICT, New York,
Teachers College Press, 1973

153. Wallace, Michael D., 'Power, Status and International War',
JOURNAL OF PEACE RESEARCH, Volume 8, 1971, pp. 23–25

154. Wallace, Michael D., WAR AND RANK AMONG NATIONS,
Lexington Mass., D.C. Heath, 1973

155. Wallensteen, Peter, STRUCTURE AND WAR: ON INTER-
NATIONAL RELATIONS 1920–1968, Stockholm, Räben &
Sjögren, 1973

156. Walton, Richard E., INTERPERSONAL PEACEMAKING: CON-
FRONTATIONS AND THIRD PARTY CONSULTATION,
Reading, Mass., Addison Wesley, 1969

157. Walton, Richard E. and McKersie, Robert B., A BEHAVIOURAL
THEORY OF LABOR NEGOTIATIONS, New York, McGraw
Hill, 1965

158. Waltz, Kenneth N., 'International Structure, National Force and
the Balance of Power', JOURNAL OF INTERNATIONAL
AFFAIRS, XXI, (2), 1967, pp. 215–231

159. Waltz, Kenneth N., MAN, THE STATE AND WAR, New York,
Columbia University Press, 1963

160. White, Ralph K., NOBODY WANTED WAR: MISPERCEPTION

IN VIETNAM AND OTHER WARS, Garden City, N.Y.,
Doubleday & Co., 1970

161. Wright, Quincy, A STUDY OF WAR, (Abridged edition),
Chicago, University of Chicago Press, 1964, (First edition
published in 1942)

162. Wulf, Christoph (ed.), HANDBOOK ON PEACE EDUCATION,
Frankfurt/Oslo, I.P.R.A. (Education Committee), 1974

163. Young, Oran R., THE INTERMEDIARIES: THIRD PARTIES
IN INTERNATIONAL CRISES, Princeton, N.J., Princeton
University Press, 1967

164. Zartman, I.W. (ed.), THE 50% SOLUTION, Garden City,
New York, Doubleday/Anchor Press, 1976

165. Zawodny, J.K. (ed.), MAN AND INTERNATIONAL RELATIONS,
(2 vols.), San Francisco, Chandler Publishing Co., 1966

166. Zinnes, Dinna A., North, Robert C. and Koch, Howard E.,
'Capability, Threat and the Outbreak of War' in J.N. Rosenau
(ed.), INTERNATIONAL POLITICS AND FOREIGN
POLICY, (1st edition), New York, The Free Press, 1961

Chapter VIII

STRATEGY

by A.J.R. Groom
University of Kent

Strategy is an integral part of the social sciences and not least of International Relations. By strategy is meant the study of the causes, modalities and effects of power politics and especially the threat of, the application of and the effects of overtly coercive measures — the 'sharp end' of power politics. In this bibliography the subject has been divided into 'conflict', 'war' and 'strategy'. The distinction is, of course, artificial and its chief *raison d'être* is convention and the organization of university courses along these lines. However, the reader cannot be urged too strongly to complement the references which follow with those of the chapter on conflict and war.

   Those writers of the classical epoch who are read for their insights as well as for their historical value knew well the importance of relating their analyses of the military events of the day to basic political and social problems and processes. Indeed, their ability to do so accounts for their continued relevance. They addressed themselves to the problems of deterrence, alliance, civil-military relations and the like, problems and processes which are the concern of contemporary strategists although clearly, then as now, there are important unique aspects of such questions. There is then a 'classical' literature. However, until the establishment of courses in and research institutes of International Relations after the First World War, it was largely a literature that lacked an appropriate niche in social science outside the confines of military academies.

104

The creation of International Relations as an academic 'discipline' owed much to rationalist-progressive thought and the reaction to the horrors of the Great War. It was much concerned with the founding and activities of the League of Nations and thus it is not surprising that the strategists of this period concentrated on questions such as collective security and the arms race; in short, on the prevention of war. Later, as the international climate changed in the thirties, culminating in the Second World War, the concern became more one of waging war. The strategists of the League's activities had an internationalist or pro-League outlook; those that followed analysed and wrote about strategic matters more from the standpoint of a particular country or government. Such a tendency has continued to the present day and it is a disturbing characteristic of the contemporary literature on strategy. An example of this is the literature on arms control and disarmament which, apart from that which emanates from sources such as SIPRI, is much more likely to examine problems from the point of view of a participant than to analyse the phenomenon as a whole.

Contemporary literature is to a considerable extent *engagé*, whether on the side of the *status quo* or of the revisionist. There is also a tendency, which in part arises out of this, for it to lack conceptual depth. Indeed, the literature is rich in highly technical analyses of the 'strategic balance' (which are not our present concern) but relatively weak in empirically-based theory dealing with the conceptual underpinnings of such analyses. This conceptual weakness helps to explain the remarkable waxing and waning of the literature on nuclear deterrence. For a decade or more beginning in the early fifties monographs and articles on nuclear deterrence abounded, inspired by a realization of the enormous power of nuclear weapons, the likelihood of their proliferation and the fact of universal vulnerability — defence was no longer possible and deterrence was the order of the day. Then the flow stopped, not because the issues had been resolved, but because they were not resolvable. The major options of some form of massive retaliation or graduated deterrence had emerged but there was no empirical theory at any systems level which could decide the issue and thus further attempts at conceptual development were futile or, in some cases, frivolous. The literature on nuclear deterrence is, therefore, essentially that of the late fifties and early sixties and, pending the development of empirical theory, it is likely to remain so.

There are two other areas of conceptual interest which feature prominently in the current literature — revolutionary warfare and the arms race and disarmament. The purpose of a revolution is to change the personnel of government, the policies of a government or the structures of a social unit. It is usually achieved by coercive means against the will of some of the other relevant actors. Political, sociological, economic and psychological variables thus play an important role and it is rare indeed that the phenomenon presents itself in a purely military guise even at the tactical or micro-level. The dramatic success of some revolutionary movements, often at the expense of militarily strong and sophisticated adversaries, has focused analytical attention on the phenomenon of revolutionary warfare. While arms control and disarmament is not a new subject it is one of renewed interest, especially as arms control and disarmament are now being perceived in the light of new models of the arms race, new theories of decision-making and analyses of the military-industrial complex. This has also led strategists to give more regard to military sociology.

Strategy is concerned with change — with coercive attempts either to promote it or to repel it. Its is thus one aspect of the political process at all levels of social intercourse. This has not been fully acknowledged in the literature in the past. This literature has concentrated on the military relations between states and has reflected the 'billiard ball' model of world society which sees states as the major actors with their relationships being hierarchically organized on a basis of power. Slowly this is altering as the influence of non-state actors such as multinational corporations or putative state actors such as the Palestinians or IRA makes itself felt in power politics. Other systems levels and different units of analysis are slowly changing the conceptual framework for the study of strategy. However, the change is but slow and the present literature is still far from providing an adequate conceptual framework for the analysis of power politics in contemporary world society.

Philosophical Aspects

General Beaufre (5) had a varied career as an active soldier and as a military diplomat before being instrumental in the development of strategic studies in France. His writings bear witness to his practical experience and display a range of intellectual qualities, such as logic, clarity and intellectual independence, not always characteristic of military men. His INTRODUCTION TO STRATEGY, together with Michael Howard's work (70, 71, 72), are an admirable *entrée* into traditional strategy.

Philip Green's volume (51) is a strong, indeed, many would say a vitriolic criticism of such doyens of traditional strategy as Herman Kahn and Thomas Schelling. The criticisms are in many cases well-founded although Green does sometimes weaken his case by 'overkill', by too much *reductio ad absurdum* and by a failure to concentrate on essentials. This book assumes a prior knowledge of the literature under consideration. To a certain degree Green's work can be considered as 'in-house' criticism while that of Anatol Rapoport (119) is more fundamental. Rapoport sees the whole subject as having such glaring moral and practical deficiencies as to be of little worth. Instead he proposes a more scientific approach and offers some rather prosaic, and by now dated, prescriptions for the East-West relationship of the day. It remains, however, a noteworthy historical work.

Boulding's CONFLICT AND DEFENCE (14) has stood better the test of time and it is a serious and partly successful attempt to bridge the gap between strategy and conflict studies. This writer's forthcoming volume (59) is in a similar vein.

The moral issues are touched upon in the Osgood-Tucker work (113) and the papers Kaplan has edited (82). Of the latter, that by Philip Green is well worth reading even if, as always, Green irritates almost as much as he illuminates. There have recently been several articles (19, 107, 108, 114) in the journals on moral and philosophical problems and a rather more substantial monograph by Ted Honderich (69) on the philosophical arguments regarding terrorism — a subject which was aired by the anarchists and others in the last century. Indeed it is a 'classical' topic of political philosophy. The Waltz book (152) has the status of a minor classic and all students of strategy should certainly read it.

Classical Doctrine

It is a moot point the extent to which the strategic writings from antiquity to the Second World War are of relevance to the contemporary world. Some writers still exert a very obvious influence and Clausewitz (24) is a case in point. But, even Clausewitz needs a good editor to sort out the historical chaff from the conceptual wheat. For this reason Earle's (32) edited volume is very useful, with a chapter for each major historical figure by a well-known expert with indications for further reading. In a different vein Bernard and Fawn Brodie's volume makes a pleasurable and instructive 'read'. They wear their learning lightly as they explore aspects of the relationships between the defence system and the social systems from the CROSSBOW TO A-BOMB (18).

Deterrence Theory

Deterrence involves the manipulation of threats in such a way as to prevail upon a target to choose options which, but for the threat, it would not have done, since the criteria upon which the choice is now made are not acceptable to the target. It thus involves a complicated relationship between stake, sanction and the likelihood of the application of the sanction which raises difficult problems of communication and credibility. At no level of analysis is deterrence derived from a well-tested empirical theory. This is especially so at the 'high politics' level between predominantly state-actors when military capabilities which can utterly destroy contemporary world society are readily available. Nevertheless, the manipulation of threat systems is central to power politics and to strategy. Despite the speculative nature of the literature, the subject cannot be ignored.

Of the general works covering the major aspects of the subject as it has traditionally been conceived (6, 17, 41, 42, 43, 51, 83, 84, 85, 86, 100, 119, 128, 131, 132, 136, 140, 141), Garnett's edited volume (42) is the best starting point. It is a set of reprints well chosen from the writings of such major nuclear strategists as Schelling, Brodie and others. Although the selections were sometimes written in the fifties they are somewhat more authorative than those Garnett and his colleagues have produced recently in a volume of original conceptual essays (4). On the other hand the new volume does include short essays on the defence policies of selected major Powers. For students who want a 'quick crib' the night before the examinations, Roy Jones has a felicitous way of meeting their needs (83).

The nuclear debate developed in the mid-fifties due to the testing of the hydrogen bomb and the beginnings of mutual deterrence. Very quickly it became evident that there were three broad options — non-nuclear status, massive retaliation and graduated deterrence. Only the latter two options were considered seriously by the major Powers. The literature reflected this and unilateralism was treated more as an emotional slogan than as a serious policy option. There was no analysis of unilateralism worthy of name. Unilateralism involves acting in an unreciprocated manner to remove what potential adversaries consider to be a major threat. Usually this carries the risk of easy, costless, and effective exploitation by the adversary against which there can be no real defence. Indeed, it is more effective if it is clear to all that such a risk is being knowingly run. The purpose is to change the nature of a power relationship towards a legitimized one by breaking stereotypes, interrupting the cycle of self-fulfilling prophesies of hostility and altering cognitive structures. It is a notion not to be dismissed even though it might be considered generally as imprudent. The nuclear debate, however, concentrated on massive retaliation and graduated deterrence. It flourished from the mid-fifties to the early sixties and then, once the major options had been delineated, it petered out since there was no empirical evidence to settle the argument and it was a futile and boring exercise merely to elaborate ever more complicated scenarios.

Of the seminal works of the period, Snyder's theoretical chapters (140) still bear reading, as does Schelling's STRATEGY OF CONFLICT (133). His later ARMS AND INFLUENCE (132) shows the imprint of Vietnam. Although the major ideas were first developed by British thinkers (56), their later exposition was dominated by writers in the United States, with a continuing British contribution. British and American writers shared a transnational community of ideas which was challenged by French writers. Beaufre's DETERRENCE AND STRATEGY (6) is his finest work and strongly recommended, as is General Gallois' STRATEGY IN THE NUCLEAR AGE (41). It is salutary to note that we have not really advanced substantially beyond the ideas of Snyder, Schelling, Beaufre and Gallois, nor can we decide definitively on the respective merits of their notions.

Two writers deserve to be included for their historical significance. Herman Kahn's books (84, 85, 86) certainly caused a stir, but hindsight suggests that it was more because of their mode of presentation than because of their intrinsic merit. They are essentially exercises in fantasy — the flaw of all deterrence theory due to its lack of an empirical base — but in 'glorious technicolour'. Albert Wohlstetter's influence was more practical and prosaic, if more far-reaching, and he has recently reflected on the 'Legends of the Strategic Arms Race' (154). A current article by Albert Langer has something of Wohlstetter's style (92). The sort of strategic calculation that characterized the work of Kahn and Wohlstetter is put admirably into perspective by McGeorge Bundy in his justly celebrated article 'To Cap the Volcano' (21).

The debate between the rival advocates of massive retaliation and graduated deterrence touched upon the tactical use of nuclear weapons and its effect on deterrence generally, and credibility and escalation in particular. Moreover, it raised the question of whether the destructive effects in the battle theatre of the tactical use of nuclear weapons would be tantamount in all likelihood to those of a strategic war. The debate still continues and recent contributions can be found in Brenner, Davis, Enthoven, and Record (16, 26, 35, 120).

The practice of nuclear deterrence has now been an integral part of 'high politics' between major Powers for at least a quarter of a century. Empirical evidence, or at least a body of experience and impressions, however ill-formed, is thus available even if its codification and utilization is difficult. Nuclear proliferation, so long 'promised' horizontally, has sneaked up vertically, as the super Powers have expanded their capabilities at an astonishing and frightening rate in the seventies. Technological developments may also now presage horizontal proliferation. George and Smoke (43) have sought to restate deterrence theory in terms that allows them to examine it in the light of United States foreign policy since the Second World War. Their volume can be recommended, as can the ADELPHI PAPER of Richard Rosecrance (128), for a cogent contemporary view of deterrence theory. This writer's forthcoming volume attempts to put deterrence theory in a wider setting of different systems levels and also to analyse the nature of limited nuclear war and conventional war in the nuclear shadow (59). Finally, there is a vast Soviet literature on the subject. Much of this has been translated into Western languages but it is not always readily accessible. However, Marshal Sokolowksy's SOVIET MILITARY STRATEGY (141) and a recent article by Milstein and Semeiko (102) provide a starting point.

Alliances

Little or no conceptual literature exists on the theory of alliances. There are many descriptive monographs, particularly on NATO, but they usually lack an explicit conceptual base and are so concerned with the issues of the day that they are of no more than passing interest. There are, of course, some exceptions. George Liska's volume (94) illustrates the traditional approach to alliances emanating from the mainstream of political thought, whereas Francis Beer has attempted to apply propositions from integration theory to NATO (8, 9) and Karl Deutsch (29, 30) has examined NATO more from a communications-transactions point of view. While Beer's and Deutsch's analyses deal with the North Atlantic area they are illustrative of ways in which the study of alliances can be integrated into the mainstream of conceptual developments in International Relations. William Riker's (123) work serves to remind that small group experiments may also shed light on the nature of coalitions and facilitate the development and testing of conceptual notions. Finally, Ole Holsti and his colleagues (68) have attempted a welcome generalization of the study of alliances.

Conventional War

The study of conventional war is very much the preserve of military colleges and does not spill over into the more general strategic, political and International Relations literature. One major exception to this is conventional war in the nuclear shadow, for which some of the literature in a previous section on limited nuclear war is relevant. Heilbrunn's volume (66) also considers this theme. However, the literature on the role of sea power is more abundant than that of land power, perhaps because the great alliances seem unlikely to clash in a purely conventional war in Europe — the prime area of confront-ation — whereas at sea they have had, literally, some close scrapes. The expansion of Soviet naval power has also focussed attention on sea power as has the problematic role of conventional sea power in a nuclear war. Booth (12), Cable (22) and Luttwak (96) and the several contributors to the ADELPHI PAPERS (160) cover various aspects of these problems. The Soviet expansion of naval power has been given a rationale by Admiral Gorshkov (46) and analyzed in MccGwire, Booth and McDonnell's edited volume (106).

The real interest in conventional warfare is in the third world. After all, the largest tank battle in history was fought between Egypt and Israel in October 1973. Many new innovations are changing the nature of conventional war from that familiar in the Second World War and new conventional Powers of the first rank have arisen. The implications of developments have not been thoroughly analyzed or incorporated into thinking within the two major alliances, but Geoffrey Kemp and his colleagues (88) have provided a basis for consideration of these issues. Given the unlikelihood of a conventional clash in Europe but the relative frequency of conventional war in the Third World and the historical ties with the former colonial Powers, the intervention of Powers from the alliances in such wars either through the supply of weapons, actively with troops or perhaps covertly by providing infor-mation or air cover, has been, and is likely to remain not uncommon. Richard Little (95) has analyzed the problems raised by this phenomenon in a thorough and cogent study and Vincent's work (149) is also relevant

111

on this topic. It will be interesting to see the degree to which differing types of intervention (such as hegemonial intervention, colonial intervention and Third World intervention of the type by Cuban forces in Angola) can be accommodated in the same framework and give rise to the same effects.

Revolutionary War

One of the most striking phenomena of the postwar world has been the plethora of revolutionary wars. There have been several types, such as those which are strictly anti-colonial, those against a hegemonial Power, and those against a local cosmopolitan elite, involving a wide range of political, economic, psychological and sociological variables. Clearly there are many situations which include elements from more than one category. Moreover, a revolution can be more or less thoroughgoing and more or less violent. A revolution – a palace revolution – may merely involve a change in personnel, but it may go further and also be concerned with a change in policies or be more thoroughgoing still and have as its aim a change in structures. The intensity and form of coercion can vary in each instance. In the postwar world the form of violence has been fairly low level and unconventional, involving guerrilla tactics, as befits what was often a 'poor man's war', although the intensity has been high. The great engines of war have been comparatively unused and the great military Leviathan's have, to a surprising degree, been muscle bound. The most effective forms of coercion in revolutionary war situations have often not proved to be the classical military ones and many new lessons have been learned the hard way. Yet the successes themselves have been spectacular, although it should not be forgotten that most revolutionary movements fail.

On considering the writers on revolutionary war, pride of place should perhaps be given to the Asian practitioners. In the light of his experience Mao Tse Tung was able to develop a general framework for revolutionary war (99, 52) which had a great deal of influence on Vietnamese revolutionaries (44). However, General Nasution had a different, if equally successful experience in the Dutch East Indies (110). In the Arab World the great figure was President Nasser and although his writing was *ex post facto* (109), like that of several other practitioners, the example of the Egyptian revolution and Nasser's philosophy was a considerable inspiration. Equally inspiring were the practitioners of Latin America but, after the rather fortuitous experience in Cuba, they were markedly less successful. Ché (60) and Régis Debray (27) were, and are, widely read but the empirical evidence suggests that Mao's rather different precepts for a successful revolution have greater validity even in a Latin American context. Nevertheless, the Latin American experience has given rise to several studies (47, 117), perhaps because the United States is usually involved either directly or indirectly. Franz Fanon (38) does not fit easily into pigeon holes — Caribbean in origin, working in Algeria, a trained social scientist yet a practitioner — but his THE WRETCHED OF THE EARTH should not be ignored, either for its analysis or for its prescriptions, since it is, and is likely to remain a seminal work, if a highly controversial one.

There is, of course, a practitioners' literature from the other side of the ideological fence — that of the counter-revolutionary. Sir Robert Thompson (145) is a leading writer in this field. His best work relates to his experience in Malaya rather than to his later forays in Vietnam. Frank Kitson has also written of his experiences and the lessons he has drawn from them in a career that includes not only Malaya but Kenya, Cyprus and elsewhere. His work (90) is chiefly noted for the application he made of his ideas to Britain in the early 1970s. The British way has usually been to stress political factors — at least in theory. A diametrically opposed view is that advocated by two RAND Corporation specialists, Leites and Wolf (93), who lambast the politically oriented 'hearts and minds' approach. Their argument is almost an economic rational actor model based on the pricing by coercive means of options open to the population. Attitudes are discounted and it is believed that behaviour can be coerced successfully irrespective of the value preferences of the target. The population will choose options contrary to its values if the price of pursuing its values is made too high. Required behaviour in the short term is the prime goal. The adoption of policies based on such views was not successful in Vietnam.

Leites and Wolf's volume is something of a half-way house between the practitioners and the political scientists on revolutionary war. Their pretention is to be scientific and their purpose was to elaborate a practical strategy. Other political scientists have not been so immediately policy oriented. Harry Eckstein's edited volume (33) wears its years well and Ted Robert Gurr's work is always worth reading (61). It is he who has put the notion of 'relative deprivation' to good use. He has also examined some of the modalities of the uses of coercive violence along the lines suggested by Leites and Wolf. Looked at from the other end of the spectrum David Baldwin's article 'The Power of Positive Sanctions' (3) is especially seminal. Thus the central issue of

POLITICAL ORDER IN A CHANGING SOCIETY (75), as Samuel Huntington calls his excellent book, is evident. Will there be a process of adjustment in which society and its institutions respond to change or will there be REVOLUTIONARY CHANGE (82) as 'multiple dysfunction meets an intransigent elite'? Both Huntington and Chalmers Johnson are good value on these themes, particularly Johnson, since he attempts to view the problem in a systems perspective. For an historian's view of such phenomena, Stone's article (142) can be recommended. This writer has attempted to incorporate their findings into his own work (58, 59).

When a system is no longer characterized by response to feedback and a high level of legitimized adjustment procedures, and thus confrontation and coercion become the order of the day, then there is often a tendency of one or other party to call upon sympathetic outsiders for help. This literature has already been mentioned (95, 149). It is particularly common in revolutionary war situations with results that are, according to classical power politics, counter-intuitive. Andrew Mack has offered suggestions (97, 98) why this might be so. France has had a long experience of this phenomenon and the reflections of French writers and practitioners on the subject can be found in Trinquier (146).

Pacification programmes in revolutionary warfare situations have often involved the civilian use of military forces. But in such situations, although the use of the military is civilian, it is part of a counter-insurgency technique in a conflict situation. Civilian use can also be made of military forces outside of a conflict situation as, for example, in the case of air-sea rescue teams. Hugh Hanning has provided an annotated inventory of such activities (65).

Unconventional Warfare

The success of the non-violent techniques of a Gandhi or a Martin Luther King in the pursuance of their aims is well-known. These experiences and analogous ones are analyzed in Sharp's works (134, 135). Sharp is concerned with the practicality of such techniques and an even more hard-nosed and less ideological consideration of the practical use of such techniques in the pursuance of power politics can be found in Boserup and Mack's excellent WAR WITHOUT WEAPONS (13) and Roberts' work (125, 126, 127).

The recent spate of terrorist activities and the more sustained urban guerrilla campaigns have focussed attention on such unconventional warfare techniques. The literature has been of a very varied quality and from a variety of ideological points of view (103, 112, 114). Wilkinson has attempted to analyze POLITICAL TERRORISM (153) in a scholarly conceptual framework and Walter's volume (151) is a brilliant analysis of regimes of political terror. This literature is surveyed in a review article by the writer (58).

A form of unconventional warfare that has remained 'unconventional' to a certain degree for a considerable time is chemical and biological warfare. The 'unconventional' is essentially conceptual since the actual use is, unhappily, frequent. It is striking, given their frequent application, that such techniques are not considered to be normal. SIPRI has published several works in this field (137, 138).

Arms Control and Disarmament

Historically, unconventional weapons have frequently, if gradually, been incorporated into the military inventories of the leading military Powers of the day. The submarine is a case in point in recent times. Their 'unconventionality' declines as their use becomes more widespread and frequent. This is a sad commentary on the efficacy of measures of arms control and disarmament. This failure is not, however, for the want of trying, since negotiations and the flow of literature on the subject has never dried up from the beginning of the century. Much of it, however, like that on alliances, has concentrated on the practical issues of the day. It is, therefore, not relevant here. The conceptual literature is, given the interest in the practical everyday aspects of arms control and disarmament, surprisingly limited. Perhaps this lack of an adequate conceptualism goes some way to explaining the failures of the pragmatic approach.

Among the works that have been widely read and quoted over the last fifteen years are those of Singer and Bull (136, 20). Wayland and Elizabeth Young have been writing in this field for a considerable period of time (157, 159). Much of the literature of this period has been based in an action-reaction model whereby the arms race was generated by one state reacting to the actions of another which it interpreted as inimical to its security and interests. Such a model is clearly inadequate in a situation in which the arms race is going full tilt yet political *détente* is being consolidated. To many peace researchers in the Federal Republic and in Scandinavia this suggested the malevolent influence of the military-industrial complex, while to others it suggested that procurement processes, once initiated, developed a life of their own and an ability to sustain themselves. Elements on this debate can be found in Gray's work (49, 50). There has been little discussion of ways in which control of the procurement process can be re-established (59).

A different approach to analyzing the arms race is the application of mathematical models. Lewis Richardson pioneered this work and two of his volumes have been published posthumously (121, 122). A more recent effort in the same direction has been published by Saaty (130).

At an anecdotal but nevertheless revealing level is Herbert York's RACE TO OBLIVION (156). After holding high positions in the United States Administration concerned with the procurement of weapons systems, York has since been a leader among those scientists who are seeking to promote arms control. His volume is partly auto-biographical, but it does offer many graphic illustrations of the manner in which the arms race progresses which tend to support those who attribute greater importance to domestic factors of a 'non-rational actor' character than to the notion of an action-reaction sequence. Another practitioner, Alva Myrdal (104), has drawn on many years of discussion at the negotiating table in her THE GAME OF DISARMAMENT. An element of dispair and bitterness can be found in William Epstein's monograph (36) and Marek Thee's article (143).

Peacekeeping

There has been a considerable amount of literature on peacekeeping, but as with disarmament and arms control, it has usually concerned itself with particular United Nations operations. Bloomfield's volume (10) reflects thought during the early years of UN operations and Gordenker's study (45) is a valuable insight into the role of the UN Secretary-General during those years. Boyd, Fabian, Groom and Wainhouse (15, 37, 53, 55, 150) relate and reflect upon the crises that UN peacekeeping went through in the mid-sixties, and ways in which in future similar difficulties might be avoided. Rikhye (124) and his colleagues give both a recent view and a practitioner's slant since they all had experience as officers posted to a peacekeeping force. The volumes of Higgins (67) are invaluable reference works for all the UN peacekeeping operations and indispensable in any library on the subject.

Of the monographs treating the subject conceptually, that of James (77) is representative of the traditional International Relations approach whereas this writer's essay (55) is a plea for the reconsideration of peacekeeping in the wider context of conflict research. In particular, it advocates that greater thought should be given to the relationship between peacekeeping and peacemaking. This theme has also been examined by Young (158). In achieving this goal, institutions other than the UN may have a significant role to play. Already there is some experience with regional organizations which Joseph Nye has analyzed empirically (64) and conceptually (113).

Civil-Military Relations

The study of strategy cannot ignore soldiers, for the personnel of the Services are often those who interpret conceptual notions in an empirical setting. Thus the sociology of the military themselves is of great interest. There seem to be no purely conceptual studies of this question but Janowitz's THE PROFESSIONAL SOLDIER (78) is an example of a pioneering study that is nationally based. More recently Abrahamsson has produced an excellent volume on MILITARY PROFESSIONALISATION AND POLITICAL POWER (1). Of course, the psychological literature is relevant, and Adorno (2) is an example of this. An interest in participants also raises questions on civil-military relations and the military-industrial complex.

Morris Janowitz and Jacques Van Doorn (78, 79, 80, 81, 147, 148) are among the leading figures of an international group who have studied many aspects of the relationship between the armed forces and society. Interest in the subject generally was sparked by the role of the military particularly in the newly independent states. Finer's THE MAN ON HORSEBACK (39) had considerable influence, and is often referred to. More recent studies include articles by Mazrui, Price and Putman (101, 116, 117) and monographs by Decalo and Kennedy (28, 89). Nor can the role of the military in developed countries be taken for granted, since societal values are changing and moving away from traditional military values; and the military are becoming more professional and so can no longer be perceived as merely a reflection of the nation in arms. In addition to this, (apart, perhaps, from the United States forces) they have mostly lost their colonial role and *raison d'être*. Some of these issues are touched upon in contributions to Beaumont and Edmonds (7), Wolfe and Erickson (155) and in the writer's little piece (54). Huntington's POLITICAL ORDER IN CHANGING SOCIETIES has already been recommended in a different context but it is a recommendation worth repeating, to which can be added an edited volume and his pioneering SOLDIER AND STATE (73, 74, 75). A little known,

117

but rewarding work is that of Coates and Pellegrin, notwithstanding its empirical examples being limited to experience in the United States (25). As prejudice recedes, analyses are beginning to be made on a comparative basis of the performance of military and non-military regimes (105). The study of the military-industrial complex was given great prominence by no less a figure than President Eisenhower in his farewell address to the people of the United States (34). Since then there has been a variety of studies from many ideological points of view, usually confined to the empirical experience of one country and most often the United States. Although it may be difficult to obtain, Slater and Nardin's paper is an excellent summary of some of the different conceptual issues (139). Finally, Lang has produced a helpful bibliographical essay covering the literature until the early 1970s (91).

Collective Security

As we noted at the beginning of this essay, collective security was one of the earliest topics with which strategy was concerned in the context of the emerging discipline of International Relations. There was a voluminous literature on the subject in the inter-war period and the drafting of the Charter of the United Nations also gave rise to many analyses. Since then the literature has been relatively sparse, although such major figures in the field as Inis Claude (23), Ernst Haas (62, 63), Joseph Nye (111) and Kenneth Thompson (144) have written on the subject. Otto Pick and Julian Critchley (115) have provided an introductory volume and the Finkelsteins (40) edited a volume in the mid-sixties. Collective security involves the willingness of the members of a system to elaborate a set of rules of behaviour in high politics for that system and to make sure that all members adhere to such rules, if necessary through the application of sanctions. On sanctions Margaret Doxey (31) has written a major treatise and a 'classical' statement can be found in the Royal Institute of International Affairs' (129) study in the late thirties. Collective security is often confused *nolens volens* with alliances, but alliances are not primarily concerned with member states. Rather, they seek to influence the behaviour of non-members, although some contemporary bodies such as the Arab League have both function.

Reference

This annotated bibliography is primarily concerned with the literature available in the English language. Even within the English language there

118

are considerable differences in usage and meaning for the same word. There are many valuable works in other languages that have not been translated, especially in French and Russian, but the reader is helped in coming to terms with them by the fact that often the specialist technology used in those languages is borrowed from or based upon an English term. This is also a potential pitfall as in the examples of 'arms control' and 'contrôle des armaments' or 'deterrence' and 'dissuasion' where the seeming similarity masks considerable conceptual differences. The differences and similarities between the English languages and foreign use of English terms is catalogued in Urs Schwarz and Laszlo Hadik: STRATEGIC TERMINOLOGY: A TRILINGUAL GLOSSARY, Dusseldorf, Econ. Verlag, 1966.

Bibliography

1. Abrahamsson, Bengt, MILITARY PROFESSIONALISATION AND POLITICAL POWER, Beverly Hills, Sage, 1971
2. Adorno, T.W. et al, THE AUTHORITARIAN PERSONALITY, New York, Harper, 1950
3. Baldwin, David, 'The Power of Positive Sanctions', WORLD POLITICS, XXIV (1), October 1971, pp. 19–38
4. Baylis, John, Booth, K., Garnett, J. and Williams, P., CONTEMPORARY STRATEGY, London, Croom Helm, 1975
5. Beaufre, A., INTRODUCTION TO STRATEGY, New York, Praeger, 1965
6. Beaufre, A., DETERRENCE AND STRATEGY, London, Faber, 1965
7. Beaumont, R.A. and Edmonds, M. (eds.), WAR IN THE NEXT DECADE, London, Macmillan, 1975
8. Beer, F.A., INTEGRATION AND DISINTEGRATION IN NATO, Columbus, Ohio, Ohio State University Press, 1969
9. Beer, F.A. (ed.), ALLIANCE: LATENT WAR COMMUNITIES IN THE CONTEMPORARY WORLD, New York, Holt, Rinehart and Winston, 1970
10. Bloomfield, L.P., INTERNATIONAL MILITARY FORCES, Boston, Little, Brown, 1964
11. Bloomfield, L.P. and Leiss, A.C., CONTROLLING SMALL WARS, New York, Alfred Knopf, 1969
12. Booth, K., NAVIES AND FOREIGN POLICY, New York, Crane Russak, 1977

13. Boserup, A. and Mack, A., WAR WITHOUT WEAPONS, London, Frances Pinter, 1974
14. Boulding, K.E., CONFLICT AND DEFENCE, New York, Harper Row, 1963
15. Boyd, J.M., U.N. PEACEKEEPING, London, Praeger, 1972
16. Brenner, Michael, 'Tactical Nuclear Strategy and European Defence', INTERNATIONAL AFFAIRS, 51(1), January 1975, pp. 23—42
17. Brodie, Bernard, WAR AND POLITICS, London, Cassell, 1974
18. Brodie, Bernard and Fawn, CROSSBOW TO A-BOMB, New York, Dell, 1962 (revised 1973)
19. Bull, H., 'Strategic Studies and its Critics', WORLD POLITICS, XX (4), July 1968, pp. 593—605
20. Bull, H., CONTROL OF THE ARMS RACE, London, Weidenfeld & Nicholson, 1961
21. Bundy, McGeorge, 'To Cap the Volcano', FOREIGN AFFAIRS, 48 (1), October 1969, pp. 1—20
22. Cable, J., GUNBOAT DIPLOMACY, London, Chatto and Windus, 1971
23. Claude, I.L., POWER AND INTERNATIONAL RELATIONS, New York, Random House, 1962
24. Clausewitz, Carl Von., ON WAR (ed. and trans. Michael Howard and Peter Paret), Princeton, N.J., Princeton University Press, 1976
25. Coates, Charles H. and Pellegrin, R.J., MILITARY SOCIOLOGY, University Park Md., Social Science Press, 1965
26. Davis, Lynn, 'Limited Nuclear Options', ADELPHI PAPERS, No. 121, London, International Institute for Strategic Studies, Winter 1975—76
27. Debray, R., REVOLUTION IN THE REVOLUTION, Harmondsworth, Middx., Penguin, 1967
28. Decalo, Samuel, COUPS AND ARMY RULE IN AFRICA, New Haven, Conn., Yale University Press, 1976
29. Deutsch, K.W., Burrell, S.A. and Kann, R., POLITICAL COM-MUNITY AND THE NORTH ATLANTIC AREA, Princeton, N.J., Princeton University Press, 1957
30. Deutsch, K.W., Burrell, S.A. and Kann, R., ARMS CONTROL AND THE ATLANTIC ALLIANCE, New York, John Wiley, 1967
31. Doxey, Margaret, ECONOMIC SANCTIONS AND INTER-NATIONAL ENFORCEMENT, New York, Oxford University Press, 1971

32. Earle, E.M. (ed.), MAKERS OF MODERN STRATEGY, New York, Atheneum, 1966
33. Eckstein, H. (ed.), INTERNAL WAR, New York, The Free Press, 1964
34. Eisenhower, D.D., 'President Eisenhower's Farewell to the Nation', U.S. Dept. of State, DEPT. OF STATE BULLETIN, 44, No. 1128, 1961
35. Enthoven, Alain C., 'US Forces in Europe', FOREIGN AFFAIRS, 53 (3), April 1975, pp. 513–532
36. Epstein, William, THE LAST CHANCE: NUCLEAR PROLIFER-ATION AND ARMS CONTROL, London, Collier-Macmillan, 1976
37. Fabian, L.L., SOLDIERS WITHOUT ENEMIES, Washington, D.C., Brookings Institution, 1971
38. Fanon, F., THE WRETCHED OF THE EARTH, Harmondsworth, Middx., Penguin, 1967
39. Finer, S.E., THE MAN ON HORSEBACK, London, Pall Mall, 1962
40. Finkelstein, M. and L. (eds.), COLLECTIVE SECURITY, San Francisco, Chandler, 1966
41. Gallois, P., BALANCE OF TERROR, Boston, Houghton Mifflin, 1961
42. Garnett, J.C. (ed.), THEORIES OF PEACE AND SECURITY, London, Macmillan, 1970
43. George, A.L. and Smoke, R., DETERRENCE IN AMERICAN FOREIGN POLICY, New York, Columbia University Press, 1974
44. Giap, V.N., PEOPLE'S WAR, PEOPLE'S ARMY, New York, Praeger, 1961
45. Gordenker, L., UN SECRETARY-GENERAL AND THE MAINTENANCE OF PEACE, New York, Columbia University Press, 1967
46. Gorshkov, S.G., SEA POWER AND THE STATE, Washington, D.C., U.S. Naval Institute Press, 1976, (Trans. U.S. Naval Institute)
47. Gott, Richard, GUERRILLA MOVEMENTS IN LATIN AMERICA, London, Nelson, 1970
48. Gray, C.S., 'The Arms Race Phenomenon', WORLD POLITICS, XXIV (1), October 1971, pp. 39–79
49. Gray, C.S., 'The Urge to Compete: Rationales for Arms Racing', WORLD POLITICS, XXVI (2), January 1974, pp. 207–233
50. Gray, C.S., THE SOVIET-AMERICAN ARMS RACE, Lexington, Mass., Lexington Press, 1976
51. Green, P., DEADLY LOGIC, Columbus, Ohio, Ohio State

University Press, 1966

52. Griffiths, S.B., MAO TSE-TUNG ON GUERRILLA WARFARE, London, Cassell, 1965

53. Groom, A.J.R., 'Prospects for Peacekeeping', INTERNATIONAL AFFAIRS, 47 (2), April 1971, pp. 340–352

54. Groom, A.J.R., 'The Guards are Home', CONTEMPORARY REVIEW, 221 (1278), July 1972, pp. 34–37

55. Groom, A.J.R., PEACEKEEPING, Bethelem, Penn., Lehigh University International Relations Monograph No. 4, 1973

56. Groom, A.J.R., BRITISH THINKING ABOUT NUCLEAR WEAPONS, London, Frances Pinter, 1974

57. Groom, A.J.R., 'Security by Association', CONTEMPORARY REVIEW, 227 (1315), July 1975, pp. 96–104

58. Groom, A.J.R., 'Coming to Terms with Terrorism', BRITISH JOURNAL OF INTERNATIONAL STUDIES, 4 (1), April 1978, forthcoming

59. Groom, A.J.R., STRATEGY IN THE MODERN WORLD, forthcoming

60. Guevara, C., GUERRILLA WARFARE, London, Pelican, 1969

61. Gurr, T.R., WHY MEN REBEL, Princeton, N.J., Princeton University Press, 1970

62. Haas, E.B., 'Types of Collective Security: An Examination of Operational Concepts', AMERICAN POLITICAL SCIENCE REVIEW, 49 (1), March 1955, pp. 40–62

63. Haas, E.B., COLLECTIVE SECURITY AND THE FUTURE OF INTERNATIONAL SYSTEM, Denver, University of Denver, Monograph Series in World Affairs, Vol. 5, 1967–1968

64. Haas, E.B., Butterworth, R.L. and Nye, J.S., CONFLICT MANAGEMENT BY INTERNATIONAL ORGANISATIONS, Morristown, N.J., General Learning Press, 1972

65. Hanning, H., PEACEFUL USES OF MILITARY FORCES, New York, Praeger, 1967

66. Heilbrunn, O., CONVENTIONAL WAR IN THE NUCLEAR AGE, London, Allen & Unwin, 1965

67. Higgins, R., UN PEACEKEEPING, 1946–67, Vol. I, Middle East; Vol. II, Asia, London, Oxford University Press, 1969

68. Holsti, O.R. et al, UNITY AND DISINTEGRATION IN INTERNATIONAL ALLIANCES, London, Wiley, 1973

69. Honderich, Ted, POLITICAL VIOLENCE; A PHILOSOPHICAL ANALYSIS OF TERRORISM, Ithaca, Cornell University Press,

1977

70. Howard, M., THEORY AND PRACTICE OF WAR, London, Cassell, 1965

71. Howard, M., STUDIES IN WAR AND PEACE, New York, Viking, 1971

72. Howard, M., 'The Relevance of Traditional Strategy', FOREIGN AFFAIRS, 51 (2), January 1973, pp. 253—266

73. Huntington, S.P., SOLDIER AND STATE, Cambridge, Mass., Harvard University Press, 1957

74. Huntington, S.P. (ed.), CHANGING PATTERNS OF MILITARY POLITICS, New York, The Free Press, 1962

75. Huntington, S.P., POLITICAL ORDER IN CHANGING SOCIETIES, New Haven, Yale University Press, 1968

76. Iklé, F.C., EVERY WAR MUST END, New York, Columbia University Press, 1971

77. James, A., POLITICS OF PEACEKEEPING, London, Chatto and Windus, 1969

78. Janowitz, M., THE PROFESSIONAL SOLDIER, New York, The Free Press, 1960

79. Janowitz, M., THE NEW MILITARY, New York, Russell Sage Foundation, 1964

80. Janowitz, M. and Van Doorn, J. (eds.), ON MILITARY INTERVENTION, Rotterdam, University Press of Rotterdam, 1971

81. Janowitz, M. and Van Doorn, J. (eds.), ON MILITARY IDEOLOGY, Rotterdam, University Press of Rotterdam, 1971

82. Johnson, C., REVOLUTIONARY CHANGE, London, University of London Press, 1968

83. Jones, R.E., NUCLEAR DETERRENCE, London, Routledge & Kegan Paul, 1968

84. Kahn, H., ON THERMONUCLEAR WAR, Princeton, N.J., Princeton University Press, 1960

85. Kahn, H., THINKING ABOUT THE UNTHINKABLE, London, Weidenfeld & Nicholson, 1962

86. Kahn, H., ON ESCALATION, London, Pall Mall Press, 1965

87. Kaplan, M.A. (ed.), STRATEGIC THINKING AND ITS MORAL IMPLICATIONS, Chicago, University of Chicago Press, 1973

88. Kemp, G., Pfaltzgraff, R.L. and Ranan, Uri, THE OTHER ARMS RACE: NEW TECHNOLOGIES AND NON-NUCLEAR CONFLICT, Lexington, Mass., D.C. Heath & Co., 1975

89. Kennedy, Gavin, THE MILITARY IN THE THIRD WORLD,

London, Duckworth, 1974

90. Kitson, Frank, LOW INTENSITY OPERATIONS, London, Faber, 1971

91. Lang, Kurt, MILITARY INSTITUTIONS AND THE SOCIOLOGY OF WAR, London, Sage, 1972

92. Langer, Albert, 'Accurate Submarine Launched Ballistic Missiles and Nuclear Strategy', JOURNAL OF PEACE RESEARCH, Vol. XIV, 1977, pp. 41–58

93. Leites, N. and Wolf, C., REBELLION AND AUTHORITY, Chicago, Markham, 1970

94. Liska, G., NATIONS IN ALLIANCE, Baltimore, Johns Hopkins University Press, 1962

95. Little, Richard, INTERVENTION, London, Martin Robertson, 1975

96. Luttwak, Edward, THE POLITICAL USES OF SEA POWER, Baltimore, Johns Hopkins University Press, 1974

97. Mack, Andrew J., 'Why Big Nations Lose Small Wars', WORLD POLITICS, XXVII (2), January 1975, pp. 175–200

98. Mack, Andrew J., 'Counterinsurgency in the Third World', BRITISH JOURNAL OF INTERNATIONAL STUDIES, I (3), October 1975, pp. 226–253

99. Mao Tse-Tung, BASIC TACTICS, New York, Praeger, 1966

100. Maxwell, S., 'Rationality in Deterrence', ADELPHI PAPERS, No. 50, London, International Institute for Strategic Studies, August 1968

101. Mazrui, A.A., 'The Lumpen Proletariat and the Lumpen Militariat', POLITICAL STUDIES, XXI (1), March 1973, pp. 1–12

102. Milstein, M.A. and Semeiko, L.A., 'Problems of the Inadmissibility of Nuclear Conflict', INTERNATIONAL STUDIES QUARTERLY, XX (1), March 1976, pp. 87–104

103. Moss, R., URBAN GUERRILLAS, London, Temple Smith, 1972

104. Myrdal, Alva, THE GAME OF DISARMAMENT, New York, Pantheon, 1977

105. McKinley, R.D. and Cohan, A.S., 'Performance and Instability in Military and Non-Military Regime Systems', AMERICAN POLITICAL SCIENCE REVIEW, LXX (3), September 1976, pp. 850–864

106. MccGwire, M., Booth, K. and McDonnell, John (eds.), SOVIET NAVAL POLICY, New York, Praeger, 1975

107. Nardin, Terry, 'Philosophy and International Violence, AMERICAN

POLITICAL SCIENCE REVIEW, LXX (3), September 1976,
pp. 952—961

108. Nardin, Terry, 'The Laws of War and Moral Judgement', BRITISH
JOURNAL OF INTERNATIONAL STUDIES, 3 (2), July 1977,
pp. 121—136

109. Nasser, G.A., PHILOSOPHY OF THE REVOLUTION, Washington,
Public Affairs Press, 1965

110. Nasution, A.H., FUNDAMENTALS OF GUERRILLA WARFARE,
New York, Praeger, 1965

111. Nye, J.S., PEACE IN PARTS, Boston, Little, Brown, 1971

112. Oppenheimer, M., THE URBAN GUERRILLA, Chicago,
Quadrangle Books, 1969

113. Osgood, R.E. and Tucker, R.W., FORCE, ORDER AND JUSTICE,
Baltimore, Johns Hopkins University Press, 1967

114. Paskins, Barrie, 'What's Wrong with Torture?', BRITISH
JOURNAL OF INTERNATIONAL STUDIES, 2 (2), July 1976

115. Pick, O. and Critchley, J., COLLECTIVE SECURITY, London,
Macmillan, 1974

116. Price, R.M., 'A Theoretical Approach to Military Rule', WORLD
POLITICS, XXIII (3), April 1971, pp. 399—430

117. Putnam, R.D., 'Towards Explaining Military Intervention in Latin
American Politics', WORLD POLITICS, XX (1), October 1967,
pp. 83—110

118. Quester, George, OFFENCE AND DEFENCE IN THE INTER-
NATIONAL SYSTEM, New York, Wiley, 1977

119. Rapoport, A., STRATEGY AND CONSCIENCE, New York,
Harper Row, 1964

120. Record, Jeffrey, US NUCLEAR WEAPONS IN EUROPE,
Washington, D.C., Brookings Institution, 1974

121. Richardson, L.F., STATISTICS OF DEADLY QUARRELS,
London, Stevens, 1960

122. Richardson, L.F., ARMS AND INSECURITY, London, Stevens,
1960

123. Riker, William, THE THEORY OF POLITICAL COALITIONS, New
Haven, Conn., Yale University Press, 1967

124. Rikhye, I.J., Harbottle, M. and Egge, B., THE THIN BLUE LINE, New
Haven, Conn., Yale University Press, 1974

125. Roberts, Adam (ed.), THE STRATEGY OF CIVILIAN DEFENCE,
London, Faber, 1967

126. Roberts, Adam, 'Civil Resistance to Military Coups', JOURNAL

OF PEACE RESEARCH, Vol. XII, 1975, pp. 19—36

127. Roberts, Adam, NATIONS IN ARMS, London, Chatto & Windus, 1976

128. Rosecrance, Richard, 'Strategic Deterrence Reconsidered', ADELPHI PAPERS, No. 116, London, International Institute for Strategic Studies, November 1975

129. Royal Institute of International Affairs Study Group, INTER-NATIONAL SANCTIONS, London, Oxford University Press, 1938

130. Saaty, T.L., MATHEMATICAL MODELS OF ARMS CONTROL AND DISARMAMENT, New York, Wiley, 1968

131. Salmon, Trevor C., 'Rationality and politics: the case of strategic theory', BRITISH JOURNAL OF INTERNATIONAL STUDIES, 2 (3), October 1976, pp. 293—310

132. Schelling, T.C., ARMS AND INFLUENCE, New Haven, Yale University Press, 1966

133. Schelling, T.C., THE STRATEGY OF CONFLICT, New York, Oxford University Press, 1963

134. Sharp, G., EXPLORING NON-VIOLENT ALTERNATIVES, Boston, Porter Sargent, 1971

135. Sharp, G., THE POLITICS OF NON-VIOLENT ACTION, Boston, Porter Sargent, 1973

136. Singer, J.D., DETERRENCE, ARMS CONTROL AND DIS-ARMAMENT, Columbus, Ohio, Ohio State University Press, 1962

137. SIPRI, THE PROBLEMS OF CHEMICAL AND BIOLOGICAL WARFARE, New York, Humanities Press, 1973

138. SIPRI, C.B. WEAPONS TODAY, London, Paul Elek, 1973

139. Slater, J. and Nardin, T., ' "The Military-Industrial" Complex Muddle', INTERNATIONAL STUDIES ASSOCIATION CON-FERENCE PAPER, New York, 1973, mimeo.

140. Snyder, G.H., DETERRENCE AND DEFENSE, Princeton, N.J., Princeton University Press, 1961

141. Sokolowsky, V.L. (ed.), SOVIET MILITARY STRATEGY, (3rd edition), New York, Crane Russak, 1975

142. Stone, L., 'Theories of Revolution', WORLD POLITICS, XVIII (2), January 1966, pp. 159—178

143. Thee, Marek, 'Arms Control: The Retreat from Disarmament', JOURNAL FOR PEACE RESEARCH, Vol. XIV, 1977, pp. 155—184

144. Thompson, K., 'Collective Security Re-examined', AMERICAN

POLITICAL SCIENCE REVIEW, XXVII (3), September 1953, pp. 753–772

145. Thompson, R., DEFEATING COMMUNIST INSURGENCY, London, Chatto & Windus, 1967
146. Trinquier, R., MODERN WARFARE: A FRENCH VIEW OF COUNTER-INSURGENCY, London, Pall Mall, 1964
147. Van Doorn, J. (ed.), ARMED FORCES AND SOCIETY, The Hague, Mouton, 1968
148. Van Doorn, J. (ed.), MILITARY PROFESSION AND MILITARY REGIMES, The Hague, Mouton, 1969
149. Vincent, J., NONINTERVENTION AND INTERNATIONAL ORDER, Princeton, N.J., Princeton University Press, 1974
150. Wainhouse, D.W., INTERNATIONAL PEACEKEEPING AT THE CROSSROADS, Baltimore, Johns Hopkins University Press, 1973
151. Walter, E.V., TERROR AND RESISTANCE, Oxford, Oxford University Press, 1969
152. Waltz, K.N., MAN, THE STATE AND WAR, New York, Columbia University Press, 1959
153. Wilkinson, Paul, POLITICAL TERRORISM, London, Macmillan, 1974
154 Wohlstetter, Albert, 'Legends of the Strategic Arms Race', FOREIGN POLICY, 15, Summer 1974, pp. 2–30; 16, Fall 1974, pp. 48–81
155 Wolfe, J. and Erickson, J. (eds.), ARMED SERVICES AND SOCIETY, Edinburgh, Edinburgh University Press, 1971
156. York, H., RACE TO OBLIVION, New York, Simon & Schuster, 1970
157. Young, E., A FAREWELL TO ARMS CONTROL?, Harmondsworth, Middx., Penguin, 1972
158. Young, O.R., THE INTERMEDIARIES, Princeton, N.J., Princeton University Press, 1967
159. Young, W., EXISTING MECHANISM OF ARMS CONTROL, Oxford, Pergamon Press, 1966
160. Various, 'Power at Sea', ADELPHI PAPERS, Part I, No. 122, Part II, No. 123, Part III, No. 124, London, International Institute for Strategic Studies, Spring 1976

Chapter IX

ORDER AND CHANGE

by J.W. Burton and Hedda Ramsden
University College, London

Until about the nineteen fifties there was a tendency — which still per-
sists in some schools — for international studies to concern itself with
means of achieving stability and preserving the international system
with the least necessary change: power balances, institutions, law,
strategy and other such topics were studied from this point of view.
The inter-state system and thinking about it moved from national
defence to alliance structures, to collective security, to attempts at
disarmament. But these changes in thought and policy were, over time,
no more than superficial variations on the continuing theme of the
state being the main, if not the sole, actor on the international stage,
and relative power being the influence which determined relationships
and policies. The 'billard ball' model of international relations which
implies that world politics is enacted by states containing relatively
homogenous, integrated societies within their clearly defined boundaries,
also implies that the preservation of states and their institutions, and
the inter-state system and its institutions, are the prime concern of
policy. It accepts the order imposed by state and inter-state authorities
as the necessary pre-condition of social stability and peaceful relations
between and within states. The literature of the time reflected this
'realist' approach to international politics; the Second World War,
the climate of the Cold War and bi-polar politics, and the development of nuclear weapons demanded a strong preoccupation with
security and stability. Bi-polarity was intended to guarantee at least a

minimum of stability, but it also meant that any change in the balance of power, any divergence from this ideology, had to be seen as a threat to the international system as a whole. Political, military and economic stability was seen as the only way to achieve security, and the only means of preventing the potential destruction of the world through a nuclear war between the great Powers.

However, another development began at about the same time: the Second World War created a climate of change. It precipitated independence movements throughout Asia and Africa, and a communications explosion which made people everywhere conscious of the possibilities for development. Thus, the literature of the late 'fifties and 'sixties has been far more concerned with the problem of modernization and development; with the nature of change, the reasons for it, its processes, the consequences of change and also the consequences of preventing it. Hence, the interest in cybernetic processes, in movements seeking independence and development, in the human needs and values reflected therein, in the nature of authority, and in conflict as a means of change.

Accompanying this shift in focus, and as a consequence of it, there is an increased interest in what is being studied in other disciplines that are also concerned with the behavioural problems associated with change. Problems of conflict, opposition to authorities, and processes of change occur at all social levels, and what is discovered at one level is of interest to those investigating at others. The processes by which change takes place, and some of the resistances to change, such as role defence are probably much the same at all levels. As a result, the literature that is now relevant to international studies, and to the general topic of order and change, cannot be confined to a strict and narrow definition of any particular discipline. The study of international conflict relies on studies of conflict generally, as do the studies of institutions and decision-making.

However, the concentration on change has not been the only influence breaking down disciplinary boundaries. Another, perhaps greater, influence has been a methodological one. The question is whether our descriptions and theories of behaviour, be it of states or of units at other levels of analysis, are based on reliable observations, or merely reflect vague impressions about aggression, power, authority, national interests, law and order, deviance or other political-sociological phenomena. While International Relations was descriptive and inductive, there was little incentive to refer to studies at other social levels.

129

Indeed, it was usually argued that there was a distinct difference between relations at the inter-state level and the domestic level, and that there could not be anything learnt reliably from the other studies. But the last twenty years have seen important advances in methodology, and studies have become far less descriptive, and far more analytical and deductive. There is now a greater awareness that description pre-supposes a theory, and it is necessary to articulate theories explicitly and to deduce falsifiable propositions, before case studies can usefully be undertaken. Once general theories of conflict and other aspects of behaviour developed, the inter-disciplinary nature of all behavioural studies became self-evident. In this sense, we are now witnessing the ending of the epoch of separate disciplines, which are circumscribed by arbitrarily drawn intellectual boundaries, and the introduction of whole fields of study and research, such as conflict, deviance and others.

The end result of this process is that International Relations has more and more to say of interest to those working at other levels. The erosion of authority within states, the diminishing importance of state boundaries and the increasing significance of systems of trans-actions, have finally exposed the traditional fallacy that international relations are characterized by anarchy, and domestic relations by order under a central authority; the international scene is probably as orderly as the domestic, with its increasing violence and the growing inability of central governments to enforce their will and norms. The study of International Relations offers a set of assumptions and a framework which is being found more and more relevant at the domestic level; this is particularly the case in the area of order and change. To the extent that the influence of governments is limited by the erosion of authority generally, and by the growth of systems of transactions which cut across national frontiers, the international model has relevance at the domestic level. Indeed, since it is no longer possible to draw arbitrary boundaries between academic disciplines, or distinctions between what is international and what is domestic, quite different models or ways of viewing international and domestic relations are called for.

Some aspects of the general topic, order and change, are dealt with elsewhere. This chapter concentrates on the following topics:

    (i)   The Study of World Society
   (ii)   Motivations and Values
  (iii)   The Erosion of Authority

130

(iv)   Deviance
(v)   Role Defence
(vi)   Problem Solving

However, none of these can be examined in isolation from the others. Books and articles inevitably touch on all when dealing with any one.

(i) The Study of World Society

In the introductory section of this chapter we referred to two fundamentally different models of international society. The literature on 'Order and Change' is concerned with the impact of the trans-national, or world society model, on the study of International Politics. The perception of political reality indicates the direction research will take: if states are the dominant actors, then some reliable predictions could be made about the inter-state system merely by adequate descriptive studies of diplomatic history, trading relations, international institutions, alliances and other aspects of the interactions of states. If, on the other hand, transactions across national boundaries that are not wholly initiated and controlled by state authorities are considered to be more influential on the behaviour of states and other social units, then reliable studies must be made of behaviour at other social levels; of the nature of authority and responses to authority; of human values and needs, of ethnic and other sympathy relationships that cross national boundaries; and of the spillover into the wider political environment of social and political unrest within states.

The study of world society seeks to focus on some high levels of interaction, but in the perspective of the whole of behaviour. It seeks to define and to explain the field and problems of special interest to International Relations scholars, but by reference to behaviour at all social levels. It is essentially a dynamic model, the features of which include the increase in the level of communications and trans-national organizations, responses to relative deprivation, the struggles for ethnic identity and the resolution of post-colonial problems of boundaries and control, the competition of ideologies, and many others.

(ii) Motivations and Values

The behaviour that gives rise to these features cannot be described usefully in broad terms such as aggression, revolutions, and breakdown of law and order. Such terms do not reflect adequately the dynamic

131

nature of political behaviour. The study of Politics, including World Politics, is the study of perceptions that the actors within a society have of that society and of each other, and the values (that is, the objectives and preferences that are the drives to behaviour) which each holds. Perceptions are a stimulus to action. They are responsible for expectations and for fears. Studies that concentrate on institutional, structural and decision-making aspects of society, but which neglect the influences that were responsible for this apparatus, must fail in giving the complete picture of world politics. Hence there is now an interest in motivations, human needs and values. In examining social-psychological values from the point of view of Political Science, and especially Political Science concerned with world society, we are not concerned only, or even mainly, with individually held values that are acquired and subject to change. Our interest is in those that are fundamental in human behaviour, and for this reason presumably universal. There is a distinction to be made between, on the one hand, values that people of one culture or ideology believe they should share, and, on the other hand, values that are held by people within all cultures and ideological systems, simply by virtue of the fact of belonging to the human race.

We are just beginning to understand the significance of values and motivations as a catalyst for change. There has been an important shift in emphasis over the last few decades from a normative approach, to one that endeavours to understand political responses, and analyses them as reactions to an environment, a major part of which is the behaviour of other actors. The values of political actors are beginning to be analyzed, even though we have not fully grasped their importance and scope, as yet; but it is this which has made Political Science both more realistic and more complex as a subject. The study of Politics is no longer History or the study of organizations. It is now the study of human behaviour in all its aspects.

(iii) The Erosion of Authority

All societies, all cultures, exhibit inequalities, relative power positions, privileged and under-privileged. The formulation of the rules of social relationships has been traditionally within the power of those who have acquired influence. Consequently, the structure and the authorities in control are considered 'natural' and attract explanations of natural order. Entailed in this traditional notion of authority is the belief that some persons are entitled to require the obedience of others, who in turn have a moral obligation to acknowledge this authority. This authority relationship can be applied at all levels; the individual and the state, the small state and the large one, the colonial people and the colonial Power.

There are few more frequent and universal political declarations by governments than those concerning 'law and order': established authorities see themselves as the guardians of law and order, that is the guardians of well integrated, harmonious societies. Governments, when confronted with illegal strikes, riots, race disturbances or the like are quick to employ the phrase as both description and justification of policy. Presumably they believe they reflect majority view-points when they claim that the objective and duty of government is to maintain 'law and order'. There is implied a moral overtone: those who do not uphold law and order are acting against the interests of society. But this consensual proposition clearly invites consideration of the type of law and the type of order that is being given support. The erosion of authority reflects a reaction against institutions that appear to frustrate human needs and values, and in circumstances in which this becomes clear, public sympathy is with those who confront authorities. This is the nature of the challenge to authority with which we are familiar.

Authority succeeds when it is based on legitimized relationships. Traditional and legal authority have gradually been eroded, giving way to a condition in which only legitimized role-differentiation (and authority derived from it) is acceptable. Traditionally, legality and legitimacy had their sources in foreign recognition, effective control, heredity, constitutional processes and other such tests. Now we must draw a clear distinction between the two terms: legitimized authority, seemingly the only type now fully accepted, is that authority which is derived from those over whom it is exercised. The test of legitimized authorities is not an ability to preserve law and order; it is the ability to accomplish planning and problem solving, adaptive change and generally to perform the role of leadership effectively.

(iv) Deviance

Deviant behaviour, and the failure of policies to prevent it, let alone to harness it for creative purposes, is a practical problem that attracts much attention. Deviance is behaviour that does not conform with certain norms. It cannot be defined or conceptualized outside a framework of norms. Social norms change, and therefore behaviour that is classified as deviant or conforming must be reclassified from time to time. A

133

constant re-examination of social norms is taking place within societies. In the interest of stability and harmony it is expedient to ask questions about the nature of authority, of its erosion, of law and order, of inequalities and of all structures and institutions that could be relevant to challenges to authority and to deviant behaviour.

We arrive at the position that the individual in society will pursue his needs and desires to the extent that he finds this possible within the confines of his environment, his experience and knowledge of options, and all other capabilities and constraints. He will use the norms common within society, and push against them to the extent necessary to ensure that they work in his interest; but if the norms of society inhibit and frustrate to the degree that he decides they are no longer useful, then, subject to values he attaches to social relationships, he will employ methods outside the norms, and outside the codes he would in other circumstances wish to apply to his behaviour. So also with the nation and the state. From this standpoint, explanations of deviant and normal behaviour have the same theoretical base: the difference is one of definition. What makes the particular individual or state deviant is not the particular characteristics of the individual, but the total situation in which the unit operates.

This does not, however, argue for the abolition of authorities, as anarchists and some functionalists would desire. Looking at the problem of deviance, not from a structural or environmental point of view, but from that of the deviant himself, the need for effective, adaptive leadership is evident. Deviance can be seen as a dynamic input into social change. It is protest, it is a vote of no confidence in social and political systems, it is the warning that structures and institutions require reconsideration, it is the signal that rates of change and stresses are greater than actors can tolerate. It is both in itself and by its influence on authorities the motivation for change. The deviant does not necessarily possess the qualities that would enable him to give direction to the desired change. He may know why he is a deviant, he may feel suppressed by a condition of un-warranted inequality, injustice or deprivation, but he may not necessarily know the conditions under which he would not be a deviant. It follows that, for deviance to lead to changes in society such that individual development can take place, it must be mediated by some agent; that is, by effective leadership.

(v) Role Defence

A power oriented approach to political and social relationships assumes that societies have evolved from primitive tribal conditions to their present form of centralized authorities, governed by the relatively powerful, as individuals or groups seek their own immediate and longer-term interests. Authority role positions have consequently emerged reflecting racial and class interests, and elite values have been promoted and internalized into consensual norms for behaviour. Frequently, human needs and desires have been denied as institutions have been preserved from change by the power and influence of elites. The essential point of this position is that even though problems were not being solved, and societies were seen to be non-adaptive and self-destructive in many ways, these structures would still be preserved in the interests of the elites who hold power. The justification for this normative point of view is the belief that the interests of most citizens, over the long term, are best catered for by the preservation of social institutions and structures, even though in the short term, and in some particular cases, there may be some curb on freedom and development. This mode of thought seems to be universal: most authorities and the elites which support them, tend to take this view, as do usually those whom they govern.

There is a direct connection between role defence and resistance to structural change. Political leadership in all societies finds change in policy, and still more change in political philosophy, hard to make. Power may be defined as the capacity not to have to adjust to changing environments, and traditionally ruling elites have been inclined to meet demands for change by resistance to such demands. Policies that have failed to achieve their objectives tend to be defended, and pursued with ever more vigour. In most conflict situations a role defence situation ultimately emerges. We are familiar with the leaders of independence movements who have defended their role positions even after independence, when a less charismatic and more analytical type of leadership is required to accomplish economic and social tasks. Where role maintenance involves a way of life for a large community, as in some parts of Africa where there is role defence on the basis of colour and tribe, this tenacity leads to open conflict on a large scale. Within societies, elite values and structures are defended, even though they may easily lead to inequalities, underprivilege, class and race discrimination and other conditions conducive to deviant behaviour. The injustice is accepted as a price that is necessary to preserve elite interests.

135

This process is in evidence in all modern societies, including socialist ones in which deviance and dissent are also present. There are resistances to change, and there are drives towards change. It is likely in many, if not most, contemporary situations, that they will in practice be determined as the result of deviant and dissident behaviour on the one side, and the use of power on the other, at least until there are consensual changes in thought about problem solving approaches.

(vi) Problem Solving

What are the processes by which society can avoid conflict between the various groups within it? What are the processes of peaceful change? The power of authorities is reflected in their ability to ensure conforming behaviour, and their ability to preserve social norms. It is they who define what is acceptable social behaviour. Thus they may define all that behaviour which is a threat to them and which militates against their interests as deviant. In this view, if authorities experience problems arising from change or conflict situations, then this must be seen as a lack of power on their part. If power, or the ability to coerce, is available, this is traditionally considered the easiest and most efficient way to deal with social problems and deviance. But experience shows that, in the long term, power is not a useful means of controlling behaviour. To enforce a certain, desired behaviour pattern may lead to deviance at another point in society; it can be self-defeating in that it may generate resistence elsewhere. No amount of coercion or threat of force can prevent determined dissent. For these reasons, the assumptions on which authority roles have been based are in doubt; namely, that there exist consensual norms that are generally accepted by individuals and groups. An alternative hypothesis is that individuals and groups pursue their own defined needs and interests and will not be frustrated permanently by other sets of norms, save at the cost of social upheaval and eventual disintegration. In the long term it is impossible to preserve authorities and institutional structures against the demands of human needs. Consistent with this is a demand for leadership to create those structures which will promote social and individual needs. Authorities are required to be adaptive and receptive to changes in the environment, rather than being protective merely of their own role interests.

Coercion versus problem solving is *the* contemporary issue. Problem solving in open systems is yet underdeveloped as a study. The literature is limited but growing. The techniques are slowly being

136

explored.

As stated earlier, none of these themes can be discussed adequately without reference to others. The following are among the most useful references, and in turn they give further references. In a developing study, as in 'Order and Change', an element of such detective work is essential.

Bibliography

1. Apter, David, SOME CONCEPTUAL APPROACHES TO THE STUDY OF MODERNISATION, Englewood Cliffs, N.J., Prentice Hall, 1968
    Modernization and development relate directly to processes of change, and thinking in these areas is altering rapidly. Development and modernization are becoming defined as an ability to be flexible, and this is a useful introductory book.
2. Bell, Daniel, THE COMING OF POST-INDUSTRIAL SOCIETY, Harmondsworth, Middlesex, Penguin, 1973
    There appears to be a growing reaction against traditional Marxist views, and an interest in the way in which bureaucratic decision-making defeats political ideologies. In the context of processes of change, this is an important book.
3. Barkun, Michael, LAW WITHOUT SANCTIONS, New Haven, Conn., Yale University Press, 1968
    This book stimulates thinking about coercive and value approaches to social organization and problems of order. It is a sociological approach to a legal problem.
4. Bennis, W., Benne, R. and Chin, R. (eds.), THE PLANNING OF CHANGE, New York, Holt, Rinehart & Winston, 1970
    Of all books, this is probably more directly appropriate to problems of order and change than any: its conscious focus is change, how it is brought about, how it is resisted. It is well written and firmly based on available sources.
5. Burton, John W., PEACE THEORY, New York, Alfred Knopf, 1962
    A study of conditions of peace, built around the notion of change and resistance to change.
6. Dahrendorf, Ralf, CLASS AND CLASS CONFLICT IN AN INDUSTRIAL SOCIETY, London, Routledge & Kegan Paul, 1959
    In a sense, the relevance of this book is that it is a theory about stability: the author belongs to the coercion school of thought

which argues that societies are, and must be, held together within a coercive framework.

7. Davies, James C. (ed.), WHEN MEN REVOLT AND WHY, New York, The Free Press, 1971
A reader with a wide variety of articles, covering theory and practice, traditional and modern. There are several articles of relevance to order and change. The bias is towards the control of violence.

8. Enloe, Cynthia H., ETHNIC CONFLICT AND POLITICAL DEVELOPMENT, Boston, Little, Brown, 1973
Control theorists are suggesting that there are certain human motivations that finally under-pin or destroy institutions and policies. In this book it is argued that the struggle for identity may be more influential than any drive toward integration. If this is the case, there are important policy implications in areas of community relations and regional relationships, and some significant predictions could be made.

9. Grinker, Roy R. (ed.), TOWARDS A UNIFIED THEORY OF HUMAN BEHAVIOUR, New York, Basic Books, 1956
A reader to which many significant scholars have contributed. It serves as the basis for discussion of the introductory point made above; that methodological and philosophical considerations have changed the study of International Relations, especially in regard to problems of Order and Change.

10. Gurr, Ted R., WHY MEN REBEL, Princeton, N.J., Princeton University Press, 1970
A title such as this presupposes some behavioural patterns that cut across all cultures — all men. It is a study of relative deprivation, but has wider implications for International Relations.

11. Johnson, Chalmers, REVOLUTIONARY CHANGE, Boston, Little, Brown & Company, 1966
An attempt to bring together coercion theory and value theory on the assumption that societies exist as entities, and include a mix of coercion and consensual values. This is an assumption that transactionalism may not accept: perhaps the assumption that societies are or should be integrated wholes is the source of many failed policies. A useful text, because it surveys past thinking.

12. Krislov, S., Boyum, K.O., Clarke, J.N., Shaefer, R.C. and White, S.O. (eds.), COMPLIANCE AND THE LAW, Beverly Hills, Sage Publications, 1966

A useful aspect of the total problem: what is the nature of compliance in conditions where change is being demanded, prevented, promoted?

13. Levine, R.E. and Campbell, D.T., ETHNOCENTRISM, New York, John Wiley, 1972
A study of relationships, and values attached to them, which throws light both on integration and independence processes, and therefore on causes of disorder and directions of change.

14. Sites, Paul, CONTROL: THE BASIS OF SOCIAL ORDER, New York, Dunellan Publishing Company, 1973
Control theory is most relevant to the study of order and change: are actors 'socialized' or do they use social norms and conventions as tools only when appropriate to their needs, and invent others when it is necessary? And what are these needs that all policies must take into account?

15. Thomas, John and Bennis, W.G., MANAGEMENT OF CHANGE AND CONFLICT, Harmondsworth, Middlesex, Penguin, 1972
A useful introductory book to problems of change, designed to stimulate thought in the area of control.

Chapter X

INTEGRATION*

by A.J.R. Groom
University of Kent

Integration and disintegration are age-old concerns of politics, political
science and, indeed, all social thought, for integration can be conceived
in terms of a single dimension, such as the economy, groups of
dimensions, or the totality of relationships. It is relevant at all levels
of analysis from two persons or a family to world society at large.
Moreover, it can be seen as a state of affairs or as a process. When seen
as a state of affairs criteria are set and integration has occurred when
these requirements are met. Disintegration occurs when the criteria
which were formally met are no longer fulfilled. The criteria themselves are usually specified by the observer or participant since there is
no generally accepted essentialist definition of integration. Integration
as a state of affairs is not incompatible with the notion of integration
as a process. It is a process whereby units move between conditions
of complete isolation and complete integration. Here the focus is upon
the process of moving towards one or the other end of the spectrum
rather than uniquely upon its integrative end. Thus integration involves
movement towards or away from collective action based upon consensual values for the achievement of common goals in which the
parties have long run expectations of mutually compatible and acceptable behaviour and in which the process is self-maintaining. Integration

*This essay is an adaptation of a chapter in Taylor P. and Groom A.J.R. (eds.),
   INTERNATIONAL ORGANISATION: A CONCEPTUAL APPROACH, London,
   Frances Pinter, 1978

is ubiquitous in that no actor can exist in total isolation so that the process of integration and disintegration provides an organizing theme at all levels of society and between all 'disciplines' of the social sciences.

Integration, as a state of affairs, has not traditionally been conceived as the dominant characteristic of world society. On the contrary, world society and, in particular, inter-state relations are often described as being anarchic in nature — a situation which has been consecrated in the doctrine of sovereignty. Indeed, it is this very anarchy, and especially the absence at the world level of a central governing body with a virtual monopoly of organized force ruling a constituency that has accepted a set of rights and duties in relation to that body, that was used to justify the study of International Relations being separated from that of Political Science. But the dichotomy is not that stark. Consensus is not always the dominant characteristic of domestic relations within states either in the developed or developing world. Nor is it entirely absent between states, as the work of many functional institutions attests, or within world society at large where the growth of 'one world' problems, such as population or the environment involving state and non-state actors of a variety of kinds striving to arrive at a consensus, is clearly evident.

Integration is not, however, the dominant characteristic of world society nor of inter-state relations. Profusion would perhaps be a better term: a profusion of systemic ties, whether power dominated or legitimized, in the widest variety of functional dimensions involving a range of actors at and between various levels and involving world, regional, local and aterritorial ties. This profusion, which offers an abundance of possibilities, is due to a number of factors of which the industrial and French revolutions are especially important. The industrial revolution brought about the makings of a world economy and it led to a tremendous growth in transactions, whereas the French Revolution was the harbinger of the nation-state which gradually imposed controls on such transaction flows. This has given rise to a plethora of international institutions designed, for the most part, to facilitate the smooth flow of transactions across state boundaries; that is, to harmonize systemic demands with national and state affiliations and institutions. But this profusion of systemic ties and institutions does not make a whole. There is no grand design of the type so-beloved by the advocates of world government. Perhaps this is not a bad thing, since the rate and the magnitude of change are such that a variety of possible responses may make it more likely that the present repertoire of possibilities will contain an appropriate response to change. Rigidity or a restricted range of capabilities does not auger well for the future. Indeed, the extent to which integration is to be encouraged is an open question. Although there seems to be an assumption in the liberal Western democratic value structure that integration is a 'good thing', contemporary world society also gives many examples where 'independence', 'devolution', 'non-alignment', 'neutralism' and the like are prized values. Moreover, it is not a question of all or nothing, integration or isolation, but a question of more integration in one sphere and not so much in another.

Studies of integration have been given a fillip by two factors in the postwar world — the example of the European Communities and the emancipation of the colonial world. The European Communities have attracted an inordinate amount of attention, particularly from scholars in the United States, perhaps to the neglect of other, more important forms of organization in terms of practical integration, such as parallel national action in Scandinavia. The emancipation of the colonial world has given prominence to the question of integration in two ways. Firstly, there is the issue of integration within states, such as Nigeria or Pakistan; and then that of integration between states, as in the West Indies or Africa, either generally or in particular dimensions. It is interesting to note that while federalism as a means of integration had a modicum of success in an earlier round of decolonialization in the United States, Australia, Canada and South Africa, it has a dismal record both within and between states in the postwar era in both the developed and developing worlds. Nevertheless, interest is provoked by problems, by failure as much as by success.

'One world' or a 'shrinking world' are epithets often used to describe the contemporary world. They are not inaccurate: one world problems abound — population, food, environment, development, even women — to name but a few, and they have been recognized as such. The shrinking world is reflected in the prodigious movement and interdependence of goods, services, ideas and people. How can and should such developments best be conceptualized? This is hardly a subject for an annotated bibliographical essay which is more concerned with the way in which such developments have actually been conceptualized in the literature. However, it is relevant to note that the literature is, in fact, rather heavily weighted in favour of certain integration theories — in particular neofunctionalism, regionalism and federalism — to the neglect of other approaches such as anarchism, cooperation or

142

harmonization. Although a bibliography must perforce reflect the literature, in order to create an element of balance this introductory survey concludes with a brief comment on a wider range of modes of integration than is readily available in the literature.

Co-operation can be seen as an attempt to adjust policies in a way that does not involve any immediate structural impact. The intention is to make agreements in specific areas for specific purposes in situations where task expansion and spillover are neither expected nor desired. In *co-ordination* there is policy alignment which may range over various areas of a functional dimension such as trade and stretch into cognate dimensions, but the structural impact of such arrangements is limited. *Harmonization*, on the other hand, involves institutionalized policy adjustment and alignment often on the basis of some superordinate norm or standard. *Parallel national action* provides a different format that can lead to a surprising level of practical and effective integration through extensive routine policy adjustment. Parallel legislation or practices are separately instituted by different actors in such a way as to be compatible with each other in order to reduce the impact of boundaries. The scope of such activities can be very considerable and although there is little formal institutionalization there may be much informal contact and con-sultation.

Informality, diversity and flexibility are the hallmarks of *networks* which are closely related to the *transactionalist approach*. Both are concerned with the waxing and waning of systems of transactions and the facilitation of intensely responsive institutional arrangements. *Association*, on the other hand, has greater structural impact as it is embodied in a formal agreement. Such agreements may be of an interim character or to link otherwise disparate actors who, neverthe-less, have complementary interests in some areas. Paradoxically association can be a form which enables both integration and separation to be pursued at the same time. Thus the purpose of such an agreement may be to promote integration in certain domains but to restrict it in others, in short, to deny the 'functional imperative' of task expansion and spillover. In *commonwealth* relationships policies are managed in such a way that although the scope and level of integration may be high, it stops short of a direct challenge to the independence of the units.

Functionalism has no fixed territorial base for organization; rather, in advocating that form should follow function in an aterritorial

143

manner, it is closely akin to networks and transactionalism. There is no end-state in functionalism, such as occurs in neofunctionalism, since the evolution of institutional forms is open-ended in response to changes in patterns of relationships, although the degree of integration may be very substantial in some systems. However, like neofunctionalists, functionalists stress the learning process whereby habits of co-operation in one area spill over into others as a result of the functional imperative. Functionalists see the growth of cross-cutting ties leading to a working peace system as being fairly automatic, whereas neofunctionalists stress that it needs an act of political will. They differ, too, in that functionalists conceive spillover systemically whereas neofunctionalists see it as a means to inter-state integration in a new polity. Thus *neofunctionalism* has been developed in the context of a regional or putative federal body coming to possess authority over national sub-systems, function by function. While it has wide scope, at least in aspiration, and a high level of integration, it is firmly tied to a particular regional context. The end-goal of neofunctionalism is in fact a federation. *Federalism* stresses the importance of a constitutional instrument setting out the relationship and competences of the federal and local bodies within a defined territorial area. The scope and level of integration may be high. This is also the aspiration in *regionalism*. Region is a geographical concept and the doctrine of regionalism must be based on the assertion that geographical variables are a prime influence on behaviour. This is an empirical question and, although the notion of region may be helpful in particular dimensions, it does not appear to be the great organizing principle when considering multi-dimensional phenomena.

Finally some approaches which are being given new or revived attention should be mentioned. *Interdependence* has become an 'in' word, but one which has a distinct meaning. It describes a situation in which independent or autarkic action has become 'unthinkable' and recognized as such; and, although formal independence remains, it is not a practical option, for better or for worse. This can mask a situation of imperialism or a hegemonial relationship — the subject of a different section and one which is separate from integration since it is based primarily on coercion — as well as one of legitimized role differentiation. *Anarchism* proposes mutual dependencies of the latter sort but without formal institutions. It has much in common with networks, transactionalism and functionalism except that it is chiefly operative at the micro-level.

Perhaps the circle can be completed by returning to 'one world' problems. Recently a notion borrowed from economics, that of *collective goods*, has been used to analyse some of the aspects of these problems. In particular 'one world' problems give rise to assets from which it is not possible to exclude 'free riders' or for which the consumption by one does not diminish availability to another. In such cases the theory of collective goods is apposite.

General Works

There are a number of general works in the field of integration which cover several different approaches. Sometimes these are by a single author but often they are collections of original articles or more frequently collections of reprints. At the risk of gross immodesty the author of this chapter would like to draw attention to a volume (47) which he has edited with Paul Taylor called INTERNATIONAL ORGANISATION: A CONCEPTUAL APPROACH which contains an original contribution on most of the approaches mentioned in the preceeding paragraphs. It is designed as a textbook giving a survey of different conceptual approaches to international organization and institutions.

Three other volumes are particularly recommended in this category. An anthology (27) entitled INTERNATIONAL POLITICAL COMMUNITIES has been widely used as a course text in the United States and, although the selection of reprints is now dated, it still comprises a judicious selection from the literature of the day. R.J. Harrison's EUROPE IN QUESTION (25) is an excellent survey of the functionalist, neofunctionalist and federalist literature in reference to the European experience. Despite its title, it is essentially a theoretical work. Jacob and Toscano's volume (28) is older but wears its years well. It is particularly useful in that it does not restrict itself to international integration but also considers integration in cities and other fora.

There is a considerable additional literature that merits attention, not least Paul Taylor's introductory INTERNATIONAL CO-OPERATION TODAY (46) and Amatai Etzioni's rather ponderous POLITICAL UNIFICATION (13) in which the case studies are poorly done. De Vree (11) and Pentland (40) cover much of the same ground as Harrison but EUROPE IN QUESTION (25) leads the field. Hodges' EUROPEAN INTEGRATION (26) would be a strong rival except that, as a reader of reprints, it is neither as coherent nor as up-to-date. Nevertheless, it is a worthwhile selection. Finally, no reader will regret taking Cobb and Elder (8) or Ake (1) off the shelf particularly as the latter offers an African perspective on the subject.

Functionalism

While it is usually a futile exercise to try to attribute to any one writer the development of such a seminal theory as functionalism, the name of David Mitrany does spring to mind in this case. His classic essay, A WORKING PEACE SYSTEM (35), the ideas of which were first published in the inter-war period, has had great influence over the years, since it is a cogent and powerful statement proposing an alternative to power politics in international relations. Mitrany died in 1975, a few weeks after the publication of some old and new essays entitled THE FUNCTIONAL THEORY OF POLITICS (36). He continued writing until his death at the age of 87, some of his last contributions being among his best. A case in point is his justly celebrated article 'The Prospect of Integration: Federal or Functional' revised from Groom and Taylor's edited volume FUNCTIONALISM: THEORY AND PRACTICE IN INTERNATIONAL RELATIONS (17). This is a collection of otherwise original essays on the theoretical aspects of functionalism, followed by some case studies. The views expressed range from the committed to the opposed, together with the agnostic and the sceptical. There has been a revival of interest in functionalism in the last decade, one of the earlier expressions of which was a Bellagio conference (18). A more recent attempt to relate the theory to developments in East-West relations in Europe can be found in an article in the JOURNAL OF COMMON MARKET STUDIES (16). Most students of international organization are introduced to the theory of functionalism by Inis Claude through the critique he offers in his much-read SWORDS INTO PLOWSHARES (7). Functionalism, as Claude has admitted, is a very seductive approach to the problems of international organization. Nowhere can this be more clearly seen than in the neofunctionalist school which, despite denying the functionalist approach by being territorial, teleological, and state-centric, nevertheless owes much to Mitrany's notion of a learning process giving rise to task expansion and spillover in order to create a working peace system.

146

Neofunctionalism

The 'guru' of the neofunctionalists is undoubtedly Ernst Haas. Much influenced by Mitrany, but with a pressing and meritorious drive to be more rigorous in his methodology, he has pioneered and led the American study of European integration (21). In addition, he has applied the same approach to the ILO (19). More recently he has expressed doubts about the whole neofunctionalist enterprise (20, 22) but, whatever the current assessment of the neofunctionalist paradigm – and it is increasingly critical – the impetus given to the study of integration by Ernst Haas must be handsomely acknowledged. Leon Lindberg and his colleague Stuart Scheingold have followed in the footsteps of Haas. Lindberg's study of the early years of the Common Market was a major contribution to the literature (32) but his later work with Scheingold (33) was less felicitous, perhaps because of an obstupefying use of jargon and a rigorous attempt at measurement which did not yield as much in precise observation as it lost in a sense of substance. A later volume edited by Lindberg and Scheingold first appeared as a special issue of INTERNATIONAL ORGANISATION and then as a book. In many ways it could be taken as representative of the neofunctionalist approach (34). The neofunctionalists wrote prolifically in the journals of the field and their articles have a prominent place in the readers and anthologies in integration. One other work that grew out of Mitrany's initial impetus is Sewell's FUNCTIONALISM AND WORLD POLITICS (44). Sewell put Mitrany into a testable form in a rather different way from the Haas-Lindberg school and his case study was on the World Bank group rather than the European Communities. Sewell's work certainly deserves mention and it falls nearest to the neofunctionalist rubric but more in the style of Haas' BEYOND THE NATION STATE (20) than Lindberg's work.

Regionalism

Regionalism as a doctrine has been written into the security and economic provisions of the UN Charter. It was viewed as a half-way house between world government and the sovereign state, as a means whereby states with interests in common that were less than universal could work together and as a form of hegemonial control for great Powers. Few, if any, of these hopes and fears have been realized but John Burton has related the early philosophy to functionalism and the degree to which such regional bodies are associative or dis-associative (3). More recently, theories of regionalism have concentrated on integration in the neofunctionalist mode, but not always. The regionalist — neofunctionalist literature has been reviewed above but Joseph Nye has had a foot in both camps. His edited volume INTERNATIONAL REGIONALISM (37) reprints several papers in the neofunctionalist mode, while his PEACE IN PARTS (38) is a sterling effort to analyze the role of regional institutions in the handling of conflicts between members. This study, and his later work with Haas and Butterworth (23), is worthwhile both from the conceptual and empirical points of view. To a certain degree, it is more concerned with the ideas about regionalism which permeat the UN Charter than later neofunctionalist interpretations. Cantori and Spiegel (4), like Nye, have tried to give a firm empirical basis to the concept of regionalism as an analytical tool. That they have failed is perhaps more to do with the geographical basis of regionalism and its single factor explanation of behaviour than the particular short-coming of their research. Russett, on the other hand, proceeded inductively (42) and received a famous rap over the knuckles from Young (50) for his pains. His findings, however, suggest that the notion of region is not a multidimensional concept. Hypotheses and findings abound in Thompson's very useful article which reviews the literature in the field (48).

Federalism

There is a voluminous literature on federalism within states, fuelled not least by the doctrine being more or less assimilated to holy writ in the United States. However, the emphasis here is more on federation as a means to integration (or, as in the case of the UK, perhaps eventually to disintegration) between state actors. Empirically federation has been tried and failed since 1945, yet the doctrine is a very powerful one. Sir Kenneth Wheare has had a hand in the design of several constitutions and his FEDERAL GOVERNMENT (49) is a classic. In the United States Carl Friedrich occupies a similar role, and his TRENDS IN FEDERALISM IN THEORY AND PRACTICE (15) is a fairly recent statement of his views. Earle (12) and Franck (14) have compiled useful collections, and Birch has provided students with an excellent crib in an article summarizing the different approaches to the subject (2).

Other approaches and miscellaneous works

The conceptual literature on some of the other approaches is indeed

148

sparse. For co-operation, harmonization, co-ordination, parallel national action, association and commonwealth the reader is referred to the volume edited by Taylor and the writer (47), where there is a chapter on each, and additional bibliographical references and footnotes. For the rest, transactionalism is rather better represented, particularly by the excellent pioneering work of Karl Deutsch (9, 10). More recently Keohane and Nye have sponsored research on transnational integration some of which has appeared in various issues of their house journal, INTERNATIONAL ORGANISATION (30), and later in book form. They have also pointed to the importance of transgovernmental relations (31). Transactionalism, transnationalism and networks are closely related, and Anthony Judge has written several articles on the latter in his house journal INTERNATIONAL ASSOCIATIONS (29) as well as contributing to the Groom and Taylor volumes (17, 47). Of considerable relevance in this context is a thought-provoking UIA symposium, entitled OPEN SOCIETY OF THE FUTURE (39).

Herbert Spiro has tried to come to grips with the notion of interdependence in a symposium article (45), while April Carter's work on anarchism is a fine introduction (5) to that elusive subject. On collective goods there is an excellent introductory article by Russett and Sullivan (43), supplemented by one by Ruggie (41). Finally, no bibliographical survey on integration would be complete without that misguided classic on WORLD PEACE THROUGH WORLD LAW (6). In a different category is Michael Haas' bibliography (24) which together with a perusal of the past issues of INTERNATIONAL ORGANIZATION and the JOURNAL OF COMMON MARKET STUDIES is a prerequisite for any serious reading in the field of integration.

Bibliography

1. Ake, Claude, A THEORY OF POLITICAL INTEGRATION, Homewood, Ill., The Dorsey Press, 1967
2. Birch, A.H., 'Approaches to the Study of Federalism', POLITICAL STUDIES, XIV (1), February 1966, pp. 15–33
3. Burton, J.W., 'Regionalism, Functionalism and the U.N. Regional Arrangements for Security', in M. Waters (ed.), THE UNITED NATIONS, New York, Macmillan, 1967
4. Cantori, Louis and Spiegel, Steven C., THE INTERNATIONAL

POLITICS OF REGIONS, Englewood Cliffs, N.J., Prentice-Hall, 1970

5. Carter, April, THE POLITICAL THEORY OF ANARCHISM, London, Routledge & Kegan Paul, 1971

6. Clark, G. and Sohn, L.B., WORLD PEACE THROUGH WORLD LAW, Cambridge, Mass., Harvard University Press, 1966

7. Claude, Inis L., SWORDS INTO PLOWSHARES, New York, Random House, 1956

8. Cobb, R.W. and Elder, C., INTERNATIONAL COMMUNITY, New York, Holt, Rinehart & Winston, 1970

9. Deutsch, Karl W., NATIONALISM AND SOCIAL COMMUNI- CATION, (2nd edition), Cambridge, Mass., Harvard University Press, 1966, (First published in 1953)

10. Deutsch, Karl W. et al, POLITICAL COMMUNITY AND THE NORTH ATLANTIC AREA, Princeton, Princeton University Press, 1957

11. De Vree, J.K., POLITICAL INTEGRATION, Paris, Mouton, 1972

12. Earle, Valerie (ed.), FEDERALISM, Itasca, Ill., Peacock, 1968

13. Etzioni, Amatai, POLITICAL UNIFICATION, New York, Holt, Rinehart & Winston, 1965

14. Franck, Thomas M. (ed.), WHY FEDERALISM FAILS, New York, New York University Press, 1968

15. Friedrich, Carl J., TRENDS OF FEDERALISM IN THEORY AND PRACTICE, New York, Praeger, 1968

16. Groom, A.J.R., 'The Functionalist Approach and East/West Co- operation in Europe', JOURNAL OF COMMON MARKET STUDIES, Vol. XIII, Nos. 1 & 2, 1975, pp. 21–60

17. Groom, A.J.R. and Taylor, P. (eds.), FUNCTIONALISM: THEORY AND PRACTICE IN INTERNATIONAL RELATIONS, London, University of London Press, 1975

18. Groom, A.J.R. and Taylor, P. (rapporteurs), FUNCTIONALISM, New York, Carnegie, 1969

19. Haas, E.B., BEYOND THE NATION STATE, Stanford, Calif., Stanford University Press, 1964

20. Haas, E.B., THE OBSOLESCENCE OF REGIONAL INTEGRATION THEORY, Berkeley, Institute of International Studies, 1976

21. Haas, E.B., THE UNITING OF EUROPE, London, Stevens, 1958

22. Haas, E.B., 'Turbulent Fields and the Theory of Regional Integration', INTERNATIONAL ORGANISATION, XXX (2),

Spring 1976, pp. 173–212

23. Haas, E.B., Butterworth, R. and Nye, J., CONFLICT MANAGE-
    MENT IN INTERNATIONAL ORGANIZATIONS, Morristown,
    N.J., General Learning Press, 1972
24. Haas, Michael, INTERNATIONAL ORGANIZATION: AN
    INTERDISCIPLINARY BIBLIOGRAPHY, Stanford, Hoover
    Institute, 1971
25. Harrison, R.J., EUROPE IN QUESTION, London, Allen & Unwin,
    1974
26. Hodges, M. (ed.), EUROPEAN INTEGRATION, Harmondsworth,
    Middx., Penguin Books, 1972
27. INTERNATIONAL POLITICAL COMMUNITIES: AN
    ANTHOLOGY, New York, Doubleday, 1966
28. Jacob, P.E. and Toscano, J.V., INTEGRATION OF POLITICAL
    COMMUNITIES, Philadelphia, J.B. Lippincott Co., 1964
29. Judge, A.J.N., 'The World Network of Organizations', INTER-
    NATIONAL ASSOCIATIONS, 24 (1), 1972, pp. 18–24
30. Keohane, Robert and Nye, J.S., TRANSNATIONAL RELATIONS
    AND WORLD POLITICS, Cambridge, Mass., Harvard University
    Press, 1972 and Special Issue of INTERNATIONAL ORGANIS-
    ATION, XXV (3), Summer 1971
31. Keohane, Robert and Nye, J.S., 'Transgovernmental Relations and
    International Organizations', WORLD POLITICS, XXVII (1),
    October 1974, pp. 39–62
32. Lindberg, Leon, THE POLITICAL DYNAMICS OF EUROPEAN
    ECONOMIC INTEGRATION, Stanford, Calif., Stanford University
    Press, 1963
33. Lindberg, L. and Scheingold, S., EUROPE'S WOULD-BE
    POLITY, Englewood Cliffs, N.J., Prentice Hall, 1970
34. Lindberg, L. and Scheingold, S. (eds.), REGIONAL INTEGRATION,
    Cambridge, Mass., Harvard University Press, 1971, and Special
    Issue of INTERNATIONAL ORGANISATION, XXIV (4),
    Autumn 1970
35. Mitrany, David, A WORKING PEACE SYSTEM, Chicago,
    Quadrangle Books, 1966
36. Mitrany, David, THE FUNCTIONAL THEORY OF POLITICS,
    London, Martin Robertson, 1975
37. Nye, Joseph S. (ed.), INTERNATIONAL REGIONALISM, Boston,
    Little, Brown, 1968
38. Nye, Joseph S., PEACE IN PARTS, Boston, Little, Brown, 1971

39. OPEN SOCIETY OF THE FUTURE, Brussels, Union of International Associations, 1973
40. Pentland, Charles, INTERNATIONAL THEORY AND EUROPEAN INTEGRATION, London, Faber & Faber, 1973
41. Ruggie, J.G., 'Collective Goods and Future International Collaboration', AMERICAN POLITICAL SCIENCE REVIEW, LXVI (3), September 1972, pp. 874—893
42. Russett, Bruce M., INTERNATIONAL REGIONS AND THE INTERNATIONAL SYSTEM, Chicago, Rand McNally, 1967
43. Russett, Bruce M. and Sullivan, J., 'Collective Goods and International Organization', INTERNATIONAL ORGANIZATION, XXV, No. 4, Autumn 1971, pp. 845—865
44. Sewell, J.P., FUNCTIONALISM AND WORLD POLITICS, Princeton, Princeton University Press, 1966
45. Spiro, H., 'Interdependence: A Third Option Between Sovereignty and Supranational Integration', in Ghita Ionescu (ed.), BETWEEN SOVEREIGNTY AND INTEGRATION, London, Croom Helm, 1974
46. Taylor, Paul, INTERNATIONAL CO-OPERATION TODAY, London, Elek, 1971
47. Taylor, Paul and Groom, A.J.R. (eds.), INTERNATIONAL ORGANIZATION: A CONCEPTUAL APPROACH, London, Frances Pinter, 1978
48. Thompson, W.C., 'The Regional Subsystem', INTERNATIONAL STUDIES QUARTERLY, 17 (1), March 1973, pp. 89—117
49. Wheare, Kenneth, FEDERAL GOVERNMENT, (4th edition), Oxford, Oxford University Press, 1963
50. Young, Oran R., 'Professor Russett: Industrious Tailor to a Naked Emperor', WORLD POLITICS, XXI (3), April 1969, pp. 486—511

Chapter XI

FOREIGN POLICY ANALYSIS

*by Christopher Hill, London School of Economics
and Margot Light, University of Surrey*

Foreign Policy Analysis is one area of the subject of International
Relations which has flourished over the last two decades, in the sense
of producing a body of informative and stimulating literature. Yet it
has not developed a generally coherent and validated set of theories, as
the spirit of scientific advance requires. To be sure, theoretical writing
has abounded, and there have been persistent exhortations (particularly
from James Rosenau (138)) to seek systematic progress through the
stages of classification, hypothesis-construction, testing, and
reformulation. But as one might expect in an attractive new area,
collective self-discipline has been lacking, and 'theory' has taken many
contrasting forms, being subject to the whims of individual researchers
following their own interests. It also has to be searched for mainly
among empirical works with analytic forms, since 'pure' foreign
policy theories are uncommon.
 On the other hand, it would be wrong to give the impression that
intellectual anarchy has prevailed. An effective consensus has emerged
on the basic concepts and framework to be used when analyzing
foreign policy. Broadly speaking, these draw on the distinctions made
in systems theory between actors and their various environments. The
overall environment in which decision-makers work is broken down
into the 'external' or 'international', the 'domestic', and the 'psychological', which is an umbrella term for the set of *images* held by decision-
makers of their world, both internal and external, in contrast to its

'operational' actuality. These categories are themselves also broken down into the many variables to be found in any process as complex as that of policy-making. Agreement is now fairly general on the identity of the variables and on the boundaries to be drawn around the analysis of foreign policy, although the recent interest in transnationalism has complicated matters, while 'the next steps' are still unclear and subject to dispute. The achievement of a taxonomy can in large part be attributed to Frankel and Rosenau, who have both thought through and clearly articulated the early development of the subject. Their two standard texts (49, 138), are still the best introduction available.

Foreign Policy Analysis is essentially the study of decision-making in the context of foreign policy, and as such it is hardly the child of International Relations theory alone. Therefore 'Pure Decision Theory' or the study of the intrinsic logic of choice-making, regardless of circumstances, is of obvious importance. One of its principal sub-areas is that of game theory, which examines decisions primarily in terms of win/lose calculations. Insofar as students of international relations have found this approach useful, it has been largely in the context of strategic theory, which tends to treat nation-states as black boxes whose internal workings can be taken for granted as being identical . Yet although this assumption is questionable, any student of bargaining within the policy-making process would be well-advised to consider whether game theory can provide helpful insights. S.J. Brams (19) provides a recent treatment, slanted towards the political scientist. Shubik (144) is also useful.

The areas of Welfare Economics and Voting Behaviour are other important branches of decision theory, dealing with the problem of the relationship between collective and individual preferences. The debates engendered in these fields relate clearly, if not always directly, to foreign policy, for the latter has always raised difficult questions about the summing of the many different 'national interests' and has now inevitably taken on board many quantifiable economic goals to add to the traditional totems of security, prestige and the like. The classic texts, repaying attention by all social scientists, are those by Arrow (7) and Downs (40), while Barry (15) provides a critical and fairly recent commentary on the implications for general political theory of this kind of work.

Analysts of foreign policy have reacted against 'rational actor' models, which assume that government decisions are judicious strategies calculated by united decision-makers who have the principal

motive of maximizing power and security, and who are fully aware
of the means available to them, and of the prevailing policies of other
states. Policy-making distortions and competing domestic interests
hardly impinge on this model. The same is true of the approach
known as the 'billiard ball model' in which states' foreign policy
positions are seen as being primarily determined by the interplay of
international forces. To some extent these models are straw men. It
is extremely difficult to find statements of overt adherence to their
philosophy, and the pure form of the models is probably an over-
statement of their narrowness, and the extent to which they are used
as dogma. Nonetheless, most diplomatic historians, and many
students of current affairs, military strategy and the international
system implicitly accept such assumptions about state behaviour,
particularly when considering the behaviour of states other than their
own. Morgenthau (114) comes closest to open avowal, and both
Allison (4) and Steinbruner (157) reconstruct the 'rational' paradigm
from the writings of the 'school'.

Despite the obvious difficulties, there have been fairly regular
attempts by proponents of the Decision-Making Approach to construct
overall theories, even if it has not always been clear how much these
theories could explain. Of these overview models, only a few stand out
as having come originally from the discipline of International
Relations. Snyder, Bruck and Sapin (155) was an influential early
attempt, concentrating on the *perceptions* of decision-makers as the
key to understanding policy stances, although it has only been taken
up in the most indirect ways. The works of H. and M. Sprout (156)
have similarly focused on the operational/psychological distinction,
but they have also been highly sensitive to the role of 'milieux' external
to the small group of inner decision-makers, particularly the
geographical elements. They have outlined, indeed, the whole series
of problems associated with causation and determination that any
policy analysis must ultimately face. Brecher (21, 22) constructs a
model which is virtually all-inclusive and certainly takes account of
the external environment, since it stresses the importance of the concept of 'feedback' (or the impact of the consequences of one's actions
back on one's own policy process) in explaining foreign policy. To the
extent that Brecher's approach succeeds, it does so because it does not
posit a static decision-making process.

Organizational Process and Cybernetic Theory should be taken
together because they both deal with the nature of routine, a central

155

attribute of any bureaucracy and one perhaps particularly pertinent to Foreign Offices, with their traditional conservatism and (in modern conditions) heavily increased inflows of information. Deutsch's (38) is the classic treatment of communications theory for the International Relations specialist, while Lindblom (95) will always be associated with 'incrementalism', or the notion that policy proceeds necessarily by small, disjointed steps, almost by default, rather than by co-ordinated strategy. Steinbruner (157) has recently formulated a 'cybernetic paradigm' that is closely related to the organizational process paradigm (itself, incidentally, also well articulated by Allison (4)). This perspective sees policy as very often being the result of automatized procedures, on the analogy of the instinctive reactions of a tennis player at the net, developed as the only way to deal with un-certainty or information overload.

A more familiar, if less subtle, approach to bureaucracy and foreign policy is that of Bureaucratic Politics. Here, the central preoccupation is with the competition and conflict which takes place between administrative departments concerned more with their own vested interests and particular views of the world than with 'the national interest' or the merits of an issue. However, the extent to which this constitutes, or is intended to constitute, a single-factor explanation of foreign policy, is very arguable, and the two main spokesmen for the theory, Allison (4, 159) and Halperin (60, 159), vary somewhat in their own treatments. In any case, it should not be forgotten that their work owed a good deal to the pluralist school of American thought and in particular to Neustadt (119), the keynote of whose work has been the political quality of top-level decision-making. Keohane and Nye have extended this approach to transgovernmental relations and international organizations (85).

In terms of theory which can be used to explain actual cases con-vincingly, one of the most successful areas of Foreign Policy Analysis has been that dealing with Psychological Variables. Ideas have been borrowed from psychologists, but not indiscriminately, nor without regard for the particular context of international relations. The behaviour of individual statesmen has been effectively scrutinised, first by De Rivera (133), but particularly by Jervis (78) in an important recent book. Equally the collective psychology of the small groups that tend to make major foreign policy decisions has been entertainingly portrayed by Janis (73), who stresses the power of consensus in suppressing full consideration of available options. Dixon (39) is, like

156

Janis, a psychologist fallen among policy analysts, but his work is of
equal relevance, with its argument that distortions of judgement are a
particular occupational hazard of the military profession, because of
the rituals and rigid formalities that easily become associated with it.
Although policy analysis owes a good deal to systems theory, it will
be clear from what has gone before that most work has concentrated
on individual variables or sets of variables rather than on the totality
of interactions involved, as a proper systems approach might demand.
It has been left to the defence analysts to use systems theory in
the round, although paradoxically only within their own rather narrow
field. (This literature is reviewed in Chapter IV.)

Theory is perhaps too grandiose a term to describe the considerable
work that has been done on the Instruments of Foreign Policy.
Nevertheless, it has not been without conceptual content, and a number
of middle-range hypotheses have been produced. This has been less the
case with Diplomatic Practice than with other areas, but McKenna's
(106) book provides a systematic study of the uses of diplomatic
protest, while Burton (29) argues for a more scientific diplomacy in the
context of an increasingly complex and interdependent international
system. Holsti (66) gives an up-to-date survey of literature.

As far as Military Techniques are concerned, George, Hall and
Simons (55) indicate the limitations of the use of force even for a
great Power, while Knorr (88, 89, 90) has demonstrated that there is
far more to the successful exercise of military capabilities than the
mere possession of great arms. In this respect also, Brodie (24) has
written one of the better books in International Relations as a whole.
However, he is not concerned with theory in the scientific sense, but
with the political and philosophical issues arising from civil-military
relations, and decisions to embark upon war.

The debate over imperialism is so closely relevant to any discussion
of the Economic Means open to states in the pursuit of foreign policy,
that readers should turn to Chapter V of this bibliography for
supplementary documentation. Here the focus is on the individual
state contemplating how to use its economic strength for international
goals, and this, in turn, largely means the question of foreign aid.
Magdoff (108) interprets the thrust of US foreign policy as being
fuelled by the vested interest of domestic capitalism in foreign exploitation. Aid and foreign investment are only the most obvious
manifestations of this tendency. Goulet (57) is passionately
persuasive about the need for an ethic of development. A treatment

which aspires to be more dispassionate is that of White (164), who gives a detailed account of both donors' and recipients' perspectives on aid. Finally, the separate and more self-contained question of the use of economic sanctions in the service of foreign policy, is dealt with by Doxey (41) in the standard work on the subject.

It is a truism that Propaganda, Persuasion and Public Relations have become increasingly common elements of international relations in this 'age of ideologies'. The assumptions behind such activity is always that the population of a hostile state can be appealed to and influenced directly, thus constraining the target government's freedom of action. Radio is now the most usual medium of propaganda, and Hale (59) is very illuminating on the extent of its use and potential influence. 'Informal penetration', however, also consists of the traditional methods of espionage and subversion, and Scott (142) pioneered the theoretical analysis of these phenomena, usually the preserve of journalists and thriller-writers. In addition, Phillips Davison (35) gives an up-to-date summary of findings on the role of mass media in inter-state relations, and outside the strict area of comparative foreign policy there is, of course, a large sociological literature on propaganda, of which Whitson and Larson (165) is an example.

It is a short conceptual distance from the area of persuasion by means of public relations, to that of the actual process of Negotiation and Bargaining between states. Negotiation and bargaining are an obvious subject for a more formal type of analysis, based on game theory. Schelling's (140) influential book considers the ways in which decision-makers can 'rationally' weigh up the likely consequences of various levels of threat within a context of deterrence. But his approach does not dominate the study of negotiation. Iklé (72), Jervis (77) and Fisher (47) centre their interest on the complexities of actual diplomatic behaviour.

Iklé and Fisher show in some detail the methods open to statesmen, and how they vary according to conditions: both aim to be 'handbooks' for political success. Jervis concentrates on the distinction between 'signals' (sent deliberately by states to each other), and 'indices' (information of all kinds used by one state to infer the intentions of another), and his overall treatment of communication in foreign policy falls largely within this framework. Moving into a more explicitly normative dimension, Burton (28) suggests procedures of 'controlled communication', through which a perceived zero-sum conflict may be reappraised by those in dispute, and be seen to be a variable-sum problem to be solved with positive gains for both parties.

No-one interested in international relations, including those who decry the 'power-politics' model, can help but be drawn towards the notion of Crisis, for even those states which do not hold the fate of the whole system in their hands, inevitably often have to act under conditions of stress and uncertainty. In consequence there now exists a compact collection of works which examines the extent to which patterns of behaviour under conditions of crisis are distinctive or peculiar. Of those writing in this area, Hermann (63) is probably the best known, for his systematic attempts to define crisis and to formulate relevant hypotheses for testing. Ole Holsti (67, 68) and his colleagues have investigated the crisis of 1914 using a content analysis designed to answer specific questions derived in turn from a theoretical approach to decision-making; and their results, on such matters as the spiralling of perceptions of mutual hostility, are important. Paige's (127) work also takes the form of testing hypotheses about crisis against a specific case-study, as does that of Brecher (21) (although the latter has a wider basis of comparison), and both show that progress can be made if painstaking research is coupled with conceptual clarity.

It is undoubtedly all too easy to spend a great deal of energy discussing problems of pure method, without reference to empirical work. On the other hand, the nature and scope of Comparative Foreign Policy is a vital issue, requiring definition. Uncommensurable, and ultimately unnecessary work will proliferate unless its purpose and potential are thought through from first principles. There are many books and collections of essays which have something to say on these issues, and the reader will be as well off with one as with many, since what is needed is an initial stimulus for anyone concerned with the subject to *think* about the theoretical problems, and not to take the answers for granted. Hanrieder (61) and Jones (79) may be taken as good starting points.

More specifically, however, there exists a special group of authors who explicitly believe in the feasibility of making wide, factually based generalizations about foreign policies, and organize their research methods accordingly. Rosenau (134) and McGowan (104, 105) have been in the forefront of the campaign for focusing on the 'genotype' rather than the 'phenotype', and it is certainly not implausible to argue that certain classes of states (e.g. large, small, 'democratic',

159

'totalitarian') may be associated with certain types of behaviour (initiatory, dependent, oscillating, inflexible). These issues have always been of interest to students of international relations, as the more traditional works of London (98) or Brzezinski and Huntington (25) demonstrate.

Whatever the sense of looking for an overall theory of foreign policy, many writers have limited the scope of their work to Special Classes of States in terms of their foreign policy-making patterns. One of the most prominent of these special classifications (whether it is right or wrong to proceed in this way is another matter) is that of the Less Developed Countries (LDCs). As yet there is more assumption than empirical evidence on the question of whether the LDCs possess different policy-making processes from the developed states, but the distinction does not seem unreasonable. Both Weinstein (163) and Singer (150) state the case economically. Using more detail, Dawisha (36) applies a decision-making framework of the kind used by Brecher (21) to the case of Egypt. Yet, in that the framework is applied successfully, it should lead us to ask whether the peculiarity of the LDCs lies more in their substantive problems than in the concepts needed to analyze their decision-making machineries. Supporters of this view would certainly be both Galtung (53) and Jenkins (74), who, in their different ways, take a structuralist perspective, emphasizing both dependency, and what more orthodox students of foreign policy would call the 'external environment', as the main determinants of foreign policy in the poor countries.

The other category of states that American political science, (which dominates the field of international theory) is ill-suited to serve, is that of the Developed Socialist Countries. In spite of an enormous literature on Soviet foreign policy, theoretical approaches are rare, and the student of foreign policy finds it difficult to escape from culture-bound US literature. In a recent monograph, Horelick, Johnson and Steinbruner (69) survey those studies which attempt to apply theoretical models to Soviet foreign policy, while Kanet (81) includes behavioural approaches to domestic policy-making. Zimmermann (173) describes the development of the study of international relations within the Soviet Union. Triska and Finley (161) provide the best and most ambitious attempt at a decision-making perspective of Soviet foreign policy, while Aspaturian (10) contains the more interesting of earlier, traditional work on the subject.

An area of topical concern is the degree to which developed socialist states share the same political processes as liberal democratic states, through natural 'convergence'. While few would now argue that the USSR is a monolith, manipulated in all its complexities by the small ruling cadre at the top, the opposite argument, that the USSR has been made into a pluralist society by the emergence of interest-groups, is also far from being the orthodoxy. Whatever position is taken, the debate itself owes a good deal to Skilling (152), who has been arguing for many years that the concept of the interest-group is applicable outside Western countries. But here, as elsewhere in foreign policy analysis, the healthy tension between qualifiers and generalizers is likely to continue for a long time to come.

Bibliography

1. Abel, Elie, THE MISSILES OF OCTOBER, (2nd edition), London, MacGibbon & Kee, 1969
2. Alger, Chadwick F., 'The Impact of International Organisation on the Practice of Diplomacy', JOURNAL OF CONFLICT RESOLUTION, VIII (1), March 1964, pp. 79–82
3. Alger, Chadwick and Brams, Steven, 'Patterns of Representation in National Capitals and Intergovernmental Organizations', WORLD POLITICS, XIV (4), July 1967, pp. 646–63
4. Allison, Graham T., ESSENCE OF DECISION, Boston, Little, Brown, 1971
5. Almond, Gabriel A. and Coleman, James S., THE POLITICS OF DEVELOPING AREAS, Princeton, N.J., Princeton University Press, 1960
6. Apter, David E., THE POLITICS OF MODERNIZATION, Chicago, University of Chicago Press, 1965
7. Arrow, Kenneth, SOCIAL CHOICE AND INDIVIDUAL VALUES, New York, John Wiley, 1951
8. Art, R.J. and Waltz, K.N., THE USE OF FORCE: INTERNATIONAL POLITICS AND FOREIGN POLICY, Boston, Little, Brown, 1971
9. Ashby, W. Ross, AN INTRODUCTION TO CYBERNETICS, London, Chapman & Hall, 1970
10. Aspaturian, Vernon V. (ed.), PROCESS AND POWER IN SOVIET FOREIGN POLICY, Boston, Little, Brown, 1971
11. Axelrod, Robert (ed.), THE STRUCTURE OF DECISION, Princeton, N.J., Princeton University Press, 1976
12. Bachrach, Peter and Baratz, Morton, 'Decisions and Non-Decisions:

An Analytic Framework', AMERICAN POLITICAL SCIENCE REVIEW, LVII (3), September 1963, pp. 633—642

13. Banks, Michael H., 'Professionalism in the Conduct of Foreign Policy', INTERNATIONAL AFFAIRS, 44 (4), October 1968, pp. 720—733

14. Barber, James and Smith, Michael, THE NATURE OF FOREIGN POLICY: A READER, Edinburgh, Holmes McDougall (in association with The Open University Press, Milton Keynes), 1974

15. Barry, Brian M., SOCIOLOGISTS, ECONOMISTS AND DEMOCRACY, London, Collier-Macmillan, 1970

16. Bauer, Raymond and Gergen, Kenneth J. (eds.), THE STUDY OF POLICY FORMATION, New York, Free Press, 1968

17. Blau, Peter M., EXCHANGE AND POWER IN SOCIAL LIFE, New York, John Wiley, 1964

18. Boulding, Kenneth E., THE IMAGE: KNOWLEDGE IN LIFE AND SOCIETY, Ann Arbor, Michigan, University of Michigan Press, 1961

19. Brams, Steven J., GAME THEORY AND POLITICS, New York, The Free Press, 1975

20. Braybrooke, David and Lindblom, Charles E., THE STRATEGY OF DECISION, New York, The Free Press, 1963

21. Brecher, Michael, THE FOREIGN POLICY SYSTEM OF ISRAEL, London, Oxford University Press, 1972

22. Brecher, Michael, DECISIONS IN ISRAEL'S FOREIGN POLICY, London, Oxford University Press, 1974

23. Brecher, Michael, INDIA AND WORLD POLITICS: KRISHNA MENON'S VIEW OF THE WORLD, London, Oxford University Press, 1968

24. Brodie, Bernard, WAR AND POLITICS, London, Cassell, 1973

25. Brzezinski, Zbigniew and Huntingdon, Samuel P., POLITICAL POWER: USA/USSR, London, Chatto & Windus, 1964

26. Buchanan, James M., THE DEMAND AND SUPPLY OF PUBLIC GOODS, Chicago, Rand McNally, 1968

27. Buchanan, James M. and Tullock, Gordon, THE CALCULUS OF CONSENT, Ann Arbor, Michigan, University of Michigan Press, 1962

28. Burton, John W., CONFLICT AND COMMUNICATION: THE USE OF CONTROLLED COMMUNICATION IN INTER-NATIONAL RELATIONS, London, Macmillan, 1969

29. Burton, John W., SYSTEMS, STATES, DIPLOMACY AND RULES, Cambridge, Cambridge University Press, 1968

30. Caplow, T., TWO AGAINST ONE: COALITIONS IN TRIADS, Englewood Cliffs, N.J., Prentice Hall, 1968
31. Castles, Francis G., Murray, David J., Potter, David C. and Pollitt, C.J. (eds.), DECISIONS, ORGANISATIONS AND SOCIETY, (2nd edition), London, Penguin (with the Open University), 1976
32. Chayes, Abram, THE CUBAN MISSILE CRISIS, London, Oxford University Press, 1974
33. Cyert, Richard M. and March, James G., A BEHAVIORAL THEORY OF THE FIRM, Englewood Cliffs, N.J., Prentice Hall, 1963
34. Dahl, Robert A. and Lindblom, Charles E., POLITICS, ECONOMICS AND WELFARE, New York, Harper Bros., 1953
35. Davison, W. Phillips, 'Mass Communication and Diplomacy' in James N. Rosenau, Kenneth W. Thompson and Gavin Boyd (eds.), WORLD POLITICS: AN INTRODUCTION, New York, The Free Press, 1976
36. Dawisha, E., EGYPT AND THE ARAB WORLD: THE ELEMENTS OF FOREIGN POLICY, London, Macmillan, 1976
37. Destler, I.M., PRESIDENTS, BUREAUCRATS AND FOREIGN POLICY: THE POLITICS OF ORGANISATIONAL REFORM, (2nd edition), Princeton, N.J., Princeton University Press, 1974
38. Deutsch, Karl W., THE NERVES OF GOVERNMENT, New York, The Free Press, 1966
39. Dixon, N.F., ON THE PSYCHOLOGY OF MILITARY IN-COMPETENCE, London, Jonathan Cape, 1976
40. Downs, Anthony, AN ECONOMIC THEORY OF DEMOCRACY, New York, Harper & Row, 1957
41. Doxey, Margaret, P., ECONOMIC SANCTIONS AND INTER-NATIONAL ENFORCEMENT, London, Oxford University Press, 1971
42. Dror, Yehezkel, PUBLIC POLICY MAKING RE-EXAMINED, San Francisco, Chandler, 1968
43. East, Maurice A., 'Foreign Policy-Making in Small States: Some Theoretic Observations Based on a Study of the Ugandan Ministry of Foreign Affairs', POLICY SCIENCES, 4 (4), December 1973, pp. 491–508
44. Ermarth, Fritz, INTERNATIONALISM, SECURITY AND LEGITIMACY: THE CHALLENGE TO SOVIET INTEREST IN EAST EUROPE 1964–1968, (RM-5909-PR), Santa Monica, Calif., Rand Corporation, 1969

45. Farrell, John C. and Smith, Asa P. (eds.), IMAGE AND REALITY IN WORLD POLITICS, New York, Columbia University Press, 1968
46. Farrell, R. Barry (ed.), APPROACHES TO COMPARATIVE AND INTERNATIONAL POLITICS, Evanston, Ill., Northwestern University Press, 1966
47. Fisher, Roger, BASIC NEGOTIATING STRATEGY, London, Allen Lane, The Penguin Press, 1971
48. Fleron, Frederick J., Jnr. (ed.), COMMUNIST STUDIES AND THE SOCIAL SCIENCES, Chicago, Rand McNally, 1969
49. Frankel, Joseph, THE MAKING OF FOREIGN POLICY, London, Oxford University Press, 1967
50. Frankel, Joseph, NATIONAL INTEREST, London, Pall Mall, 1970
51. Frei, Daniel (ed.), INTERNATIONAL CRISES AND CRISIS MANAGEMENT, Farnborough, Teakfield, 1978
52. Gallagher, Matthew P. and Spielman, Karl F., Jnr. (eds.), SOVIET DECISION-MAKING FOR DEFENSE: A CRITIQUE OF US PERSPECTIVES ON THE ARMS RACE, New York, Praeger, 1972
53. Galtung, Johan, 'A Structural Theory of Imperialism', JOURNAL OF PEACE RESEARCH, Volume 8, 1971, pp. 81–117
54. George, Alexander, PROPAGANDA ANALYSIS, Evanston, Ill., Row, Peterson & Co., 1959
55. George, Alexander, Hall, David K. and Simons, WIlliam E., THE LIMITS OF COERCIVE DIPLOMACY: LAOS-CUBA-VIETNAM, Boston, Little, Brown, 1971
56. Glassman, Jon D., 'Soviet Foreign Policy Decision-Making' in COLUMBIA ESSAYS IN INTERNATIONAL AFFAIRS: VOL. III, THE DEAN'S PAPERS, 1967, New York, Columbia University Press, 1968
57. Goulet, Denis, A. THE CRUEL CHOICE, New York, Atheneum, 1973
58. Greenstein, F.I., PERSONALITY AND POLITICS, Chicago, Markham, 1969
59. Hale, J., RADIO POWER, London, Elek, 1975
60. Halperin, Morton H., BUREAUCRATIC POLITICS AND FOREIGN POLICY, Washington, D.C., Brookings Institution, 1974
61. Hanrieder, Wolfram F., COMPARATIVE FOREIGN POLICY: THEORETICAL ESSAYS, New York, McKay, 1971
62. Helleiner, G.K., A WORLD DIVIDED: THE LESS DEVELOPED COUNTRIES IN THE WORLD ECONOMY, Cambridge, Cambridge

University Press, 1976

63. Hermann, Charles F. (ed.), INTERNATIONAL CRISES: INSIGHTS FROM BEHAVIORAL RESEARCH, New York, The Free Press, 1972

64. Hoffman, Arthur S. (ed.), INTERNATIONAL COMMUNICATION AND THE NEW DIPLOMACY, Bloomington, Indiana, Indiana University Press, 1968

65. Hoffman, Erik P. and Fleron, Frederic J. Jr.,(eds.), THE CONDUCT OF SOVIET FOREIGN POLICY, Chicago, Aldine-Atherton, 1971

66. Holsti, Kalevi J., 'The Study of Diplomacy' in James N. Rosenau, Kenneth W. Thompson and Gavin Boyd (eds.), WORLD POLITICS: AN INTRODUCTION, New York, The Free Press, 1976

67. Holsti, Ole R., CRISIS, ESCALATION,WAR, Montreal, McGill-Queen's University Press, 1972

68. Holsti, Ole R., 'The 1914 Case', AMERICAN POLITICAL SCIENCE REVIEW, LIX (2), June 1965, pp. 365–378

69. Horelick, Arnold L., Johnson, A. Ross and Steinbruner, John D., THE STUDY OF SOVIET FOREIGN POLICY: DECISION-THEORY-RELATED APPROACHES, Beverly Hills, Sage Publications, 1975

70. Horelick, Arnold and Rush, Myron, STRATEGIC POWER AND SOVIET FOREIGN POLICY, Chicago, University of Chicago Press, 1966

71. Hough, Jerry F., 'The Bureaucratic Model and the Nature of the Soviet System', JOURNAL OF COMPARATIVE ADMINISTRATION, 1973, pp. 134–168

72. Ikle, Fred C., HOW NATIONS NEGOTIATE, New York, Harper & Row, 1964

73. Janis, Irving L., VICTIMS OF GROUPTHINK, Boston, Houghton Mifflin, 1972

74. Jenkins, Robin S., EXPLOITATION, London, MacGibbon & Kee, 1970

75. Jenkins, Robin S., 'Perception in Crisis', (IPRA Papers, 2nd Conference, Vol. 1), The Hague, Van Gorcum, 1968

76. Jervis, Robert, 'Bargaining and Bargaining Tactics' in J. Roland Pennock and John W. Chapman (eds.), COERCION, Chicago, Aldine-Atherton, 1972

77. Jervis, Robert, THE LOGIC OF IMAGES IN INTERNATIONAL RELATIONS, Princeton, N.J., Princeton University Press, 1970

78. Jervis, Robert, PERCEPTION AND MISPERCEPTION IN

165

INTERNATIONAL POLITICS, Princeton, N.J., Princeton
University Press, 1976

79. Jones, Roy E., ANALYSING FOREIGN POLICY: AN INTRO-
DUCTION TO SOME CONCEPTUAL PROBLEMS, London,
Routledge & Kegan Paul, 1970

80. Juviler, Peter H. and Morton, Henry W. (eds.), SOVIET POLICY
MAKING, New York, Praeger, 1967

81. Kanet, Roger E. (ed.), THE BEHAVIOURAL REVOLUTION
AND COMMUNIST STUDIES, New York, The Free Press, 1971

82. Katz, Daniel and Kahn, Robert L., THE SOCIAL PSYCHOLOGY
OF ORGANIZATIONS, New York, John Wiley, 1966

83. Keller, Suzanne, 'Diplomacy and Communication', PUBLIC
OPINION QUARTERLY, XX (1), Spring 1956, pp. 176–182

84. Kelman, Herbert C. (ed.), INTERNATIONAL BEHAVIOUR: A
SOCIAL-PSYCHOLOGICAL ANALYSIS, New York, Holt,
Rinehart & Winston, 1965

85. Keohane, Robert O. and Nye, Joseph S., 'Transgovernmental
Relations and International Organizations', WORLD POLITICS,
XXVII (1), October 1974, pp. 39–62

86. Kilson, Martin (ed.), NEW STATES IN THE MODERN WORLD,
Cambridge, Mass., Harvard University Press, 1975

87. Kintner, William R. and Klaiber, Wolfgang, EASTERN EUROPE
AND EUROPEAN SECURITY, New York, Dunellen, 1971

88. Knorr, Klaus, MILITARY POWER AND POTENTIAL, Lexington,
Mass., D.C. Heath, 1970

89. Knorr, Klaus, 'Military Statecraft' in James N. Rosenau, Kenneth
W. Thompson and Gavin Boyd, WORLD POLITICS: AN
INTRODUCTION, New York, The Free Press, 1976

90. Knorr, Klaus, THE POWER OF NATIONS, Princeton, N.J.,
Basic Books, 1975

91. Lall, A.S., MODERN INTERNATIONAL NEGOTIATION IN
PRINCIPLE AND PRACTICE, New York, Columbia University
Press, 1966

92. Lee, John (ed.), THE DIPLOMATIC PERSUADERS, New York,
John Wiley, 1968

93. Leifer, Michael, THE FOREIGN RELATIONS OF THE NEW
STATES, Camberwell, Australia, Longman, 1974

94. Leites, Nathan, KREMLIN MOODS, (RM-3535-ISA), Santa
Monica, Calif., Rand Corporation, 1964

95. Lindblom, Charles E., THE POLICY-MAKING PROCESS,

Englewood Cliffs, N.J., Prentice Hall, 1968

96. Liska, George, THE NEW STATECRAFT: FOREIGN AID,
Chicago, University of Chicago Press, 1962

97. Lodge, Milton C., SOVIET ELITE ATTITUDES SINCE STALIN,
Columbus, Ohio, Bell & Howell, 1969

98. London, Kurt, THE MAKING OF FOREIGN POLICY: EAST
AND WEST, Philadelphia, Philadelphia University Press, 1965

99. Lovell, John P., FOREIGN POLICY IN PERSPECTIVE, New
York, Holt, Rinehart & Winston, 1970

100. Luce, Duncan, INDIVIDUAL CHOICE BEHAVIOR, New York,
John Wiley, 1959

101. Luce, Duncan and Raiffa, Howard, GAMES AND DECISIONS,
New York, John Wiley, 1957

102. McClelland, Charles A., 'The Acute International Crisis', WORLD
POLITICS, XIV (1), October 1961, pp. 182–204

103. McClelland, Charles A.,"Decisional Opportunity and Political
Controversy', JOURNAL OF CONFLICT RESOLUTION,
VI (3), September 1962, pp. 201–212

104. McGowan, Patrick J. (ed.), THE SAGE INTERNATIONAL
YEARBOOK OF FOREIGN POLICY STUDIES, (Vols. I & II),
Beverly Hills, Sage Publications, 1973 and 1974

105. McGowan, Patrick J. and Shapiro, Howard B., THE COMPARATIVE
STUDY OF FOREIGN POLICY: A SURVEY, Beverly Hills, Calif.,
Sage Publications, 1973

106. McKenna, J.C., DIPLOMATIC PROTEST IN FOREIGN POLICY,
Chicago, Loyola University Press, 1962

107. Macridis, Roy C. (ed.), FOREIGN POLICY IN WORLD
POLITICS, (4th edition), Englewood Cliffs, N.J., Prentice Hall,
1972

108. Magdoff, Harry, THE AGE OF IMPERIALISM: THE
ECONOMICS OF US FOREIGN POLICY, London, Monthly
Review Press, 1969

109. March, James G. and Simon, Herbert A., ORGANIZATIONS, New
York, John Wiley, 1968

110. Martin, L.W. (ed.), NEUTRALISM AND NON-ALIGNMENT:
THE NEW STATES IN WORLD AFFAIRS, New York, Praeger,
1962

111. May, Ernest, 'LESSONS' OF THE PAST, New York, Oxford
University Press, 1973

112. Modelski, George A., A THEORY OF FOREIGN POLICY, New

York, Praeger, 1962

113. Morgenthau, Hans J., IN DEFENCE OF THE NATIONAL INTEREST: A CRITICAL EXAMINATION OF THE AMERICAN FOREIGN POLICY, New York, Alfred Knopf, 1951

114. Morgenthau, Hans J., POLITICS AMONG NATIONS: THE STRUGGLE FOR POWER AND PEACE, (5th edition), New York, Alfred Knopf, 1973

115. Murakami, Y., LOGIC AND SOCIAL CHOICE, London, Routledge & Kegan Paul, 1968

116. Nelson, J., AID, INFLUENCE AND FOREIGN POLICY, New York, Macmillan, 1968

117. Von Neumann, J. and Morgenstern, O., THEORY OF GAMES AND ECONOMIC BEHAVIOUR, Princeton, N.J., Princeton University Press, 1944

118. Neustadt, Richard E., ALLIANCE POLITICS, New York, Columbia University Press, 1970

119. Neustadt, Richard E., PRESIDENTIAL POWER: THE POLITICS OF LEADERSHIP, New York, John Wiley, 1960

120. Nicholson, Michael B., OLIGOPOLY AND CONFLICT, A DYNAMIC APPROACH, Liverpool, Liverpool University Press, 1972

121. Nicolson, Harold, DIPLOMACY, London, Oxford University Press, 1963

122. Niezing, J., 'Diplomacy: an organization in transition', ACTA POLITICA, V(2)

123. North, Robert C., 'Decision Making in Crises', JOURNAL OF CONFLICT RESOLUTION, VI (3), September 1962, pp. 197–199

124. North, Robert C. et al, CONTENT ANALYSIS, Evanston, Ill., Northwestern University Press, 1963

125. Northedge, F.S. (ed.), THE USE OF FORCE IN INTERNATIONAL RELATIONS, London, Faber & Faber, 1974

126. Olson, Mancur, THE LOGIC OF COLLECTIVE ACTION, Cambridge, Mass., Harvard University Press, 1971

127. Paige, Glenn D., THE KOREAN DECISION, JUNE 24–30, 1950, New York, The Free Press, 1968

128. Pinder, John, 'Economic Diplomacy' in James N. Rosenau, Kenneth W. Thompson and Gavin Boyd (eds.), WORLD POLITICS: AN INTRODUCTION, New York, The Free Press, 1976

129. Ploss, Sidney I. (ed.), THE SOVIET POLITICAL PROCESS: AIMS, TECHNIQUES AND EXAMPLE OF ANALYSIS, Waltham, Mass., Ginn, 1971

130. Raiffa, Howard, DECISION ANALYSIS, Reading, Mass., Addison-Wesley, 1968

131. Riggs, Fred (ed.), FRONTIERS OF DEVELOPMENT ADMINIS-TRATION, Durham, N.C., Duke University Press, 1970

132. Riker, William H., THE THEORY OF POLITICAL COALITIONS, New Haven, Conn., Yale University Press, 1962

133. Rivera. Joseph de, THE PSYCHOLOGICAL DIMENSION OF FOREIGN POLICY, Columbus, Ohio, Charles E. Merril, 1968

134. Rosenau, James N. (ed.), COMPARING FOREIGN POLICIES: THEORIES, FINDINGS AND METHODS, New York, John Wiley, 1974. (Distributed by Halsted Press Division)

135. Rosenau, James N. (ed.), DOMESTIC SOURCES OF FOREIGN POLICY, New York, The Free Press, 1967

136. Rosenau, James N. (ed.), INTERNATIONAL POLITICS AND FOREIGN POLICY, (2nd edition), New York, The Free Press, 1969

137. Rosenau, James N. (ed.), LINKAGE POLITICS, New York, The Free Press, 1969

138. Rosenau, James N., THE SCIENTIFIC STUDY OF FOREIGN POLICY, New York, The Free Press, 1971

139. Rourke, F.E., BUREAUCRACY AND FOREIGN POLICY, Baltimore, John Hopkins Press, 1972

140. Schelling, Thomas C., STRATEGY OF CONFLICT, New York, Oxford University Press, 1960

141. Scott, Andrew M., 'Environmental Change and Organizational Adaptation: The Problem of the State Department', INTER-NATIONAL STUDIES QUARTERLY, XIV (1), March 1970, pp. 87–99.

142. Scott, Andrew M., THE REVOLUTION IN STATECRAFT: INFORMAL PENETRATION, New York, Random House, 1965

143. Shoup, Paul, 'Comparing Communist Nations: Prospects for an Empirical Approach', AMERICAN POLITICAL SCIENCE REVIEW, LII (1), March 1968, pp. 185–205

144. Shubik, Martin (ed.), GAME THEORY AND RELATED APPROACHES TO SOCIAL BEHAVIOUR: SELECTIONS, New York, John Wiley, 1964

145. Sidjanski, Dusan (ed.), POLITICAL DECISION MAKING

PROCESSES, Amsterdam, Elsevier, 1973

146. Seigal, Sidney and Fouraker, Lawrence E., BARGAINING AND GROUP DECISION MAKING, New York, McGraw Hill, 1959

147. Sigal, Leon V., 'The "Rational Policy" Model and the Formosa Straits Crises', INTERNATIONAL STUDIES QUARTERLY, XIV (2), June 1970, pp. 121–156

148. Simon, Herbert A., ADMINISTRATIVE BEHAVIOUR, (2nd edition), New York, The Free Press, 1965

149. Simon, Herbert A., THE SCIENCES OF THE ARTIFICIAL, Cambridge, Mass., MIT Press, 1968

150. Singer, Milton, 'The Foreign Policies of Small Developing States', in James N. Rosenau, Kenneth W. Thompson and Gavin Boyd (eds.), WORLD POLITICS: AN INTRODUCTION, New York, The Free Press, 1976

151. Singer, Milton, WEAK STATES IN A WORLD OF POWERS, New York, The Free Press, 1972

152. Skilling, Gordon H. and Griffiths, Franklyn (eds.), INTEREST GROUPS IN SOVIET POLITICS, Princeton, N.J., Princeton University Press, 1971

153. Slusser, Robert, THE BERLIN CRISIS OF 1961, Baltimore, Johns Hopkins Press, 1973

154. Snyder, Glenn H., 'Conflict and Crisis in the International System' in James N. Rosenau, Kenneth W. Thompson and Gavin Boyd (eds.), WORLD POLITICS: AN INTRODUCTION, New York, The Free Press, 1976

155. Snyder, Richard C., Bruck, H.W. and Sapin, Burton, FOREIGN POLICY DECISION MAKING, New York, The Free Press, 1962

156. Sprout, Harold and Margaret, THE ECOLOGICAL PERSPECTIVE IN HUMAN AFFAIRS, Princeton, N.J., Princeton University Press, 1965

157. Steinbruner, John D., THE CYBERNETIC THEORY OF DECISION, Princeton, N.J., Princeton University Press, 1974

158. Stewart, Philip D., 'Soviet Interest Groups and the Policy Process', WORLD POLITICS, XXII (1), October 1969, pp. 29–50

159. Tanter, Raymond and Ullman, Richard H. (eds.), THEORY AND POLICY IN INTERNATIONAL RELATIONS, Princeton, N.J., Princeton University Press, 1972

160. Tatu, Michel, POWER IN THE KREMLIN: FROM KHRUSHCHEV TO KOSYGIN, New York, Viking Press, 1969

161. Triska, Jan and Finley, David SOVIET FOREIGN POLICY, New

York, Macmillan, 1968

162   Waltz, Kenneth N., MAN, THE STATE AND WAR, New York,
       Columbia University Press, 1959

163.   Weinstein, F.B., 'The Uses of Foreign Policy in Indonesia: An
       Approach to the Analysis of Foreign Policy in the Less Developed
       Countries', WORLD POLITICS, XXIV (3), April 1972, pp. 356–
       381

164.   White, J., THE POLITICS OF FOREIGN AID, London, The
       Bodley Head, 1974

165.   Whitson, J.B.K. and Larson, A., PROPAGANDA, New York,
       Oceana Publications, 1964

166.   Wilkenfeld, J. (ed.), CONFLICT BEHAVIOUR AND LINKAGE
       POLITICS, New York, McKay, 1974

167.   Wilkinson, David O., COMPARATIVE FOREIGN RELATIONS:
       FRAMEWORK AND METHODS, Belmont, Calif., Dickenson,
       1969

168.   Williams, P. and Smith, M., 'The Foreign Policies of Authoritarian
       and Democratic States', YEARBOOK OF WORLD AFFAIRS,
       1976

169.   Young, Oran R., BARGAINING, Urbana, University of Illinois
       Press, 1976

170.   Young, Oran R., THE INTERMEDIARIES: THIRD PARTIES IN
       INTERNATIONAL CRISIS, Princeton, N.J., Princeton University
       Press, 1967

171.   Zartman, I. William, INTERNATIONAL RELATIONS IN THE
       NEW AFRICA, Englewood Cliffs, N.J., Prentice Hall, 1966

172.   Zartman, I. William, 'The Political Analysis of Negotiation: How
       Who Gets What and When', WORLD POLITICS, XXVI (3), April
       1974, pp. 385–399

173.   Zimmerman, William, SOVIET PERSPECTIVES ON INTER-
       NATIONAL RELATIONS, 1956–1967, Princeton, N.J., Princeton
       University Press, 1969

Chapter XII

PSYCHOLOGICAL ASPECTS OF INTERNATIONAL RELATIONS

by A.N. Oppenheim
London School of Economics

Introduction

Since international relations are concerned with what happens to large
numbers of people, and are decided and carried out by people working
in human organizations, it is obvious that psychological factors must
enter into virtually every international process to a greater or lesser
extent; and that psychological processes will enter into every other
section of this bibliography. Moreover, the contributions by (and the
borrowings from) psychology are an ongoing and controversial process
which changes with each new publication; our bibliography will have
to be selective, but will focus on a number of relevant areas.

Part of the difficulty of choice lies in the fact that the definitions of
'psychology' vary a good deal, and that psychology overlaps with many
other disciplines, e.g. sociology, administrative science, human biology,
linguistics, communication studies, psycho-analysis, social psychiatry.
Another problem lies in the type of approach used, and the nature of
evidence which is considered acceptable: I.R. writers have sometimes
rejected psychological contributions because 'they aren't International
Relations', while psychological discussions produced by I.R. scholars
have been rejected by psychologists for being 'un-scientific'. It should
also be realized that there are numerous aspects of I.R. which no doubt
would repay psychological investigation, but to which few psychologists
have addressed themselves; in this sense, a good deal of research is still
'missing'. On the other hand, there are many broad findings and

principles current in psychology which could readily be applied indirectly to aspects of international relations, e.g. social perception, group
dynamics, stress research; in addition, *some* psychologists (and others)
have applied themselves directly to certain areas of international
relations, for example through simulation studies, research into conflict resolution, bargaining behaviour, and group decision-making. Our
bibliography will draw on both these fields: the broader, and the more
specific ones.

Apart from books and the more specialized psychological literature,
many psychological articles of relevance to I.R. students appear
regularly in the JOURNAL OF CONFLICT RESOLUTION and the
JOURNAL OF PEACE RESEARCH.

General Psychological Processes: Perception

Most of the broad determinants of human behaviour in *individuals* —
such as thinking, remembering, the unconscious, learning, perceiving,
becoming socialized, personality development, intelligence, attitudes
and values — are of relevance to I.R. in various ways, for example, in
trying to understand the behaviour of leaders and of decision-makers,
in the selection and training of diplomats, or in the study of national
stereotypes. However, in I.R. we are frequently concerned with the
behaviour of people in groups or *organizations*, in institutions or
bureaucracies or power hierarchies, and so we have to move from the
individual to the collective level. One way of linking these two levels
of analysis — of the individual on his own, and of the person as a role-
player in a sub-system — is to consider them from the point of view of
perceptual processes.

It would be very wrong to imagine that the process of perception is a
'faithful recording of reality', not unlike a film or tape recording. There
is abundant evidence to show that perception is a *dynamic* process, not
a passive one, and that the way it works is not only determined by the
outside world but also by the perceiver's culture, attitudes, expectations,
needs, experience and many other aspects. We are continuously engaged
in selecting important from unimportant stimuli, in 'recognizing' people,
things, or patterns of events, in 'interpreting' the behaviour of others
or of groups, states or organizations; we make causal or probabalistic fore-
casts and 'explanations', and select from, define, and redefine the outside
world in accordance with who we are and what we want to be, or do.
In short, perception is subjective.

The processes of perception are connected with a whole range of

173

other mental processes. The same 'subjectivity biases' which cause us to notice, to attend to, and to select, also cause us to retain (to store, to remember) and to recall selectively, to compare (to like/dislike/fear/enjoy/etc.), to communicate, and to respond in much the same biased ways. Such processes, in their turn, influence future perceptions, so that a closed circle is set up — vicious or adaptive, according to one's point of view. Most of the time, our habits-of-mind help to defend our Ego and our opinions, to find consonance rather than dissonance (see Festinger (18)) and to give meaning and predictability to the world. Since virtually all stimuli are ambiguous, to a greater or lesser extent, they offer ample scope for such self-fulfilling dynamics; divergent views or dissonant experiences can be ignored or internally overruled, so that only very occasionally are we brought up short, and have to revise the way our mind is made up.

We also perceive *ourselves*. Each of us has a 'self percept', a set of notions about who we are, what our roles are, what we are good or bad at, how we should dress, or speak, or behave. These ideas will be strongly influenced by the frequent evidence we receive of how others perceive us, though 'to see ourselves as others see us' is difficult. To understand a set of transactions or an ongoing relationship between two people, or two firms, or two states, we need to know how they see themselves as well as how they see each other; if these two sets of percepts are very different, they can be brought more into line with each other by an argument or a fight — or by trying to understand the dynamics which have led to the development of such divergent images. A considerable part of marriage guidance, for example, is taken up with such explorations, and the same processes have been tried in the field of conflict resolution between communities or between states (see Burton (12)).

If communication between individuals is sometimes difficult because they do not 'see' things from the same point of view, then communication between groups is often more difficult still. If the groups belong to different countries or cultures — as they often do, in the field of foreign affairs — then they are further divided by language, values, images, history and other factors which influence their perceptions of each other and of the situation. Inevitably, such differences will also affect the decision-makers.

A useful basic text book in Social Psychology which stresses various aspects of social perception is Secord and Backman (59); it is but one of many such texts, with varying emphases. Tagiuri and Petrullo's

174

reader (63) covers the field of person-perception, and links it to the perception of objects. The books by Festinger (18) and by Rokeach (54) are based on two different traditions of socio-psychological research — the former more oriented towards cognitive processes, the latter more concerned with personality and individual differences — but they show in greater detail some of the general mental processes which would also be found in the study of international affairs. These volumes have been followed by many more recent experimental studies in similar vein. For a more detailed experimental study of human information processing, consult Schroder, Driver and Streufert (57).

Kelman's excellent reader (34) provides many links between social psychology and the international scene; it is still full of relevant insights. For a more detailed analysis of the ways in which perceptual processes enter into decision-making in foreign affairs, see de Rivera (53), and some of the papers in Kriesberg (36). Several non-psychologists have concerned themselves with the power of images and stereotypes, for example Boulding (10), Jervis (32) and Reynolds (52). North and his colleagues have become well-known for their content analysis studies of the documents produced by decision-makers, showing their perceptual and thought processes (46).

General Psychological Processes: Organizational Behaviour

Now let us shift the level of analysis and look at organizations, especially at decision-making bureaucracies, such as government departments. Analogies between individuals and organizations must obviously not be taken too far, or too literally, but several *structural* parallels suggest themselves. For example, the embassies or foreign missions maintained by a foreign affairs ministry could be regarded as its 'eyes and ears' and sometimes as its 'mouth' — in general terms, as sensors and communicators. The links between the missions and the policy-makers could be regarded as the nerve paths; the departmental archives and its library could be likened to the human memory; the human brain, which selects, compares and processes all this information has, as its organizational counterpart, the decision-making apparatus within the foreign affairs ministry.

It is also not difficult to find *functional* equivalents in the mind to the ways in which organizational decision-making works. The incremental, cumulative ways in which positions are found to have been taken, not necessarily on the widest consideration of the relevant evidence; the selective management of information; the playing down

175

of some information sources in favour of others; the ways in which *recent* experience tends to be over-valued; the problems of overload and stress; the tendency to develop commitment; the problems of change and progression through time (see Reynolds (52)); the unwillingness to plan and look ahead, and the tendency to satisfice rather than to maximise; all these and many others are problems which are familiar to us from individual psychology, and which can readily be noted in the workings of organizations (see Janis (30)).

If this raises some questions about the ways in which these organizational procedures affect the Foreign Affairs Ministry's perceptions, it must also make us wonder about the uses that are made of these perceptions when they enter the central decision-making process. Only a handful of studies have been made of the ways in which foreign affairs ministries arrive at their decisions and their policies, but from studies of similar organizations we can suggest some of the issues that should be raised. How, for example, does the 'organizational memory' operate? Can the files and the archives be used rapidly and effectively in the process of making decisions? What is the prevailing administrative style — consensual, hierarchical, delegated, or what? In which ways does the organization try to create and maintain shared perceptual frameworks; for example, through departmentalization, by controlling selection, experience and careers? Remembering that 'knowledge is power', how is information distributed, summarized, selectively presented, checked, compared, and processed by the organization? Are the central decision-makers specially trained and experienced in their tasks, or are they diplomats on a temporary 'home-posting'? How does the ministry perceive its 'attentive publics' (Reynolds (52)), and those whom it must 'take with it', or obtain clearance from? At what hierarchical level does most 'uncertainty absorption' take place, and with what effects? How serious is the tendency (which exists in most organizations) to give attention to the here-and-now at the expense of forward planning, in the field of foreign affairs? And how resilient is the organization under crisis conditions? (See Reynolds (52).) These last two topics — anticipation of events, and crisis behaviour — are so important that we shall return to them presently.

Here we should like to stress three further points. First, that the issues we have raised have to do with the structures and the functioning of human organizations as 'bureaucratic machines', almost irrespective of the people who man them, the organization's tasks or objectives, or the country within which it operates. Second, in foreign affairs the problems of obtaining and using information, the problems of 'un-certainty-reduction', must be particularly difficult because of cultural and secrecy barriers between countries. Third, in addition to the usual interpersonal likes and dislikes, envy, clique formation, power exploitation and so on which can be found in any group of human beings, large decision-making organizations are subject to a phenomenon known as *bureaucratic politics*. This refers to the ways in which career factors and personal motives interact with the functioning of the organization. Officials will curry favour in order to get earlier promotion or a pleasanter posting, they will be tempted to produce 'sycophantic feedback' (telling their superiors what they want to hear), the old boy network will operate, and vested interests in sectors within the organiz-ation will fight each other. Here, for example, is Frederick Forsyth's biting description of a fictional Head of the France desk at the FCO:

'He possessed, or he would not have got the appointment, all the essential requirements: a long and distinguished record of service in diplomacy elsewhere than France, a history of soundness in his political judgements which, although frequently wrong, were inevitably in accord with those of his superiors of the given moment; a fine record and one of which to be justly proud. He had never been publicly wrong, nor inconveniently right, never supported an unfashionable viewpoint nor proffered opinions out of line with those prevailing at the highest levels of the Corps . . . '

(*The Day of the Jackal*, London, Corgi Books, 1971)

We should ask ourselves what *kinds* of bureaucracies are most likely to produce this type of behaviour, and what its effects may be on the long-term functioning of the organization.

There is a considerable literature on the social functioning of organizations, in particular of industrial firms and commercial or governmental bureaucracies. March's handbook (40) is fundamental to anyone studying this area, and there are several classics in this field, such as March and Simon (41), Argyris (7), Burns and Stalker (11), Herzberg (25), Katz and Kahn (33), McGregor (42), and Woodward (68), each related to 'schools' or styles of management and human relations. Likewise, there are numerous publications dealing with particular kinds of organizations (e.g. hospitals) or with particular types of problems (e.g. leadership, trade unions, information processing). Many of the more seminal contributions have first appeared in the pages of the ADMINISTRATIVE SCIENCE QUARTERLY.

It is not easy to develop suitable methods and concepts for the study of complex bodies such as organizations; Pugh et al. (50) have produced a British survey of research in organizational behaviour which amply illustrates these problems, to the solution of which they themselves have contributed. Methods of simulation have been widely used in the field, for example by Raser and Crow (51), and relevant summaries have been provided by Guetzkow et al. (22) and by Inbar and Stoll (29). Simulation techniques can provide training and valuable insights, but they lack the precision (which is not without drawbacks) of the socio-psychological experiment. The techniques of interaction analysis developed by Bales (8) present one example of the tendency to try to make observations more accurate and more reliable.

By choosing to study an organization in a certain way, the researcher is implicitly adopting a theoretical position and is making some assumptions about human behaviour. An advanced book which puts such theories and assumptions to the test is Ackoff and Emery (1). When trying to account for organizational outputs there is often a tendency — as in Political Science or in History — to stress either the role of key individuals, or the importance of certain fixed attributes of the organization. This 'personalistic' versus 'structuralistic' dilemma is well-reviewed in Lichtman and Hunt (37), and related to attempts to make prescriptive norms. The reader edited by Salaman and Thompson (56) for the Open University is also useful in this respect.

Within this general area, there is a literature concerned with political decision-making (as distinct from industrial/commercial decision-making), and a smaller literature which has tried to link organizational research with foreign policy decision-making, within the political field. The reader produced by Castles et al. for the Open University (14) makes some useful psychosociological links between administrative science and political behaviour. There are several relevant chapters in Pruitt and Snyder's reader (49), and Pruitt is also the author of an early study of the functioning of the Department of State (48), a field to which Argyris (7) has also contributed. Oppenheim and Bayley have attempted to compare industrial relations and interstate behaviour, using participant observation (47).

The internal workings of bureaucracies are well described by Downs (17), and linked to political pressures by Gawthrop (20). MacKenzie (39) gives an excellent and wide-ranging account of this whole area. Studies of bargaining and negotiation have recently come to the fore, such as those by Warr (65), Sherif (60), Deutsch (16) and by Stephenson and Morley (44).

178

Specific Psychological Processes: Political Socialization

The term 'socialization' refers to the processes of social learning whereby an individual becomes a member of his culture, and sub-culture. It
covers a very wide field, including various aspects of childhood and
adolescence as well as adult socialization (e.g. migration, and social
mobility), and complex problems of imitation, identification, intro-
jection and conformity in the family, in peer groups, at school, and in
mass media consumption.

The sub-area of *political* socialization is expanding rapidly, both in
Social Psychology, and in Political Science and Political Sociology. These
studies are obviously relevant to such issues as the development of
democracy, of support for parties and regimes, and the perception by
children of their national leaders, but few such researchers have included
items of specific relevance to International Relations. It would be
interesting to have much fuller information on the development of
children's stereotypes about other nations, their attitudes to war, to the
UN, to various modes of conflict resolution, and their national and
supranational loyalties. Several of the listed researches have touched on
one or other of these issues, but an effective cross-national summary of
children's perceptions of international affairs has yet to appear.

The Almond and Verba study (4) is an early cross-national research
which has had a seminal influence. The studies by Hess and Torney (27),
and by Jennings and Niemi (31), are good examples of studies of
American youth, while Morrison and McIntyre have been concerned
with British children (45). These studies have tried to assess the relative
influence of home and school on the children's political development.
Sear's chapter (58) amply reviews the literature and takes the matter
further, in seeking to link childhood attitudes to adult political behaviour.
The ten-nation study by Torney, Oppenheim and Farnan (64) represents
both a considerable technical achievement and several theoretical
advances; it contains some items dealing with the UN, with war and with
conflict.

Specific Psychological Processes: Aggression

The notion that war is due to man's 'animal nature' has long been part
of the stock-in-trade of commentators on international affairs, and the
study of 'aggression' has a long history in Psychiatry and Psycho-analysis.
This whole area has become more controversial with the arrival of
modern ecological studies, which show — *inter alia* — that animals rarely
kill each other except for food, and that they have highly developed

social and genetically based mechanisms for inhibiting aggression between members of the same species. Modern research by social psychologists studying aggression has thrown further doubt on the extent to which aggression is 'built in', and has shown the importance of over-crowding and other social conditions.

This complex area is well summarized by Montague (2nd edition) (43). Lorenz's study (38) has become a classic of ecological research though it has been sharply criticized for its conclusions. Robert Ardrey (6) has done much to popularize this kind of topic. The studies by Berkowitz (9) illustrate work on human aggression in the socio-psychological laboratory. The work by the Russells (55) is specifically concerned with overcrowding.

Specific Psychological Processes: Response to Stress

From the very broad area of stress research there have been several applications to International Relations, in particular the stress experienced by foreign policy makers under crisis conditions.

Crises can, of course, happen to individuals, but here we are particularly concerned with what happens to a decision-making organization under stress. Typically, the organization will experience overloads: more information is coming in, more decisions have to be made (and more rapidly, too), and more orders have to go out. Despite extra work and countermeasures, communication channels may get clogged, thus creating serious delays, and isolating the decision-makers more and more from events in the field. This, in turn, may cause them to 'go into crisis' and to engage in crisis behaviour: their perceptions become crudely polarized, they cannot think more than one or two moves ahead, they may become dominated by fear-motivated projections, they may tend to over-react and thus enter an escalation spiral. Janis (30) has coined the term 'group-think' for this kind of behaviour.

Charles Hermann's two books (23, 24), Griffin's volume (21), and the earlier book by Guetzkow (22) and his collaborators, summarize much of the findings obtained through simulation work. Tom Milburn's paper 'The Management of Crises' (in Hermann (24)), is a good example of prescriptions and advice that have emerged from research in this field. Howard Lentner's chapter illustrates the kind of measures that can be taken, for example to prevent communication overloads.

Steinbruner (62), Allison (3), Holsti (28), Snyder and Paige (61), and others, have made detailed studies of real-life crises. Robert Kennedy's book (35) gives a graphic personal account of the Cuban missile crisis.

Specific Psychological Processes: Anticipation and Surprise

The risks and dangers associated with an international crisis are much increased if the decision-makers are caught by surprise. Typically, this may well be attributed to a failure on the part of the intelligence services, but closer study may show that the information was, in fact, available at some levels within the organization, but was distrusted, or overlooked, or became swamped by other information, and therefore never reached the top decision-makers. Or the decision-makers themselves may reject the information; this may well happen when, for example, they have a strong expectation of some other events which they regard as more probable, or when they have particular attitudes of distrust or fear towards the source of the information, which in turn will affect their perceptual processes. Some kinds of organization have a tendency to want to hear only 'good' news (sycophantic feedback), while in others the harbinger of 'bad' tidings may find his career blighted; either way, the upper echelons will have deprived themselves of some information. Thus we note once again the importance of subjective perceptual factors, both in individuals and in organizations.

A group of decision-makers may also be caught by surprise through lack of anticipation. As we have seen, perception is an active, dynamic process; organizations should not merely wait passively for information to flow in, they must 'think ahead' and engage in 'information seeking'. This raises such issues as the relevant location and staffing of foreign missions, the value of political reporting, and the need for well-integrated planning departments within foreign affairs ministries. New methods for crisis forecasting are also being developed.

Janis's book (30), which deals with a number of actual crises, vividly shows how surprise factors operate, and has built on Wohlstetter's analysis of the Pearl Harbour attack (67). Another interesting case study is that of Hitler's attack on the Soviet Union, presented by Barton Whaley (66), in which he extends Wohlstetter's theoretical framework. The reasons for the Israeli's failure to anticipate the outbreak of the October 1973 war are analyzed by Herzog (26).

A well-written and informative book on British diplomats and their organization has recently been produced by Geoffrey Moorhouse, and Eric Clark has written its State Department counterpart (15). Alger and Brams (2) have studied the distribution abroad of diplomats from many countries. The entire March 1977 of the INTERNATIONAL

181

STUDIES QUARTERLY is devoted to problems of crisis forecasting.

Other Psychological Processes

Any bibliography must, of necessity, reflect the 'state of the art' at a given time. Important and useful socio-psychological books remain to be written about topics not included here, in ways that would make them relevant to international relations. For example, we urgently need field studies of the psychological interaction between foreign policy and the mass media, including special pressure groups and 'attentive publics'. Out-dated studies of national stereotypes need to be superseded by broader research on percepts and attitudes, both of members of the public, and of diplomats and decision-makers. The problems of communication and mis-communication between nations, so often highlighted in simulation studies, need to be explored in greater detail in real-life situations. We are awaiting more and better studies on information management within organizations, including polarizing, stereotyping, sychophanting, risky shifts, exploitation, and other distortive processes. We are only just beginning to study at first hand the processes of bargaining and of negotiation; in this, as in other contexts, the personality, background, and attitudes of leaders, and the whole process of leadership, are of obvious importance. Deterrence is another area that is awaiting more psychological research, and so is the study of individual attitudes to power.

In the long run, perhaps the most important psychological contributions will be those that concern themselves with social change, conflict prevention, and conflict resolution.

Bibliography

1. Ackoff, R.L. and Emery, F.E., ON PURPOSEFUL SYSTEMS Chicago, Aldine, 1972, and London, Tavistock, 1972
2. Alger, C.F. and Brams, S., 'Patterns of Representation in National Capitals and Intergovernmental Organizations', WORLD POLITICS, XIV (4), July 1967, pp. 646–663
3. Allison, G.T., ESSENCE OF DECISION, Boston, Little, Brown, 1971
4. Almond, G.A. and Verba, S., THE CIVIC CULTURE, Boston, Little, Brown, 1965
5. AMERICAN BEHAVIOURAL SCIENTIST, Vol. 20, (1), September/October 1976 (Whole issue devoted to political decision-making)

6. Ardrey, R., THE TERRITORIAL IMPERATIVE, New York, Atheneum, 1966
7. Argyris, C., SOME CAUSES OF ORGANISATIONAL INEFFEC-TIVENESS WITHIN THE DEPARTMENT OF STATE, Washington, D.C., Government Printing Office, 1967
8. Bales, R.F., INTERACTION PROCESS ANALYSIS, Reading, Mass., Addison-Wesley, 1950
9. Berkowitz, L., AGGRESSION: A SOCIAL PSYCHOLOGICAL ANALYSIS, New York, McGraw Hill, 1962
10. Boulding, K.E., THE IMAGE, Ann Arbor, Mich., University of Michigan Press, 1956
11. Burns, T. and Stalker, G.M., THE MANAGEMENT OF INNOVATION, London, Tavistock, 1961, and New York, Barnes & Noble, 1961
12. Burton, J.W., CONFLICT AND COMMUNICATION, London, Macmillan, 1969
13. Carthy, J.D. and Ebling, F.J. (eds.), THE NATURAL HISTORY OF AGGRESSION, London, Academic Press, 1964
14. Castles, F.G., Murray, D.J., Pollitt, C.J. and Potter, D.C., DECISIONS, ORGANISATIONS AND SOCIETY, (2nd edition), Harmondsworth, Middx., Penguin Books in association with the Open University, 1976
15. Clark, E., CORPS DIPLOMATIQUE, London, Allen Lane, 1973
16. Deutsch, M., THE RESOLUTION OF CONFLICT, New Haven, Conn., Yale University Press, 1973
17. Downs, A., INSIDE BUREAUCRACY, Boston, Little, Brown, 1967
18. Festinger, L., A THEORY OF COGNITIVE DISSONANCE, Stanford, Calif., Stanford University Press, 1962
19. Fisher, R., INTERNATIONAL CONFLICT FOR BEGINNERS, New York, Harper & Row, 1969
20. Gawthrop, L.C., BUREAUCRATIC BEHAVIOUR IN THE EXECUTIVE BRANCH, New York, The Free Press, 1969
21. Giffin, S.F., THE CRISIS GAME, Garden City, New York, Doubleday, 1965
22. Guetzkow, H., Kotler, P. and Schultz, R., SIMULATION IN SOCIAL AND ADMINISTRATIVE SCIENCE, Englewood Cliffs, N.J., Prentice-Hall, 1972
23. Hermann, C.F., CRISES IN FOREIGN POLICY: A SIMULATION ANALYSIS, Indianapolis, Bobbs-Merrill, 1969
24. Hermann, C.F. (ed.), INTERNATIONAL CRISES: INSIGHTS

FROM BEHAVIOURAL RESEARCH, New York, The Free Press, 1972

25. Herzberg, F., WORK AND THE NATURE OF MAN, New York, T.Y. Crowell, 1966
26. Herzog, C., THE WAR OF ATONEMENT, London, Weidenfeld & Nicholson, 1975
27. Hess, R.D. and Torney, J.V., THE DEVELOPMENT OF POLITICAL ATTITUDES IN CHILDREN, Chicago, Aldine, 1967
28. Holsti, O.R., CRISIS, ESCALATION, WAR, Toronto, McGill-Queens University Press, 1972
29. Inbar, M. and Stoll, C.S., SIMULATION AND GAMING IN SOCIAL SCIENCES, New York, Macmillan, 1972
30. Janis, I.L., VICTIMS OF GROUPTHINK, Boston, Houghton-Mifflin, 1972
31. Jennings, M.K. and Niemi, R.G., THE POLITICAL CHARACTER OF ADOLESCENCE: THE INFLUENCE OF FAMILIES AND SCHOOLS, Princeton, N.J., Princeton University Press, 1974
32. Jervis, R., THE LOGIC OF IMAGES IN INTERNATIONAL RELATIONS, Princeton, N.J., Princeton University Press, 1970
33. Katz, D. and Kahn, R.L., THE SOCIAL PSYCHOLOGY OF ORGANISATIONS, New York, John Wiley, 1966
34. Kelman, H.C. (ed.), INTERNATIONAL BEHAVIOUR, New York, Holt, Rinehart & Winston, 1965
35. Kennedy, R.F., THIRTEEN DAYS: A MEMOIR OF THE CUBAN MISSILE CRISIS, London, Macmillan, 1969
36. Kriesberg, L. (ed.), SOCIAL PROCESSES IN INTERNATIONAL RELATIONS, New York, John Wiley, 1968
37. Lichtman, C.M. and Hunt, R.G., 'Personality and organisation theory: a review of some conceptual literature', PSYCHOLOGICAL BULLETIN, 76 (4), 1971, pp. 271–294
38. Lorenz, K., ON AGGRESSION, New York, Harcourt, Brace & Jovanovich, 1966
39. MacKenzie, W.J.M., POLITICS AND SOCIAL SCIENCE, Harmondsworth, Middx., Pelican Books, 1967
40. March, J.G. (ed.), HANDBOOK OF ORGANIZATIONS, Chicago, Rand-MacNally, 1965
41. March, J.G. and Simon, H.A., ORGANIZATIONS, New York, John Wiley, 1958
42. McGregor, D., THE HUMAN SIDE OF ENTERPRISE, New York, McGraw Hill, 1960

43. Montagu, M.F.A. (ed.), MAN AND AGGRESSION, (2nd edition), New York, Oxford University Press, 1973

44. Morley, I.E. and Stephenson, G.M., THE SOCIAL PSYCHOLOGY OF BARGAINING, London, Allen & Unwin, 1977

45. Morrison, A. and McIntyre, D., SCHOOLS AND SOCIALISATION, Harmondsworth, Middx., Penguin Books, 1971

46. North, R.C., Holsti, O.R., Zaninovich, M.G. and Zinnes, D.A., CONTENT ANALYSIS: A HANDBOOK WITH APPLICATIONS FOR THE STUDY OF INTERNATIONAL CRISES, Evanston, Ill., Northwestern University Press, 1963

47. Oppenheim, A.N. and Bayley, J.C.R., PRODUCTIVITY AND CONFLICT, Proceedings of the International Peace Research Association, The Hague, Van Gorcum, 1969

48. Pruitt, D.G., PROBLEM SOLVING IN THE DEPARTMENT OF STATE, Denver, Col., University of Denver Press, 1964

49. Pruitt, D.G. and Snyder, R.C. (eds.), THEORY AND RESEARCH ON THE CAUSES OF WAR, Englewood Cliffs, N.J., Prentice-Hall, 1969

50. Pugh, D.S., RESEARCH IN ORGANIZATIONAL BEHAVIOUR, New York, Heineman, 1975

51. Raser, J.R. and Crow, W.J., 'A Simulation Study of Deterrence Theories', Ch. 21 in L. Kriesberg (ed.), SOCIAL PROCESSES IN INTERNATIONAL RELATIONS, New York, John Wiley, 1968

52. Reynolds, P., PERCEPTION AND THE PSYCHOLOGICAL ENVIRONMENT, Open University Course D.203; in press

53. Rivera, J.H. de, THE PSYCHOLOGICAL DIMENSION OF FOREIGN POLICY, Columbus, Ohio, Merrill, 1968

54. Rokeach, M., THE OPEN AND THE CLOSED MIND, New York, Basic Books, 1960

55. Russell, C. and Russell, W.M.S., VIOLENCE, MONKEYS AND MAN, London, Macmillan, 1968

56. Salaman, G. and Thompson, K., PEOPLE AND ORGANIS-ATIONS, London, Longmans (for the Open University Press), 1973

57. Schroder, H.M., Driver, M.J. and Streufert, S., HUMAN INFOR-MATION PROCESSING, New York, Holt, Rinehart & Winston, 1967

58. Sears, D.O., 'Political Behaviour', Ch. 41 in G. Lindzey and E. Aronson, THE HANDBOOK OF SOCIAL PSYCHOLOGY, Volume V, Reading, Mass., Addison-Wesley, 1969

59. Secord, P.H., and Backman, G.W., SOCIAL PSYCHOLOGY, New York, McGraw Hill, 1964
60. Sherif, M., GROUP CONFLICT AND CO-OPERATION, London, Routledge & Kegan Paul, 1967
61. Snyder, R.C. and Paige, G.D., THE UNITED STATES DECISION TO RESIST AGGRESSION IN KOREA, Evanston, Ill., Northwestern University Press, 1958
62. Steinbruner, J.D., THE CYBERNETIC THEORY OF DECISION, Princeton, N.J., Princeton University Press, 1974
63. Tagiuri, R. and Petrullo, L., PERSON PERCEPTION AND INTERPERSONAL BEHAVIOUR, Stanford, Calif., Stanford University Press, 1958
64. Torney, J.V., Oppenheim, A.N. and Farnen, R.F., CIVIC EDUCATION IN TEN COUNTRIES, Stockholm, Almqvist & Wiksell, and Wiley International, 1975
65. Warr, P., PSYCHOLOGY AND COLLECTIVE BARGAINING, London, Hutchinson, 1973
66. Whaley, B., CODEWORD BARBAROSSA, Cambridge, Mass., M.I.T. Press, 1973
67. Wohlstetter, R., PEARL HARBOUR: WARNING AND DECISION, Stanford, Calif., Stanford University Press, 1962
68. Woodward, J., INDUSTRIAL ORGANIZATION. THEORY AND PRACTICE, London, Oxford University Press, 1965

Chapter XIII

ANTHROPOLOGY AND INTERNATIONAL RELATIONS

by A. V.S. de Reuck
University of Surrey

One of the features of the 'behavioural revolution' of the 1960s in the study of International Relations was the notion that the insights from other disciplines might profitably be applied to the analysis of international behaviour. On the one hand, this meant that theories and findings from fields such as Organization Theory or Social Psychology could be transferred directly to the field of International Relations, on the grounds that similar organizational or psychological factors were at work in, for example, group decision making, whether the issue to be decided was an economic, a diplomatic or a military one. In another sense, it meant that certain generalizations might be applied — with due caution — to situations that were in relevant respects analogous, so that lessons learned at other social levels might be useful in throwing light on problems at the international level.

A potential source of insights that might be applied in this second fashion was obviously the discipline of Anthropology, as even a superficial acquaintance with this subject revealed that many of the same human situations, relationships and patterns of behaviour were discernible when simple societies were compared with international society. Both, for example, shared problems engendered by a decentralization of authority and coercive power. Both revealed a variety of efforts to institutionalize procedures for resolving conflicts between groups and individuals making up the society. Moreover, in many cases anthropological studies revealed societies that had failed to establish a formal political system fulfilling rule-making and rule-enforcing functions for its people. Other features of international society re-emerged as aspects of the traditional societies studied by anthropologists; peace keeping and mediation processes; self-help; overlapping group membership serving to dampen down the level, if not the frequency, of conflicts; the development of diplomatic norms; patterns of alliance formation, and the use of inter-personal and inter-group violence to settle disputes and rivalries.

The parallel between contemporary global society and some of the stateless social systems studied by anthropologists is most succinctly outlined by Roger Masters in his well-known paper 'World Politics as a Primitive Political System' (40), and this is further developed in the context of structural constraints on the spread of conflict by Michael Barkun in his LAW WITHOUT SANCTIONS (9). However, behavioural students of International Relations who expect to be able to borrow directly from anthropology, or to have their theoretical foundations dug for them by labourers in other disciplines, deserve to be disappointed. (Though from time to time, indeed, they may be undeservedly rewarded — Barth's famous MODELS (11, 47) and Boissevain's FRIENDS OF FRIENDS (16) are gifts indeed.) Typically, ethnographic analysis consists of a series of case studies of particular societies, each with its own individual culture, and each subject to a different ecological environment. (A good example is the famous Burmese study by Edmund Leach (34).) Both the mode of study and the resultant findings thus tend to discourage the comparison and consolidation of empirical data — and there is no lack of these in anthropology — and the building of broad-gauge theories to encompass processes across societies. Thus, when an International Relations scholar searches for a set of comparative anthropological findings about the nature of mediation, the development of legal systems (see, however, Hamnett (32)), or the origins and conduct of inter-tribal war, the best that he can expect is a useful symposium, such as Paul Bohannan's LAW AND WARFARE (15), or Bramson and Goethal's WAR: STUDIES FROM PSYCHOLOGY, SOCIOLOGY AND ANTHROPOLOGY (20) which adhere to their chosen theme, even if each paper is on a different society, differently analyzed. More usually, the result resembles Fried, Harris and Murphy's symposium (28), which is diffuse, diverse, and little help in integrating anthropological findings.

Political anthropology, on the other hand, offers a number of elegant synoptic reviews — for example, Balandier (7), Banton (8), or Mair (39), and a major theoretical essay by Morton Fried on THE EVOLUTION OF POLITICAL SOCIETY (27). For a general overview of anthropological theory, Lewis is recommended (35).

Since few anthropologists are experts in International Relations and few specialists in International Relations are also anthropologists, cross fertilization of these disciplines has been limited and there are few anthropological works that bear explicitly on international studies. Two major works by Ada Bozeman which do so (POLITICS AND CULTURE IN INTERNATIONAL HISTORY (19) and CONFLICT IN AFRICA (18)) are, unfortunately, to be viewed with caution.

Anthropology does, however, have a useful function for the study of International Relations. What it can do is to raise new questions and so give rise to scholarly cognitive dissonance: the seed of all intellectual growth. Familiar problems in unfamiliar contexts look different; unfamiliar problems in familiar contexts are disturbing; even to surprise old theories coupling with exotic data may stir the loins of the imagination. Only connect.

What follows therefore is a highly personal and idiosyncratic selection of works which make connections worthy of closer attention than they have hitherto received. There is no space here to develop these connections except to say that they relate as much to (a) conflict analysis, (b) inter-ethnic relations, or (c) modernization studies, as they do to foreign affairs. It should be added that there are doubtless many other works of equal or greater merit here neglected.

The classical definition of anthropology as the study of non-literate peoples is misleading and perhaps outdated. Anthropology essentially studies the diversity of human social systems and cultures. Human diversity is an aspect sadly neglected by scholars of International Relations, to whom it should be particularly significant. Western political science generally tends to be blindly ethnocentric and suffers the more because this is largely unrecognized.

The work that might even begin to remedy this state of affairs has yet to be written, but those who wish to attain a glimmer of what it might be like to have their sight restored are recommended to read Ruth Benedict's THE CHRYSANTHEMUM AND THE SWORD (13), Chie Nakane's JAPANESE SOCIETY (45), together with, say, Geoffrey Gorer's THE AMERICANS (31) and Louis Dumont's HOMO HIERARCHICUS (23) which discuss the Japanese, the American and the Indian people respectively. The structure and limitations of one's own language only become apparent to those who have learnt another language as well.

A similar salutary shock may be had from comparing Colin Turnbull's THE MOUNTAIN PEOPLE (53) with THE FOREST PEOPLE (52) which describe a Hobbesian and a Lockean society respectively.

The vexed question of man's alleged inheritance of an aggressive instinct from his primate forbears is discussed at length by Robert Ardrey (1, 2, 3, 4), Konrad Lorenz (38) and Ashley Montague (42, 43). Of these, only the latter may be relied upon, at least so far as human beings are concerned.

A more significant, and less hackneyed problem relates to the biological (evolutionary) basis for intraspecific co-operation (see for example O.E. Wilson's work on SOCIOBIOLOGY (56)), the nature of dominance (well discussed by Knipe and Maclay (33)) and its correlation with Chance and Larsen's very important concept of attention structure (22) and the existence of alternative modes of interaction among primates, named respectively 'agonistic' and 'hedonic' by Chance and Jolly (21).

The evolutionary progression of social formations from *Gemeinshaft* to *Gesellschaft*, originally associated with the work of Tönnies, or from mechanical or organic solidarity as discussed by Durkheim, provides the foundations for modernizing development. The cultural concomitants of this process are too varied to be summed up in one work but the classic studies by Redfield (49) and Riesman (50) deserve still to be read. Worsley (58) and Wilson (55) discuss millenarial reactions (including cargo-cults and the like) by tribal people to imperialist penetration, in works which afford a link between modern political protest and traditional religious 'politics'. In this tradition, Boissevain's SAINTS AND FIREWORKS (17), a book about Malta, might be read with profit in relation to Ulster.

One type of conflict control stressed by anthropologists is that of 'cross-cutting cleavages'. The rules of marriage and succession have so evolved in many cases that disputes cannot extend far beyond the original opponents without bringing in on each side, as natural allies of the antagonists, persons who have strong common interests (through kinship and property) which cut across the lines of conflict and create channels for communication and mediation. Conflicting parties, whoever they are, are thus sewn together by a tenacious web of social connections, and these structural constraints damp down any tendency to escalation of violence. Max Gluckman's CUSTOM AND

CONFLICT IN AFRICA (29) provides an interesting analysis of this process.

Another common device is the institutionalized mediator, who may or may not wield political power in his own right, but who has the authority to speak judiciously (but *not* judicially) for the community — or, what is much the same thing, for the gods: for instance the role of leopard-skin chief of the Sudanese Nuer outlined by E.E. Evans-Pritchard (25) or the Saint among the Swat Pathans described by Frederick Barth (12).

In a broader framework, Black-Michaud's work on the social functions of feud in the maintenance of social structure (14) and Barth's (10) on ethnic boundaries can be compared with Cynthia Enloe's analysis of modern ethnic politics (24) and E.K. Francis' general study of inter-ethnic relations (26).

The structure and function of the political system in microcosm are the subjects of Bailey's STRATAGEMS AND SPOILS (5) and GIFTS AND POISON (6). Peter Munch's CRISIS IN UTOPIA (44) is a valuable study of a small egalitarian society on Tristan da Cunha in both its domestic aspects and its external affairs.

Finally, a commendation of George Park's THE IDEA OF SOCIAL STRUCTURE (48), a book which contains the irritant grit upon which several theoretical pearls may grow — read it backwards if there is any risk that you will not reach the end. The best predictor of an actor's behaviour is his location in the social structure, and the route and the rate by which he arrived at that location. Social structures are fluid, and yet correlated with culture. Now read on . . .

Bibliography

1. Ardrey, Robert, AFRICAN GENESIS, London, Collins, 1961
2. Ardrey, Robert, THE HUNTING HYPOTHESIS, London, Collins, 1976
3. Ardrey, Robert, THE SOCIAL CONTRACT, London, Collins, 1970
4. Ardrey, Robert, THE TERRITORIAL IMPERATIVE, London, Collins, 1967
5. Bailey, F.G., STRATAGEMS AND SPOILS: A SOCIAL ANTHROPOLOGY OF POLITICS, Oxford, Basil Blackwell, 1969
6. Bailey, F.G. (ed.), GIFTS AND POISON: THE POLITICS OF REPUTATION, Oxford, Basil Blackwell, 1971
7. Balandier, G., POLITICAL ANTHROPOLOGY, London, Allen Lane,

1970

8. Banton, M. (ed.), THE SOCIAL ANTHROPOLOGY OF COMPLEX
    SOCIETIES, (ASA Monograph No. 4), London, Tavistock, 1966

9. Barkun, Michael, LAW WITHOUT SANCTIONS: ORDER IN
    PRIMITIVE SOCIETIES AND THE WORLD COMMUNITY,
    New Haven, Conn., Yale University Press, 1968

10. Barth, Frederick, ETHNIC GROUPS AND BOUNDARIES, London,
    Allen & Unwin, 1969

11. Barth, Frederick, MODELS OF SOCIAL ORGANISATION,
    London, Royal Anthropological Institute, Occasional Paper No. 23,
    1966

12. Barth, Frederick, POLITICAL LEADERSHIP AMONG THE
    SWAT PATHANS, London, Athlone Press, 1959

13. Benedict, Ruth, THE CHRYSANTHEMUM AND THE SWORD:
    PATTERNS OF JAPANESE CULTURE, London, Routledge &
    Kegan Paul, 1977, (First published in 1946)

14. Black-Michaud, Jacob, COHESIVE FORCE: FEUD IN THE
    MEDITERRANEAN AND THE MIDDLE EAST, Oxford, Basil
    Blackwell, 1975

15. Bohannan, Paul (ed.), LAW AND WARFARE: STUDIES IN THE
    ANTHROPOLOGY OF CONFLICT, New York, The American
    Museum of Natural History, 1967

16. Boissevain, Jeremy, FRIENDS OF FRIENDS: NETWORKS,
    MANIPULATORS AND COALITIONS, Oxford, Basil Blackwell,
    1974

17. Boissevain, Jeremy, SAINTS AND FIREWORKS: RELIGION
    AND POLITICS IN MALTA, London, Athlone Press, 1969

18. Bozeman, Ada, CONFLICT IN AFRICA: CONCEPTS AND
    REALITIES, Princeton, N.J., Princeton University Press, 1976

19. Bozeman, Ada, POLITICS AND CULTURE IN INTERNATIONAL
    HISTORY, Princeton, N.J., Princeton University Press, 1960

20. Bramson, L. and Goethals, G.W. (eds.), WAR: STUDIES FROM
    PSYCHOLOGY, SOCIOLOGY, ANTHROPOLOGY, (2nd edition),
    New York, Basic Books, 1968

21. Chance, M.R.A. and Jolly, C.J., SOCIAL GROUPS OF MONKEYS,
    APES AND MEN, London, Jonathan Cape, 1970

22. Chance, M.R.A. and Larsen, R.R. (eds.), THE SOCIAL STRUCTURE
    OF ATTENTION, New York, John Wiley, 1976

23. Dumont, L., HOMO HIERARCHICUS, London, Paladin, 1972

24. Enloe, Cynthia H., ETHNIC CONFLICT AND POLITICAL

DEVELOPMENT, Boston, Little, Brown, 1973

25. Evans-Pritchard, E.E., NUER RELIGION, London, Oxford University Press, 1956
26. Francis, E.K., INTERETHNIC RELATIONS: AN ESSAY IN SOCIOLOGICAL THEORY, Oxford, Elsevier, 1976
27. Fried, Morton, THE EVOLUTION OF POLITICAL SOCIETY, New York, Random House, 1967
28. Fried, M., Harris, M. and Murphy, R. (eds.), WAR: THE ANTHROPOLOGY OF ARMED CONFLICT AND AGGRESSION, New York, American Museum of Natural History, 1968
29. Gluckman, Max, CUSTOM AND CONFLICT IN AFRICA, Oxford, Basil Blackwell, 1956
30. Gluckman, Max, ORDER AND REBELLION IN TRIBAL AFRICA, New York, The Free Press, 1963
31. Gorer, Geoffrey, THE AMERICANS: A STUDY IN NATIONAL CHARACTER, London, Arrow Books, 1959
32. Hamnett, Ian (ed.), SOCIAL ANTHROPOLOGY AND LAW, (ASA Monograph No. 14), London, Academic Press, 1977
33. Knipe, H. and Maclay, G., THE DOMINANT MAN: THE PECKING ORDER IN HUMAN SOCIETY, London, Fontana/Collins, 1973
34. Leach, E.R., POLITICAL SYSTEMS OF HIGHLAND BURMA, London, Athlone Press, 1954
35. Lewis, I.M., SOCIAL ANTHROPOLOGY IN PERSPECTIVE, Harmondsworth, Middx., Pelican Books, 1976
36. Lloyd, P.C., AFRICA IN SOCIAL CHANGE, Harmondsworth, Middx., Penguin Books, 1971
37. Lloyd, P.C., CLASSES, CRISES AND COUPS: THEMES IN THE SOCIOLOGY OF DEVELOPING COUNTRIES, London, Granada, 1971
38. Lorenz, Konrad, ON AGGRESSION, New York, Harcourt Brace and World, 1966
39. Mair, Lucy, PRIMITIVE GOVERNMENT, Harmondsworth, Middx., Pelican Books, 1962
40. Masters, Roger D., 'World Politics as a Primitive Political System', WORLD POLITICS, Volume XVI (4), July 1964, pp. 595—619
41. Mitchell, J. Clyde (ed.), SOCIAL NETWORKS IN URBAN SITUATIONS, Manchester, Manchester University Press, 1969
42. Montagu, M.F. Ashley, THE NATURE OF HUMAN AGGRESSION, New York, Oxford University Press, 1976
43. Montagu, M.F. Ashley (ed.), MAN AND AGGRESSION, New

York Oxford University Press, 1968

44. Munch, Peter A., CRISIS IN UTOPIA, London, Longmans, 1971
45. Nakane, Chie, JAPANESE SOCIETY, London, Weidenfeld & Nicholson, 1970
46. Nieboer, H.J., SLAVERY AS AN INDUSTRIAL SYSTEM: ETHNOLOGICAL RESEARCHES, The Hague, Martinus Nijhoff, 1900
47. Paine, R., SECOND THOUGHTS ABOUT BARTH'S MODELS, London, Royal Anthropological Institute Occasional Paper No. 32, 1974
48. Park, George, THE IDEA OF SOCIAL STRUCTURE, New York, Doubleday, 1974
49. Redfield, Robert, THE LITTLE COMMUNITY and PEASANT SOCIETY AND CULTURE, Chicago, University of Chicago Press, 1965
50. Riesman, David, THE LONELY CROWD, New Haven, Yale University Press, 1966, (First published in 1950)
51. Schapera, I., GOVERNMENT AND POLITICS IN TRIBAL SOCIETIES, London, Watts, 1956
52. Turnbull, Colin, THE FOREST PEOPLE, London, Jonathan Cape, 1961
53. Turnbull, Colin, THE MOUNTAIN PEOPLE, London, Jonathan Cape, 1973
54. Waterbury, J., THE COMMANDER OF THE FAITHFUL. THE MOROCCAN POLITICAL ELITE — A STUDY IN SEGMENTED POLITICS, London, Weidenfeld & Nicholson, 1970
55. Wilson, Brian, MAGIC AND THE MILLENIUM: RELIGIOUS MOVEMENTS OF PROTEST AMONG THE THIRD WORLD PEOPLES, London, Paladin, 1975
56. Wilson, E.O., SOCIOBIOLOGY: THE NEW SYNTHESIS, Cambridge, Mass., Harvard University Press, 1975
57. Wittfogel, K.A., ORIENTAL DESPOTISM, New Haven, Conn., Yale University Press, 1957
58. Worsley, P.C., THE TRUMPET SHALL SOUND, London, Paladin, 1970

Chapter XIV

WAYS OF ANALYZING THE WORLD SOCIETY

by Michael Banks
London School of Economics

Previous chapters in this book have surveyed a dozen specialized sub-fields in the general discipline of International Relations. While perennial staples of the discipline, such as power, foreign policy, and war have been covered, there has been particular emphasis on those topics which have been singled out as significant in the academic debates of recent years: transnationalism, conflict theory, psychological aspects of policy-making, and problems of values and change. This final chapter will attempt a summary and overview, placing the newer trends in the perspective created by the established ones, and concentrating throughout on the theme of analysis: the how-to-do-it question in International Relations studies.

To analyze means to unravel, to take to pieces. The term 'world society' refers to the total community of mankind, four billion or so people spread across the inhabited portions of the earth. Analyzing the world society, then, is the business of taking apart the human race, dividing it into sections, noting the significant properties of each section and examining the relationships between them. But how many sections are there, and how should they be subdivided? What properties are we interested in? Which relationships matter, and for what purposes? What, in short, are the appropriate units of analysis and levels of analysis?

There is no single, comprehensive, neat and tidy answer to all these questions. Instead the discipline offers us a variety of answers, sometimes complementary, sometimes contradictory. The most notable feature is the way in which bodies of knowledge have grown up around specific topics, producing the separate clusters of writings on which the chapter headings of the Bibliography are based. But these 'islands' of theory, as they are sometimes known in the field, stand presumably in an ocean of non-theory, or ignorance. And the islands-in-the-ocean metaphor itself breaks down when one considers that the 'islands' are not composed of knowledge about comparable things, but actually belong to quite different categories. Some are about issues of method or approach (like systems); others deal with policy (strategy, for example); yet others derive from humane concern, such as conflict resolution and prevention of war.

This disparity in the assortment of pieces of knowledge that we have managed to accumulate highlights the two central weaknesses of the output of International Relations studies. Together these two weak areas are known (parochially and pejoratively) as the 'theory of theories', and some grasp of the intellectual issues they raise is of critical importance for anyone wishing to work in International Relations. They are, first, the area of general theory: what is the overall shape of our world society? Its structure? Its major processes? The other is mainstream methodology: what are the analytic techniques required for the dissection of the world society? The principal concepts? The methods best suited for testing existing theories and for creating new knowledge?

This chapter is concerned with both these groups of 'concepts and methods' problems. It will tackle them by looking first at the writings on the whole problem of general theory and how to deal with it, which is a task that the literature as a whole does remarkably badly. Then the discussion will move on to consider something that is done very much better in the field. Using the analytic knife ruthlessly, the chapter will cut into the literature in an attempt to expose four distinct and separate answers to the basic question: what *is* the structure of the world society? These are labelled here, respectively, the 'state-centric' approach, the 'international relations' approach, the 'world society' approach and the 'global class systems' approach. Each approach may also be called a paradigm, because it constitutes a distinct treatment of the issue of which are the right pieces into which the seamless web of the entire human society should be chopped. For anyone seriously interested in understanding, there is no avoiding the use of an approach, or paradigm. To make any sense of the world at all, the complex must be made simple. Patterns must be identified, and the important ones

196

separated from those thought to be trivial. The durable must be distinguished from the ephemeral. To make these simplifying judgements is to theorize, and if the individual theories are to be coherent they must fit a general scheme of some kind. That is all that is meant here by the rather grand term 'paradigm'.

General Theory: The Textbook Literature

Common sense suggests that if the competing paradigms could be put together, taking the strongest explanatory points from each, then the result would be the perfect textbook, dispensing with the need to study each approach separately. Unfortunately no such textbook exists. It seems that the task of writing it is much too hard. To some extent the paradigms are simply incompatible: they direct attention to quite different things, and attempts to merge them become messy and confusing — which is a fair description of much writing about international relations. Also, many textbook writers feel obliged to concentrate on 'the real world'. This means describing current and historical events, with the consequence that the analytic framework is swamped in a flood of facts. In some cases textbook writers who are committed to a single approach waste their efforts by belittling the insights offered by writers within other paradigms. And, as a further reason for the inadequacy of most textbooks, the authors tend to take the view that studying theory as such is an unsuitable activity for beginning students in the field. James Rosenau has recently published a thoroughgoing critique of the textbook literature (51).

A few of the textbook authors have abandoned real-world description and have attempted instead the task of surveying approaches, concepts, theories and frameworks in a comparative and critical way. Outstanding among the relatively recent publications is CONTENDING THEORIES OF INTERNATIONAL RELATIONS, by Dougherty and Pfaltzgraff (11), in which the authors aspire to such catholicity that some readers are puzzled by the wealth of ideas. Along similar lines, Patrick Morgan's THEORIES AND APPROACHES TO INTERNATIONAL RELATIONS: WHAT ARE WE TO THINK? (37) is readable and much more lively, but less substantial. Robert Lieber's and Davis Bobrow's contributions (32, 2) each concentrate on only part of the whole picture, but deal usefully with the analytic problems involved. Charles Reynolds' THEORY AND EXPLANATION IN INTERNATIONAL POLITICS (46) is a more ambitious effort, but lacks overall coherence. To read these and other recent works like that

197

by David Edwards on INTERNATIONAL POLITICAL ANALYSIS (12) can be worthwhile, but it is also heavy going. The authors are struggling with long-unsolved problems, and one becomes the more admiring of the earlier work of scholars of the calibre of Quincy Wright, whose THE STUDY OF INTERNATIONAL RELATIONS (65) appeared in 1955. In some ways the large compendium IN SEARCH OF GLOBAL PATTERNS, one of James Rosenau's many edited volumes (50), is the most helpful guide for the beginner. It includes a series of autobiographical accounts by scholars who have tried different approaches and who describe their successes and failures. Finally, the most impressive of recent analytic texts, Michael Sullivan's INTERNATIONAL RELATIONS: THEORIES AND EVIDENCE (57), displays unparalleled scholarship, but suffers badly from the author's fierce insistence on a narrow empiricism.

General Theory: Commentaries

If the writers of concepts-and-methods texts have succeeded only partially in their efforts to introduce the newcomer to the task of analyzing the world society, where else may the reader turn for general guidance? There is one body of writings which may help: the commentaries on the state of the literature, a regular feature of the learned journals and occasional symposia in International Relations. For example, Charles McClelland's paper (35) 'On the Fourth Wave' of international theory is first class, and the strong language employed in the inter-paradigm debate between F.S. Northedge (42) and James N. Rosenau (49) in the pages of MILLENNIUM in 1976 brings the subject to life in a way that only controversy can achieve. The collection of London School of Economics lectures by Rosecrance, Nye, Modelski, Haas, Russett and Claude which Geoffrey Goodwin edited with Andrew Linklater is useful (18) as are the papers by Waltz and others in volume 8 of THE HANDBOOK OF POLITICAL SCIENCE, devoted to International Relations (62). Stanley Hoffmann's treatment in DAEDALUS of International Relations as 'An American Social Science' (22) is beautifully written, even though its message is brutally discouraging for believers in almost any kind of explanation at all for world politics. Recent contributions by Lipjhart (33), Scott (52) and Inkeles (24) all provide a non-textbook alternative for the reader interested in coming to grips with the challenge of explaining the world society, rather than sinking into its factual morass.

General Theory: The State-Centric Paradigm

Beyond this, the reader has no alternative but to consider the basic expositions of the concepts which have been contributed within the four separate approaches described earlier. The simplest of these, the state-centric paradigm, is also known as the 'international politics' approach, the 'billiard-ball model', or simply as 'power politics'. Its exponents assert that all analysis must begin, and continue, and end, with the behaviour and relationships of states in their political aspect. Fundamentally, states can be reduced to units of power. Everything else is secondary, and because it is secondary then the analyst can successfully proceed with his job of explaining world events exclusively in terms of what states are, what they do, and the patterns of relationships that are formed by their actions. States, then, are defined in terms of their territoriality and their sovereignty; for the purposes of the analysis, a state and its government is the same entity, and it is the only entity that need be discussed in order to arrive at the explanation. Actions are analyzed in terms of security, power, and the rational-strategic calculation of each state's interests in relation to other states. The patterns formed by their inter-relationships are described in terms of the comparative proportions of cooperation and of conflict produced, particularly with relation to the dominant conflictual pattern, known as the balance of power. Those who emphasize the cooperative aspects of these relationships are known as 'idealists', 'liberals' or sometimes 'rationalists', whereas those who stress the hostile and competitive aspects are known as 'realists'.

As a producer of general propositions about world politics, the state-centric paradigm is undoubtedly the best understood and most widely used of the four available interpretations of the structure of the world society. Its central concepts of power, interest, bargaining, equilibrium and rank can be easily applied to make straightforward explanations of international events. In its purest form, which is strategic theory, the basic distinction between capability and intent has far-reaching implications. In foreign policy analysis, the simplifying assumption that the state can be seen as a single, unitary, self-motivated and self-reliant actor in world politics enables relatively penetrating statements to be made, both about what states actually do and, in the normative sense, about what they should do.

However, the state-centric paradigm can be subjected to strongly destructive criticism. There are three main points. First, the paradigm only deals with part of what happens in the world society, namely the

199

government-to-government relations of states, and of major states in particular. Other things (the poverty-wealth gap between south and north in the globe, for example) are not explained at all. Second, the assumptions made about the nature of the state are simply wrong. States are not billiard-balls, and they do not always, or even often, act rationally. Third, 'power' is one of those concepts that tends to dissolve under the scrutiny of careful analysis.

Given these oft-made objections, few writers have dared in recent years to write a straightforward power-politics account of the world society in the traditional style of Hans Morgenthau (38). Most writers prefer to modify their analysis and move to a greater or lesser degree towards the 'international relations' paradigm, described below. This is true for example of K.J. Holsti's INTERNATIONAL POLITICS, in spite of its title (23). It has, deservedly, been the leading textbook of the 1970's. One author who has, however, persisted with the pure form of the state-centric approach (while ignoring recent criticism and development of the theories it contains) is F.S. Northedge, whose THE INTERNATIONAL POLITICAL SYSTEM (41) is the clearest and best-written of the general books available. Hedley Bull's equally comprehensive THE ANARCHICAL SOCIETY (3) partially covers the same ground, but treats the analytic difficulties with far more circumspection, while also paying greater attention to the moral problems of international politics. For the analysis of past inter-state systems in the history of the world, Martin Wight's SYSTEMS OF STATES, published posthumously, is indispensable (63). Finally, E.H. Carr's classic, THE TWENTY YEARS CRISIS (8) is still worthwhile after forty years, especially for its treatment of realism and idealism.

Beyond these general treatments, the reader is perhaps best advised to observe the state-centric paradigm working to advantage when it is used as a basis for an assault upon woolly-minded thinking, grand schemes and over-optimistic views upon present and future happenings in the world society. An example is the writings of the realist author Robert Tucker, who makes politically conservative but intellectually forceful arguments in his THE INEQUALITY OF NATIONS (60) and (with Robert Osgood) FORCE, ORDER AND JUSTICE (43). Both books contain points that need to be countered with equal trenchancy if the visions of those who wish to make progressive changes are to carry weight. This becomes clear if one looks at the writings on comparable topics written within other paradigms, such as Denis Goulet's THE CRUEL CHOICE (19) and Richard Falk's A STUDY OF FUTURE

WORLDS (13). Each in its own terms is an excellent study but never-theless lacks full persuasiveness. Neither counters the main assertion in the state-centric paradigm: that states will be states — individualistic and selfish — and states do have power.

The International Relations Paradigm

The second paradigm for general theory is best labelled the international relations approach. It is superficially the most persuasive of the four approaches to general theory. But it is also the most confused and the least analytically powerful. It asserts that although the world is indeed composed of states, and that therefore we must first examine states in order to explain world events, there are many other phenomena to be analyzed as well. State behaviour is seen by this approach as only one of the sources of action. Alliances and other international institutions are important, non-state actors such as churches and multinational companies have a role to play, economic relationships have a significance of their own and may constrain state behaviour. And the state itself, in this perspective, turns out to be much more complicated than it is shown to be in the state-centric approach. The self-interested rationality of policy-making is reduced by morality, ideology and nationalism. States are not unitary billiard-balls, but are made up of one nation, or several nations, and of various interest groups and ethnic groups. They are affected by geographic circumstance, law, economic conditions and political leadership in such varied and complex ways that generalization about their behaviour is seen to be so difficult as to be almost impossible.

In sum, the international relations approach seeks to analyze the world society with an emphasis on state behaviour, but taking into account also everything else that seems to be related to state behaviour. In contrast to the state-centric paradigm, the simplicities of state-to-state relations vanish and in their place comes series after series of more and more factors and variables which must be considered before any explanations or predictions can be made. The focus of the approach remains fairly clear, but its boundaries are almost non-existent. Virtually everything that happens in the world appears, to the advocate of this approach, to be related to international relations, which means that the analytic choice of concepts for the examination of any single event is almost haphazard.

The strongest writing within the international relations paradigm is that which deals with features of the world which the narrower, power-focussed, state-centric approach can neither predict nor accommodate.

The growth of law in relations between states, for example, is simply an unwelcome paradox for state-centric theory. But it is a fact, and its significance is inadequately conveyed by attempts of extreme state-centric theorists to treat it as 'power politics in disguise'. Ideology is another force behind events, perhaps best approached through C.B. McPherson's lively account of the different meanings that the word 'democracy' can have in different parts of the world (36). For more elaborate treatment, Martin Seliger's IDEOLOGY AND POLITICS (54) stands in a class by itself.

No student of international relations is competent without some knowledge of nationalism and national self-determination, those political dynamisms which can either cement a state together and then urge it into forceful international behaviour, or by contrast fractionate it into a series of warring subdivisions. In this specialized topic area, Karl Deutsch's NATIONALISM AND SOCIAL COMMUNICATION is an early masterpiece (10), as also is Elie Kedourie's more philosophical treatment (26). The historian Hugh Seton-Watson has now added a wide-ranging study (55) to the already large stock of works available. Other social convictions about politics have swept across the face of the world in the past century, notably including social Darwinism and fascism in the earlier period, and developmentalism and racism more recently. Of these, it is worth picking out Hugh Tinker's pioneering but only half-successful study of RACE, CONFLICT AND THE INTERNATIONAL ORDER (58) as a likely trend-setter.

For analytic purposes, phenomena like race, ideology and nationalism effectively undermine the simplistic elegance of state-centric models of the world, but provide no comparable general framework. And so 'international relations' has come to mean merely the almost intuitive study of how all these diverse things can be fitted together into a broad appreciation of the nature of human society as a whole. Some scholars working within the international relations approach even doubt that they have a discipline at all, in the scholarly sense of using a well-understood set of theories and previous findings to explore further a well-defined subject-matter.

But other scholars within the approach, more rigorous in method and more optimistic in their convictions, have spent much energy in the past twenty years in an effort to incorporate the untidy elements of international relations within a coherent framework. The effort has been especially pronounced among those who wish to see their discipline measure up to the scientific criteria of generality, elegance

202

and testability. But their hopes have, in general, been unfulfilled: the analyses either become too complex, or 'multivariate' as the jargon term has it, or alternatively they have the unintended consequence, much discussed in the early 1970's, of moving back to a slightly less straightforward version of the classic state-centric paradigm. To illustrate this work, four of the specific problems discussed are worth brief mention here. These are the conceptual debates on the 'level of analysis problem', 'linkage politics', 'penetrated systems' and the identification of 'actors' in the international system.

The first of these, levels of analysis, was introduced to the literature as a methodological problem by J. David Singer in 1961 (56), and has been conveniently reviewed by William Moul in a 1973 paper (40). It is an attempt to clarify, separate and then somehow fit together again the ill-assorted statements often found together in writings about international politics. Typically, some statements in a single body of argument will relate to individual human behaviour, others to the properties of large-scale organizations like governments or armies, while yet others deal with macro-systemic phenomena like relations between antagonistic alliance systems. Clearly the different statements must not be confused and it is wrong to derive conclusions about, say, war, from observation of teenage hooligans.

The ultimate source of this problem is that an analysis of state-to-state relations alone runs into many difficulties, forcing the scholar to consider the effects of behaviour at other levels. If he does this, he slides into a different paradigm. 'Linkage politics', discussed by James Rosenau and others (48, 64) deals with a similar difficulty: the observable fact that political cause-and-effect relationships flow across state borders, and not always from government to government at the inter-state level. Politics within states matter for the explanation of politics between states. And a government of one state can and does manipulate the domestic politics of another state, bypassing its supposedly sovereign authorities, as Andrew Scott points out in his discussion of 'penetrated systems' (53).

These points lead naturally to the related problem of whether states are the only important 'actors' in world politics. This issue has produced one of the field's longest-running debates, argued from all sides by scholars of several different methodological persuasions. The best-known statement was presented by John Herz in his 1957 paper on 'The Rise and Demise of the Territorial State', now conveniently reprinted with a later recantation in a collection of his essays (21). Herz, like Goodwin in his 'Erosion of External Sovereignty' (17) argues, as any state-centric advocate must, that states are here, and here to stay in charge of world politics. But a simple reassertion of the conventional wisdom in order to preserve the state-centric paradigm is no answer to the tide of objections, and the reader can find a more balanced treatment of them in Oran Young's incisive paper on 'The Actors in World Politics' (66).

The World Society Paradigm

The third paradigm, the world society approach, sometimes known as the 'cobweb' model, seeks to bring some coherence and systematic order to the excessively complex picture presented by the international relations paradigm. It suggests that the source of the confusion is the continuing emphasis on the state, which should be dropped and replaced by a different analytic focus: the system. Then, for any given real-world problem to be explained, the relevant systems which affect that particular problem can be sorted out and mapped, and the flows of activity within each relevant system can be examined and (potentially) even measured. In this way, state-to-state relations can be treated systemically, much as they are in the state-centric paradigm — and so can any other self-contained set of relationships. For example, where actors such as civil insurgents or business firms or ethnic groups are involved, relationships which intimately affect them can be examined directly. There is no need to make the possibly misleading prior assumption that statehood, in all its legal, military and political aspects, is immediately relevant or important. In a broader sense, the cobweb approach also attempts to portray the world society as a whole. Its aim is to isolate and consider those patterns which give unity to the world society, not just at the level of governmental relations, but at the functional level of transnational economic and cultural relations, and also at the basic level of shared human values and aspirations.

In short, the world society answer to the question 'what is the structure?' is that the world comprises many overlapping systems, each distinct and therefore capable of being analyzed as such. Find the boundaries of each system, see what makes it tick, and an explanation of the political events it produces will begin to take shape. Unlike the first two paradigms, this cobweb model is a product of the past decade, although its roots in functionalism, in liberal international thought and in pluralist political philosophy are evident. While it is still a minority approach, its potential capacity to locate the islands of theory in a well-defined chart of the ocean of world politics seems considerable. It provides both a coherent general framework and also some suggestions for showing relationships between the parts within the framework. But while the concepts are attractive, empirical research has yet to be carried out within the paradigm, and final judgement on its merits must be deferred.

Writings on the world society paradigm are dominated by the work of John Burton, who outlined the new approach in 1965 with his INTER-NATIONAL RELATIONS: A GENERAL THEORY (4), developed it fully three years later in his major book, SYSTEMS, STATES, DIPLOMACY AND RULES (5) and has subsequently published several restatements (6) and extensions. Among them, the most useful short introduction for a newcomer to his work is his best single essay, 'International Relations or World Society?' (7) which appeared in 1974. Recently other studies using similar terminology and employing the same analytic framework have begun to appear. One of these, a multi-author work entitled THE WEB OF WORLD POLITICS (34) contains in its first three chapters the clearest statement of the approach that is available.

Beyond these few general works, the influence of the world society paradigm is perhaps best exhibited in the writings of the 'peace and conflict research movement'. This arose in the 1950's as a reaction against the prevalence of state-centric thinking in international studies, and in particular against the political conservatism, methodological amateurism and obsession with strategic and great Power affairs that inevitably accompanied the then intellectually dominant 'realist' mood of the field. Peace researchers initially set themselves to take a fresh look at conflict and war, but soon found that because most inter-state conflicts had domestic roots, the thrust of their inquiries had to shift downward from the inter-state level of analysis. In the 1960's they adopted the systems perspective with more enthusiasm than any other section of the International Relations discipline, and later in the 1970's they incorporated the fashionable concern with 'one world' problems of energy shortage, population increase, pollution and diminishing returns in food production.

From all these related concerns it became apparent in peace research that the only acceptable general perspective was that of treating the globe as a single unit, and analyzing its subsystems according to the needs of the particular research problem at hand, whether it be economic development, the arms race and the trade in arms, the operations of multinational companies or the situation of oppressed minorities.

205

As A.J.R. Groom has demonstrated in his stimulating analysis of the problems of the Middle East (20), the world society paradigm is at its strongest when it is used to analyze a particular conflict situation. Its techniques of unravelling those issues and relationships which are most important to the parties directly concerned (rather than starting with military capabilities, or with the policies of major states) provides a much superior basis for uncovering the factors which are crucial to the resolution of existing conflicts and the avoidance of future ones.

Unfortunately, the literature on peace research does not, in general, do justice to its promise. Nor, on the whole, does it enter into fruitful debate with other paradigms in International Relations so as to produce cumulative growth in the whole field. And the implicit use of the world society framework has never been articulated satisfactorily, even in the splendid work of Anatol Rapoport (45). Johan Galtung's turgid but occasionally profound work on PEACE: RESEARCH, EDUCATION, ACTION (14) shows considerable use of the world society model, but he nowhere spells it out. Juergen Dedring's RECENT ADVANCES IN PEACE AND CONFLICT RESEARCH (9), the only major survey of the field, is useful for its bibliographic guidance but fails to provide a forceful statement of the underlying analytic framework.

Where the world society paradigm does come through most forcibly, however, is in an area where most of the discussants do not intend it to. This is in the literature on transnationalism and interdependence, analyzed mostly by scholars working within the state-centric paradigm and the international relations subfield of international political economy. During the 1970's this has moved to centre stage in the International Relations discipline, as the 'real world' has exhibited symptom after symptom of its essentially cobwebbed nature. The most dramatic event was the worldwide inflationary surge following the OPEC oil price increases of 1973, but there have been many others. They have been best set forth and analyzed in the work of Edward Morse (39), and also in a series of influential writings by Joseph Nye and Robert Keohane (27, 28, 29), culminating in their POWER AND INTER-DEPENDENCE (30). Analytically, the questions these and many other authors raise are searching, topical and clearly central to any understanding of world politics. If cross-national transactions of all kinds really are increasing, as Katzenstein has argued (25), does that create a condition of general interdependence? If the domestic policy of one state is affected by the domestic policy of another state, what does that do to a model of world politics which assumes that the *foreign* policies of states should be the object of our studies? Where mutual sensitivity and vulnerability exist between states, how does this affect their sovereignty? And if governments spend much of their time nowadays debating their policies in terms of economic demands and constraints, what has happened to the traditional interpretation of policy as power, and power as a matter of potential military force?

A few writers have tackled these conceptual difficulties by simply denying either the existence, or the significance, of the facts which give rise to them. Kenneth Waltz, for example, argues in his well-known 'the Myth of National Interdependence' (61) that we can in effect safely persist with our state-centric thinking because interdependence has long existed in the world, may not in fact be on the increase and has not, so far, weakened the essential predominance of power politics. Rosecrance and Stein take a more complex position in their 'Interdependence: Myth or Reality?' (47) discussion, but are reluctant to see the new interdependencies as calling for a whole new framework for analysis. Robert Gilpin, an author well worth the attention of any student of these matters (16), starts his analysis with a squarely mercantilist line of argument: that power is wealth, and wealth is power. Both are in the interests of the nation-state, so that the undoubtedly real interdependency of today's world economy can be interpreted as something created by, and beneficial to, the strongest of current nation-states — the USA. But Gilpin also points out that just as economic relationships arise from particular political conditions, so political conditions can be changed by changing economic relationships. This is precisely the kind of relationship to which the world society paradigm draws attention, though much work remains to be done before it acquires the clarity and testability desired by its proponents.

The Global Social Class Paradigm

Fourth in the paradigm series is the Marxist or global social class analysis, taking all its forms together: classical Marxism-Leninism, contemporary Soviet and Maoist adaptations and western and third-world versions, as well as the various structuralist theories found in radical peace research, in writings about development and 'north-south' relations in world politics, and in many theories of imperialism and dependency. Together these approaches shift the primary level of analysis downward from that of government-to-government interactions to the relations between social classes. They emphasize the importance of the objective interests of classes, and analyze the methods by which one class exerts domination over another, both within states and between states, by manipulation of political institutions including governments. In contrast to the state-centric and international relations approaches, both of which emphasize the vertical divisions between states, the Marxist analysis identifies horizontal 'layer-cake' divisions in the world society.

Although classical Marxism dates back for over a century and, in various forms, constitutes orthodox international theory in many countries apart from the Soviet Union and China, its acceptance has been slow and selective in the western International Relations literature. Its stature, has, however, increased rapidly in the past decade. In international political economy, the Marxist concept of unequal exchange has been introduced to assist with the analysis of the relationship between first-world prosperity and third-world poverty. In conflict studies, the Marxist concept of structural violence has been used to develop an explanation of the latent causes of political instability and the potential acceptability of solutions to disputes. In strategic studies, the rising incidence of guerrilla warfare and terrorism has been analyzed with the help of social-class models quite foreign to the older state-centric emphasis of the field. How far the Marxist paradigm will or should extend is not yet clear. Empirical validation of Marxist theories has long been a major difficulty for many branches of social science, and International Relations is no exception.

Writings on the various branches of Marxism and Marx-inspired theory vary in quantity according to the branch of the paradigm that is considered. The central analysis is, of course, contained in the published works of the founding fathers themselves: Marx, Lenin and to some extent Hegel, Engels and others. In the contemporary literature of the International Relations discipline, this massive and fundamental body of ideas is almost completely ignored, although its influence on the other branches of the paradigm is extensive. At the moment, no analytic study of the 'international relations' concepts and methods of pure Marxism exists, although the original writings are all available in so many editions and with so many commentaries that they need no detailing here. But a forthcoming study has been promised, MARXISM-LENINISM AND THEORY OF INTERNATIONAL RELATIONS, by Vendulka Kubalkova and Albert Cruikshank. It seems likely that it will automatically become one of the major works in English-language international studies, if only because its publication will help to fill such a gigantic gap. The authors have offered an advance helping of the book in their article on 'The Double Omission' published late in 1977 (31).

Kubalkova and Cruikshank's 'double omission' points not only to the lack of systematic incorporation (and criticism) of the great Marxist classics into the western International Relations literature, but also to a lack of interest in contemporary Soviet Marxist thinking. It is very noticeable that the standard treatments of Soviet behaviour, in the foreign policy analysis literature, attempt their explanations by using state-centric theories into which the ideological dimension fits uneasily, if at all. Students, indeed, are frequently set to write essays which treat 'ideology' and 'national interest' as symmetric opposites in the analysis. In fact there does exist both a substantial body of Soviet Marxist international theory (though its relation to Soviet foreign policy is not well understood outside the USSR), and a small quantity of available writing on it. Among western authors, William Zimmerman's excellent SOVIET PERSPECTIVES ON INTERNATIONAL RELATIONS (67) deserves more attention than it has received, and Rapoport's THE BIG TWO (44) contains a useful overview of the paradigm. From Soviet authors themselves, a number of studies are now available in English, often in low-priced editions distributed in the West. Arbatov's IDEOLOGICAL STRUGGLE (1) and Tomashevskii's ON THE PEACEFUL CO-EXISTENCE OF STATES (59) are representative examples. But the reader should be warned that the style of Soviet Marxist political writing is even less palatable than the jargon-ridden product of much American Political Science.

Western studies of Chinese thinking about International Relations theory lag even farther behind than those of Soviet thinking, and there is nothing that can yet be recommended, although this gap too will probably begin to fill within a few years. The remaining branches of the global class system paradigm are all focussed on various aspects of the 'north-south' divide in the world society, between rich and poor societies. They are reviewed elsewhere in this Bibliography, under the headings of stratification and dominance-and-dependency relationships. But one publication, finally, must be highlighted: the masterly treatment by Johan Galtung of 'A Structural Theory of Imperialism' (15), in which the author set the pattern for a whole wave of writing on the problem of the relations between 'core' and 'periphery' communities in the world. Analytically, this is a piece of social science writing of a style and power to match the very best work done in the state-centric paradigm — a rare item.

Competing Paradigms

Not everyone in the field of International Relations would divide up the literature in the fashion adopted here. In particular, the distinction between 'state-centric' and 'international relations' approaches will strike some readers as a forced one. But the object of the exercise has been utilitarian: to help newcomers to the field to sort out the literature into its distinctive strands, nothing more. The strands *can* be so differentiated, and for some labourers in the dusty vineyard of studies of this complex world of ours, it seems useful to take them apart in this way. No grand meta-theoretical implications are intended.

For those new to the field, it is worth noting also that it is in the nature of paradigms for them to be incompatible one with another. There may be choice between them, but there cannot be debate. One of them may be more persuasive than another, but it cannot disprove another. Insofar as the world society paradigm really is addressing itself to new questions about hitherto unemphasized relationships, as its exponents tell us it is, then it is not contradicting the state-centric paradigm. It is passing it by, to engage in a separate conversation with the subject-matter. Similarly, there is no clash between a state-centric model of the causes of war in terms of destabilizing changes in military technology, and a model of conflict produced by 'structuralist' peace researchers (working within the global class system paradigm) who write of underlying contradictions below the surface political relationships. There is a sense in which both may be 'true' — to use that word for the first, and last, time in this concluding chapter. We can choose, and compare, and that provides stimulus, even excitement, in the demanding business of analyzing the world.

Bibliography

1. Arbatov, Y.A., THE IDEOLOGICAL STRUGGLE IN CONTEMPORARY INTERNATIONAL RELATIONS, Moscow, Progress Publishers, 1972
2. Bobrow, Davis B., INTERNATIONAL RELATIONS: NEW APPROACHES, London, Collier-Macmillan, 1973
3. Bull, Hedley N., THE ANARCHICAL SOCIETY: A STUDY OF ORDER IN WORLD POLITICS, London, Macmillan, 1977
4. Burton, John W., INTERNATIONAL RELATIONS: A GENERAL THEORY, Cambridge, Cambridge University Press, 1965
5. Burton, John W., SYSTEMS, STATES, DIPLOMACY AND

RULES, Cambridge, Cambridge University Press, 1968

6. Burton, John W., WORLD SOCIETY, Cambridge, Cambridge University Press, 1972

7. Burton, John W., 'International Relations or World Society?' in John W. Burton, A.J.R. Groom, C.R. Mitchell and A.V.S. de Reuck, THE STUDY OF WORLD SOCIETY: A LONDON PERSPECTIVE, Pittsburgh, Pittsburgh University Center for International Studies, for the International Studies Association, 1974

8. Carr, Edward Hallett, THE TWENTY YEARS CRISIS, 1919–1939: AN INTRODUCTION TO THE STUDY OF INTERNATIONAL RELATIONS, London, Macmillan, 1939

9. Dedring, Juergen, RECENT ADVANCES IN PEACE AND CONFLICT RESEARCH: A CRITICAL SURVEY, London, Sage Publications, 1976

10. Deutsch, Karl W., NATIONALISM AND SOCIAL COMMUNICATION: AN INQUIRY INTO THE FOUNDATIONS OF NATIONALITY (2nd edition), Cambridge, Massachusetts, M.I.T. Press, 1966

11. Dougherty, James E. and Pfaltzgraff, Robert L., Jr., CONTENDING THEORIES OF INTERNATIONAL RELATIONS, Philadelphia, J.B. Lippincott Company, 1971

12. Edwards, David V., INTERNATIONAL POLITICAL ANALYSIS, New York, Holt, Rinehart & Winston, 1969

13. Falk, Richard A., A STUDY OF FUTURE WORLDS, New York, The Free Press, 1975

14. Galtung, Johan, PEACE: RESEARCH, EDUCATION, ACTION, (Essays in Peace Research, Volume 1), Copenhagen, Christian Ejlers, 1975

15. Galtung, Johan, 'A Structural Theory of Imperialism', JOURNAL OF PEACE RESEARCH, Volume 8, 1971, pp. 81–118

16. Gilpin, Robert, U.S. POWER AND THE MULTINATIONAL CORPORATION: THE POLITICAL ECONOMY OF FOREIGN DIRECT INVESTMENT, London, Macmillan, 1975

17. Goodwin, Geoffrey L., 'The Erosion of External Sovereignty' in Ghita Ionescu (ed.), BETWEEN SOVEREIGNTY AND INTEGRATION, London, Croom Helm, 1974, pp. 100–117

18. Goodwin, Geoffrey L. and Linklater, Andrew (eds.), NEW DIMENSIONS OF WORLD POLITICS, London, Croom Helm, 1975

19. Goulet, Denis A., THE CRUEL CHOICE: A NEW CONCEPT IN THE THEORY OF DEVELOPMENT, New York, Atheneum, 1973

20. Groom, A.J.R., 'Conflict Analysis and the Arab-Israeli Conflict' in

POLITICS BETWEEN STATES: CONFLICT AND COOPER-
ATION, ed. by James Barber, Josephine Nigro and Michael Smith
for the Open University, Milton Keynes, Open University Press, 1975

21. Herz, John H., THE NATION-STATE AND THE CRISIS OF
WORLD POLITICS: ESSAYS ON INTERNATIONAL POLITICS
IN THE TWENTIETH CENTURY, New York, David McKay, 1976

22. Hoffmann, Stanley, 'An American Social Science: International
Relations', DAEDALUS: PROCEEDINGS OF THE AMERICAN
ACADEMY OF ARTS AND SCIENCES, 106 (3), Summer 1977,
pp. 41—60

23. Holsti, Kalevi J., INTERNATIONAL POLITICS: A FRAMEWORK
FOR ANALYSIS (3rd edition), London, Prentice-Hall
International, 1977

24. Inkeles, Alex, 'The Emerging Social Structure of the World', WORLD
POLITICS, XXVII (4), July 1975, pp. 467—495

25. Katzenstein, Peter J., 'International Interdependence: Some Long-
Term Trends and Recent Changes', INTERNATIONAL
ORGANIZATION, 29 (3), Autumn 1975, pp. 1021—1034

26. Kedourie, Elie, NATIONALISM, London, Hutchinson, 1960

27. Keohane, Robert O. and Nye, Joseph S. (eds.), TRANSNATIONAL
RELATIONS AND WORLD POLITICS, Cambridge, Massachusetts,
Harvard University Press, 1971

28. Keohane, Robert O. and Nye, Joseph S., 'International Inter-
dependence and Integration', in Nelson W. Polsby and Fred I.
Greenstein (eds.), HANDBOOK OF POLITICAL SCIENCE,
Volume 8: INTERNATIONAL POLITICS, Reading, Massachusetts,
Addison-Wesley, 1975

29. Keohane, Robert O. and Nye, Joseph S., 'Transgovernmental
Relations and International Organizations', WORLD POLITICS,
XXVII (1), October 1974, pp. 39—62

30. Keohane, Robert O. and Nye, Joseph S., POWER AND INTER-
DEPENDENCE: WORLD POLITICS IN TRANSITION, Boston,
Little, Brown, 1977

31. Kubalkova, Vendulka and Cruikshank, A.A., 'A Double Omission',
BRITISH JOURNAL OF INTERNATIONAL STUDIES, 3 (3),
October 1977, pp. 286—307

32. Lieber, Robert J., THEORY AND WORLD POLITICS, London,
George Allen & Unwin, 1973

33. Lipjhardt, Arend, 'The Structure of the Theoretical Revolution
in International Relations', INTERNATIONAL STUDIES

QUARTERLY, 18 (1), March 1974, pp. 41–74

34. Mansbach, Richard W., Ferguson, Yale H. and Lampert, Donald E., THE WEB OF WORLD POLITICS: NON STATE ACTORS IN THE GLOBAL SYSTEM, London, Prentice-Hall International, 1976

35. McClelland, Charles A., 'On the Fourth Wave: Past and Future in the Study of International Systems', in James N. Rosenau, Vincent Davis and Maurice A. East (eds.), THE ANALYSIS OF INTERNATIONAL POLITICS, London, Collier-Macmillan International, 1972, pp. 15–40

36. McPherson, C.B., THE REAL WORLD OF DEMOCRACY, London, Oxford University Press, 1966

37. Morgan, Patrick M., THEORIES AND APPROACHES TO INTERNATIONAL POLITICS: WHAT ARE WE TO THINK? (2nd edition), New Brunswick, New Jersey, Transaction Books, 1975

38. Morgenthau, Hans J., POLITICS AMONG NATIONS: THE STRUGGLE FOR POWER AND PEACE, (5th edition), New York, Alfred Knopf, 1973

39. Morse, Edward L., MODERNIZATION AND THE TRANSFORMATION OF INTERNATIONAL RELATIONS, New York, The Free Press, 1976

40. Moul, William B., 'The Level of Analysis Problem Revisited', CANADIAN JOURNAL OF POLITICAL SCIENCE, 6 (3), September 1973, pp. 494–513

41. Northedge, F.S., THE INTERNATIONAL POLITICAL SYSTEM, London, Faber & Faber, 1976

42. Northedge, F.S., 'Transnationalism: The American Illusion', MILLENNIUM: JOURNAL OF INTERNATIONAL STUDIES, 5 (1), Spring 1976, pp. 21–27

43. Osgood, Robert and Tucker, Robert W., FORCE, ORDER AND JUSTICE, London, Oxford University Press, 1968

44. Rapoport, Anatol, THE BIG TWO: PERCEPTIONS OF SOVIET-AMERICAN RELATIONS SINCE WORLD WAR TWO, New York, Pegasus, 1970

45. Rapoport, Anatol, CONFLICT IN MAN-MADE ENVIRONMENT, Harmondsworth, Middx., Penguin Books, 1974

46. Reynolds, Charles, THEORY AND EXPLANATION IN INTERNATIONAL POLITICS, London, Martin Robertson, 1973

47. Rosecrance, Richard N. and Stein, Arthur, 'Interdependence: Myth or Reality?', WORLD POLITICS, XXVI (1), October 1973, pp. 1–27

48. Rosenau, James N. (ed.), LINKAGE POLITICS: ESSAYS ON THE CONVERGENCE OF NATIONAL AND INTERNATIONAL SYSTEMS, New York, The Free Press, 1969

49. Rosenau, James N., 'International Studies in a Transnational World', MILLENNIUM: JOURNAL OF INTERNATIONAL STUDIES, 5 (1), Spring 1976, pp. 1–20.

50. Rosenau, James N. (ed.), IN SEARCH OF GLOBAL PATTERNS, London, Collier-Macmillan, 1976

51. Rosenau, James N. and others, 'Of Syllabi, Texts, Students and Scholarship in International Relations: Some Data and Interpretations on the State of a Burgeoning Field', WORLD POLITICS, XXIX (2), January 1977, pp. 263–340

52. Scott, Andrew M., 'The Logic of International Interaction', INTERNATIONAL STUDIES QUARTERLY, 21 (3), September 1977, pp. 429–460

53. Scott, Andrew M., THE REVOLUTION IN STATECRAFT; INFORMAL PENETRATION, New York, Random House, 1965

54. Seliger, Martin, IDEOLOGY AND POLITICS, London, George Allen & Unwin, 1976

55. Seton-Watson, Hugh, NATIONS AND STATES: AN INQUIRY INTO THE ORIGINS OF NATIONS AND THE POLITICS OF NATIONALISM, London, Methuen, 1977

56. Singer, J. David., 'The Level of Analysis Problem in International Relations' in Klaus Knorr and Sidney Verba (eds.), THE INTERNATIONAL SYSTEM: THEORETICAL ESSAYS, Princeton, New Jersey, Princeton University Press, 1961

57. Sullivan, Michael P., INTERNATIONAL RELATIONS: THEORIES AND EVIDENCE, London, Prentice-Hall International, 1976

58. Tinker, Hugh, RACE, CONFLICT AND THE INTERNATIONAL ORDER: FROM EMPIRE TO UNITED NATIONS, London, Macmillan, 1977

59. Tomashevskii, V.G., ON THE PEACEFUL CO-EXISTENCE OF STATES, Moscow, Novosti, 1973

60. Tucker, Robert W., THE INEQUALITY OF NATIONS, London, Martin Robertson, 1977

61. Waltz, Kenneth N., 'The Myth of National Interdependence' in Charles P. Kindleberger (ed.), THE INTERNATIONAL CORPORATION, Cambridge, Massachusetts, M.I.T. Press, 1970, pp. 205–223

62. Waltz, Kenneth N., 'Theory of International Relations' in Fred I.

Greenstein and Nelson W. Polsby (eds.), HANDBOOK OF
POLITICAL SCIENCE, Volume 8: INTERNATIONAL POLITICS,
Reading, Massachusetts, Addison-Wesley, 1975, pp. 1–85

63. Wight, Martin, SYSTEMS OF STATES (edited with an introduction
by Hedley Bull), Leicester, Leicester University Press, in association
with the London School of Economics and Political Science, 1977

64. Wilkenfeld, Jonathan (ed.), CONFLICT BEHAVIOR AND
LINKAGE POLITICS, New York, David McKay, 1973

65. Wright, Quincy, THE STUDY OF INTERNATIONAL RELATIONS,
New York, Appleton-Century-Crofts, 1955

66. Young, Oran R., 'The Actors in World Politics' in James N. Rosenau,
Vincent Davis and Maurice A. East (eds.), THE ANALYSIS OF
INTERNATIONAL POLITICS, London, Collier-Macmillan, 1972,
pp. 125–144

67. Zimmerman, William, SOVIET PERSPECTIVES ON INTER-
NATIONAL RELATIONS, Princeton, New Jersey, Princeton
University Press, 1969

NOTES ON CONTRIBUTORS

MICHAEL BANKS   graduated in 1957 with first class honours from The London School of Economics, where he has been Lecturer in International Relations since 1961. He spent four years doing post-graduate work in the USA, and has taught at University College London (1967–69), at the University of Southern California (1972–73) and for short periods in Austria, Germany, Kenya and Zambia. His publications have been on African politics, British and United States foreign policy, systems analysis, general theory of international relations, conflict theory and various aspects of peace theory.

JOHN W. BURTON   is presently a Reader in International Relations at University College, London. He was educated at the University of Sydney, and at London University where he received his Ph.D. He was Permanent Head of the Australian Department of External Affairs from 1945 to 1950, and was appointed Australian High Commissioner in Ceylon in 1951. He became Visiting Research Fellow at the Australian National University from 1960–1963, and thence moved to his present post at University College. He was awarded a D.Sc. by the University of London in 1974. Major publications include THE ALTERNATIVE (1954); PEACE THEORY (1962); INTERNATIONAL RELATIONS: A GENERAL THEORY (1965); SYSTEMS, STATES, DIPLOMACY AND RULES (1968); CONFLICT AND COMMUNICATION (1969); and WORLD SOCIETY (1972).

ANTHONY de REUCK is senior lecturer in International Studies at the University of Surrey. As a physicist he worked at Imperial College and on the International Scientific Relations staff of the Royal Society. Later he edited CONFLICT IN SOCIETY (1966); CASTE AND RACE (1967); and COMMUNICATION IN SCIENCE (1968) for the Ciba Foundation. He joined the staff of the Centre for Analysis of Conflict in 1969 and graduated again from University College London in International Relations. He has held office in the Conflict Research Society and the Royal Anthropological Institute. Current research interests include the group dynamics of conflict resolution (HUMAN CONTEXT, VI (1) 1974) and the development of a trans-action theory of international relations.

JOHN C. FAHY is a Ph.D. candidate at the University of London and a faculty member of the University of Maryland/European Division in the Department of Government and Politics. His research interests include Urban and Regional Planning, Economic Development, and Decision-Making Analysis with particular emphasis on Southern Europe.

NANCY WILSHUSEN FAHY is currently a Ph.D. candidate in International Relations at the University of London and on

217

the Editorial Board for the JOURNAL OF THE CONFLICT RESEARCH SOCIETY. She is also Assistant to the Director of the University of Southern California, United Kingdom Program in International Relations and was formerly Project Administrator of the Threat Recognition and Analysis Project (TR & A) at the International Relations Research Institute of the University of Southern California. Her research interests include problem-definition and problem solving at the global level, and in particular satisfying one of man's most basic human needs — food.

A.J.R. GROOM   teaches International Relations at the University of Kent. His publications include BRITISH THINKING ABOUT NUCLEAR WEAPONS and some thirty articles. He has edited INTERNATIONAL ORGANISATION: A CONCEPTUAL APPROACH and FUNCTIONALISM with Paul Taylor and THE MANAGEMENT OF BRITAIN'S EXTERNAL RELATIONS with Robert Boardman. His monographs include PEACE-KEEPING, and he has co-authored THE STUDY OF WORLD SOCIETY with other contributors to this present volume.

CHRISTOPHER HILL   was educated at Merton and Nuffield Colleges, Oxford, and came to the London School of Economics, where he is a Lecturer in the Department of International Relations, in 1973. His interests centre on the theory and practice of decision-making, with special reference to foreign policy and to British politics. He has published several articles on foreign policy analysis, and is completing a case-study in the making of British foreign policy.

MARGOT LIGHT   was born in South Africa and moved to London

218

in 1963. She took a degree in Russian and International Relations at the University of Surrey, and spent a year at Moscow State University. She currently teaches Russian, Soviet Foreign Policy and International Relations at the University of Surrey. Her major research interests include Foreign Policy Analysis, and Soviet-Marxist Theories of International Relations.

RICHARD LITTLE has recently moved from the Department of Politics at the University of Lancaster to become Lecturer in Government at the Open University. He has written articles on various aspects of International Relations theory and he has just completed a study of foreign aid allocation. The results of the latter will shortly be published in WORLD POLITICS and the BRITISH JOURNAL OF POLITICAL SCIENCE. He is the author of INTERVENTION: EXTERNAL INVOLVEMENT IN CIVIL WARS.

CHRISTOPHER MITCHELL was originally trained as a schoolteacher at Westminster College, London, but later returned to the University of London to take a B.Sc. and Ph.D. in International Relations. He has taught the subject at University College London and at the Universities of Southampton and Surrey. He was also a Research Associate at the Centre for the Analysis of Conflict, and, for a brief period, Senior Research Officer at the London School of Economics. Currently he is a Lecturer in International Relations at The City University, London, where his major interests are in the application of systems theory to the study of international relationships; and the role of third parties in international and transnational conflict. He has published articles in a number of journals, including INTERNATIONAL STUDIES

QUARTERLY, JOURNAL OF PEACE RESEARCH, and the BRITISH JOURNAL OF POLITICAL SCIENCE, and is currently working upon a study of the structure and processes of international conflicts.

MICHAEL NICHOLSON was born in 1933 in Yorkshire. He was educated at Trinity College Cambridge where he read economics and later took a Ph.D. in the same discipline. He subsequently held faculty positions at various universities, namely, Manchester, Massachusetts Institute of Technology, Carnegie Institute of Technology (now Carnegie Mellon University), Stockholm, Lancaster, University College London, and the University of Texas at Austin. For several years now, he has been the Director of the Richardson Institute for Conflict and Peace Research in London. He has published numerous papers in economic theory and, later in decision theory as applied to Political Science. His main work has been concerned with formal decision theory as applied to conflict problems, particularly bargaining problems and questions of decision making under uncertainty. He has made a number of contributions to the applications of probability theory to decision taking under uncertainty and the controversies involved. Following Russell's advice (not personally given) that one's first book should be incomprehensible in order to induce the appearance of wisdom, he wrote OLIGOPOLY AND CONFLICT: A DYNAMIC APPROACH (Liverpool University Press, 1972), which was a formal work in economic theory. Unfortunately, publication delays meant this plan was frustrated and it was preceded by CONFLICT ANALYSIS (English Universities Press, 1971), a readable account of the approach of the social scientist to International Relations. His interest in the philosophical presuppositions of the social sciences stems from his undergraduate days and he is completing a book-length manuscript on the subject.

A.N. OPPENHEIM was born in Israel in 1924, and has long been a Reader in Social Psychology at the London School of Economics. Among his special interests are problems in political science and international relations, and he was director of the Conflict Research Unit at the School until 1972. He has written extensively on problems of decision-making, especially under crisis conditions; at present he is concerned with a study of diplomats and ministries of foreign affairs. His early work on attitude development in adolescents, which included joint authorship of TELEVISION AND THE CHILD (London, Oxford University Press, 1958), has generated a major study of political socialisation (jointly with J.V. Torney and R. Farnen) CIVIC EDUCATION IN TEN COUNTRIES: AN EMPIRICAL STUDY (Stockholm, Almqvist and Wiksell, 1975), and his most recent monograph CIVIC EDUCATION AND PARTICIPATION IN DEMOCRACY: THE GERMAN CASE (London, Sage Contemporary Political Sociology Series, 1977). His special interest in survey methodology has led to a widely used textbook QUESTIONNAIRE DESIGN AND ATTITUDE MEASUREMENT (New York, Basic Books, 1966).

FRANCES PINTER received her B.A. from New York University, has studied at the London School of Economics, and received her Ph.D. from University College, London. She is currently research officer and tutor at the Centre for Criminological Research, University of

221

Oxford. She has worked for the Community Relations Commission in Northern Ireland and has published articles on the Northern Ireland conflict. In 1973 she founded Frances Pinter Ltd. which specializes in social science publications.

HEDDA RAMSDEN was born in Germany and has lived in Great Britain for the last twelve years. She read International Relations at the London School of Economics and Political Science and at University College London. Her current work focusses on conflict theory and on conflict resolution. As a Ph.D. student she is investigating patterns of conflict; in particular, the extent to which role defence may be a source of major political conflicts.